T0328922

Athenian Democracy

Second Edition

LACTOR Sourcebooks in Ancient History

For more than half a century, *LACTOR Sourcebooks in Ancient History* have been providing for the needs of students at schools and universities who are studying ancient history in English translation. Each volume focuses on a particular period or topic and offers a generous and judicious selection of primary texts in new translations. The texts selected include not only extracts from important literary sources but also numerous inscriptions, coin legends and extracts from legal and other texts, which are not otherwise easy for students to access. Many volumes include annotation as well as a glossary, maps and other relevant illustrations, and sometimes a short Introduction. The volumes are written and reviewed by experienced teachers of ancient history at both schools and universities. The series is now being published in print and digital form by Cambridge University Press, with plans for both new editions and completely new volumes.

Athenian Democracy

Second Edition

———

Edited by
ROBIN OSBORNE
University of Cambridge

CAMBRIDGE
UNIVERSITY PRESS

Shaftesbury Road, Cambridge CB2 8EA, United Kingdom

One Liberty Plaza, 20th Floor, New York, NY 10006, USA

477 Williamstown Road, Port Melbourne, VIC 3207, Australia

314–321, 3rd Floor, Plot 3, Splendor Forum, Jasola District Centre, New Delhi – 110025, India

103 Penang Road, #05–06/07, Visioncrest Commercial, Singapore 238467

Cambridge University Press is part of Cambridge University Press & Assessment,
a department of the University of Cambridge.

We share the University's mission to contribute to society through the pursuit of
education, learning and research at the highest international levels of excellence.

www.cambridge.org
Information on this title: www.cambridge.org/9781009383394
DOI: 10.1017/9781009383370

First edition © The London Association of Classical Teachers 2014.

Second edition published by Cambridge University Press and Assessment, © The London Association of
Classical Teachers 2023.

First published 2023

A catalogue record for this publication is available from the British Library.

A Cataloging-in-Publication data record for this book is available from the Library of Congress.

ISBN 978-1-009-38339-4 Paperback

PREFACE

There have been two previous editions of LACTOR 5. In 1973 R.W. Clayton and the LACT Ancient History Group produced a 64-page book under the title *Athenian Politics: Democracy in Athens from Pericles to Cleophon*. This was a translation – with a small number of omissions and additions – of the sources collected in M.S. Warman, I. Sutherland and C. Macdonald's *From Pericles to Cleophon* published in 1954. In 1998 John Roberts replaced this with a volume of 144 pages entitled *Athenian Radical Democracy*, the focus of which was, under the explicit influence of the work of Mogens Herman Hansen, much more institutional, and which included translations of material from Thucydides that *Athenian Politics* had excluded.

This replacement for Roberts' *ARD* includes much material from that volume, but in line with the developing LACTOR style includes more commentary and discussion, and in line with the changing demands of the sixth-form syllabus throws its net rather more widely, in particular including rather more fourth-century source material. For all that fourth-century Athenian democracy differed formally (see §4) and in other ways from fifth-century democracy, fourth-century practice nevertheless remains in many cases our best guide to what is likely to have happened in the fifth century. Although material of fourth-century date must always be used with care, it is foolish to arrive at conclusions about fifth-century democracy without being aware of what happened in the fourth century.

Given that the personal has long been the political, the relatively narrow definition of Athenian democracy reflected in this book needs some justification. The justification lies both in the utility of a relatively short book and in the existence of LACTOR 12 covering *The Culture of Athens*. In due course a replacement edition for *The Culture of Athens* is needed, not least to take account of Athenian visual culture, but in the short term the teaching need is for LACTOR 5.

I am very grateful to my successive research assistants, Dr. Kristen Leith and Dr. Philip Boyes, for their labours on this volume, and to Melvin Cooley and Terry Edwards for their careful vetting and proof-checking.

Robin Osborne
King's College, Cambridge

December 2013

TABLE OF CONTENTS
(Numbers in bold print refer to passages)

Notes and Abbreviations

All dates are BC unless otherwise stated.

'[23.1]' or 'The city [of Athens] or Peri[kles proposed]': Square brackets have been used to enclose editorial material inserted into texts. This material includes chapter and section numbers, explanatory glosses, and more or less conjectural supplements to fragmentary epigraphic texts. In the case of the latter, although I have sometimes put a square bracket part way through a proper name, in the case of words other than proper names that cannot be completely read on a stone I have decided whether or not there is serious doubt about the restoration, putting the English translation into square brackets only when such doubt exists.

'This (the restoration of democracy in 403) was the eleventh in number of the changes': Round brackets have been used to enclose editorial glosses.

Inscriptions are given by reference to ML or RO if in those selections, by reference to *IG* or relevant corpus if not.

DK   H. Diels and W. Kranz *Die Fragmente der Vorsokratiker* (Berlin 1934–54)

FGrH   F. Jacoby ed. *Die Fragmente der griechischer Historiker* (1923–)

IG   *Inscriptiones Graecae*

ML   R. Meiggs and D.M. Lewis *A Selection of Greek Historical Inscriptions to the end of the Peloponnesian War* (revised edition, Oxford, 1988)

RO   P.J. Rhodes and R. Osborne *Greek Historical Inscriptions 404–323 B.C.* (Oxford, 2003).

SEG   *Supplementum Epigraphicum Graecum*

Index of passages

Glossary

Arkhon
(pl. arkhontes)

A general word for someone holding a magistracy, but particularly used in Athens of the nine arkhons who had once been the most important of all Athenian magistrates. After 487 they were chosen by lot and had mainly religious and judicial functions. One arkhon, known by modern scholars as the Eponymous Arkhon, gave his name to the year at Athens: 'when Euthunos was arkhon...'. See also below on Basileus and Polemarkh.

Areopagos

The Rock of Ares, where the Council made up of ex-arkhons met. The powers of the Council varied from time to time and were, in particular, cut back by the reforms of Ephialtes in 462. In the Classical period the Areopagos was primarily a law-court.

Assembly (*ekklēsia*)

The meeting of the Athenian people some 40 times a year, usually on the Pnyx hill, at which all major state decisions were taken.

Basileus

The Basileus (often referred to by scholars as the 'arkhon basileus') was the chief magistrate with responsibility for religious rites.

Council (*boulē*)

Body of 500 Athenians over the age of 30 selected by lot, 50 from each of the ten Athenian tribes, to serve for a year as the committee which prepared business for the Assembly and saw that the Assembly's decisions were carried out.

Dadoukh

The title of the second-highest-ranking priest in the Eleusinian Mysteries.

Deme

One of the communities of Attica recognized as a political unit by Kleisthenes in 508/7. Demes were mostly villages, or groups of hamlets, but 'wards' of the town were also recognized as separate demes.

Eleven (*hendeka*)

The Eleven were the officials responsible for prisons and the administration of punishment to condemned criminals.

Ephebe

A young man, just enrolled as a citizen and doing military service between the ages of 18 and 20.

Epimelētēs

'Curator' or 'manager'; often translated here as 'official in charge'.

Examination   The inspection or cross-examination of a citizen to assess their
(*dokimasia*)   suitability before service either as a magistrate or in the cavalry.

Generals (*stratēgoi*) From the end of the sixth century the Athenians elected 10
                         generals each year, normally one from each of the ten tribes,
                         but from the mid fifth century to the mid fourth exceptions to
                         that rule were possible and in the second half of the fourth the
                         link to the tribes was abandoned. Individually or in groups they
                         commanded Athenian troops in war.

Gennētai   The members of a *genos*, or kinship groups into which Athenian
                         society was subdivided. Each *genos* seems to have been
                         responsible for a particular cult.

Hamippoi   Mixed infantry and cavalry.

Hēliaia   The Athenian People's court.

Hellēnotamiai   A board of 10 Athenian officials who received, recorded and
                         made payments from the tribute of the allies. In 411 their
                         number was increased to 20 and they seem to have taken on the
                         functions of the *kolakretai*.

Hieromnēmon   A secretary or registrar; particularly with responsibility over
                         religious matters.

Hierophant   The chief priest of the Eleusinian Mysteries, selected from the
                         Eumolpidai tribe.

Hieropoios   A magistrate overseeing temples and sacred rites.

Hipparkh   The commander of the cavalry.

Hippeis   'Knights' – the cavalrymen, Athens' second-highest social
                         class.

Khalkothekē   The Athenian bronze store-house, on the Akropolis.

Khoregos   The one who leads or finances a chorus.

Kleroukhy   A colony or allotment of land for citizens which remained a
                         political dependency of Athens.

Kolakretai   Treasurers, whose terms of appointment are not properly
                         understood, but who are called upon to provide money for
                         various expenses. See further on *Hellenotamiai*.

Lokhagos   A military captain.

Lykeion	A gymnasium and parade-ground, where Aristotle founded his school.
Medimnos	The standard Athenian measure of grain.
Metic	A foreigner resident in Athens for more than a month who was liable to pay the 1 dr. a month poll-tax known as the *metoikion*, and was without citizen rights.
Mna or mina	Unit of weight and value equivalent to 100 drakhmas.
Nomothetai	'Law-makers'. The members of a committee charges with drafting laws, in the fourth century.
Orgeones	Members of associations or groups dedicated to worship of a deity.
Pentakosiomedimnoi	The highest social class, made up of those whose land produced 500 *medimnoi* of barley per year.
Phratry	'Brotherhood'. A kinship group smaller than a tribe but larger than a genos.
Phylarkh	A cavalry leader elected by members of his tribe.
Pnyx	The hill in Athens, where the Assembly met.
Polemarkh	'War-leader'. One of the arkhons and traditionally the commander of the military. After this responsibility passed to generals in the early fifth century, the polemarkh in the classical period had a particular role dealing with court cases involving non-Athenians.
Polētai	'Sellers'. Officials with responsibilities for taxes, putting contracts out to tender, and dealing with confiscated property.
Probouloi	Members of a committee created in 413 to consider ideas before they were formally put to the people.
Proedroi	The presiding officers of the Assembly in the fourth century.
Prytaneis/**Prytany**	The 50 Council members from each tribe took it in turns to serve for a tenth of the year as *prytaneis*, that is as a standing committee of the Council, dealing with day to day emergencies and preparing Council business. The period of 35-36 days for which each tribe served was known as a 'prytany'.
Scrutiny (*euthunai*)	At the end of their term of office all public officials were

subjected to an official scrutiny of their conduct while in office.

Stele   A slab (of stone) on which inscriptions were carved.

Symmory   A group of men responsible for (the costs of manning) a triremeor for paying the property tax called eisphora.

Taxiarkh   The commander of a tribal contingent of hoplites.

Thesmothetai   The six junior arkhons, assisting the arkhons.

Thetes   The lowest class, essentially without landed property.

Thiasos   A group devoted to a particular cult. Also used of a sub-group of a phratry.

Tribes (*phylai*)   In the reforms which were the basis of the classical democracy Kleisthenes divided the Athenians into 10 groups, spread over Attika, on the basis of their village or ward of residence. These 10 groups took their names from old Athenian heroes: Erekhtheus gave his name to the tribe Erekhtheis, Kekrops to the tribe Kekropis, Aias to the tribe Aiantis and so on.

Trierarkh   The citizen who paid for, outfitted and in some cases commanded a trireme.

Trittyes   'Thirds'. A subdivision consisting of a third of a tribe and based in one region of Attica.

Zeugites   The third social class, reckoned originally to have had property producing 200 *medimnoi* of goods per year.

INTRODUCTION

Athens has the reputation for being the world's first democracy. The strength of that claim depends upon the sense that is given to 'democracy'. Even those who maintain Athens' priority do not agree about when Athens became a democracy – and primarily for reasons of modern politics, not because of disagreement about the facts of the Athenian case.[1] But even if one is convinced by claims that other Greek states had democracies first, or even that the first democracy was earlier still in the Near East, Athenian democracy has a special interest.[2]

What make classical Athenian democracy interesting and important are our detailed knowledge of how it worked and its success. Whereas in the case of other Greek cities (with the exception of Sparta) we have, at best, a meagre knowledge of their constitution and one or two incidents illuminating how politics worked there, in the case of Athens we have detailed constitutional knowledge and numerous particular illustrations of the machinery at work. What is more, there is little doubt that Athenian democracy worked well. Although the tragic momentum of Thucydides' history, where Athens is built up in such a way as to emphasise the magnitude of its defeat, has often led to the fourth-century being viewed as merely the pale shadow of the fifth, this is far from the case. Fourth-century Athens not only ran itself effectively, it ran for more than 20 years a significant second 'empire', and, though defeated by Philip of Macedon, continued to organize a flourishing civic life until a second defeat following the death of Alexander the Great and for long after that. The measurement of 'success' is a difficult matter, but Josiah Ober has recently argued that even in the terms used by modern social scientists, Athens must be reckoned exceptionally successful.[3]

This book attempts to bring together the ancient source material that allows us to understand how it was that Athens came to have a constitution that can be described as democratic, and how that constitution worked. This is not simply a matter of understanding the rules which the Athenians developed for who could do what, but how those rules were operated, and what the pressures were that threatened the workings either in the sense of threatening to break the rules or threatening the rules by manipulating them to achieve undesired results.

The questions that we need to ask of the source materials here fall into three groups, broadly aligned with the three sections into which the book is divided. First, there are questions of historical causation: how did Athens become democratic? what precise effect did individual changes to the rules about who could do what have? why were some changes apparently accepted without contest and others bitterly fought over? Second, there are questions of how the democracy operated: what exactly was the balance of power between the council and the assembly? or between the assembly and the lawcourts? what rôle did the generals play? how was it possible to run a large and complicated city when most of the officials were selected by lot? what rôle did the sub-divisions of the people play – the tribes, *trittyes* and demes, and the older descent groups, the phratries and *genē* (singular: *genos*, 'clans')? Thirdly, there are questions of what happened when particular individuals tried to use the machinery of democracy to achieve particular ends and of how democracy coped with the particular events and

---

1. See Osborne (2006).
2. Robinson (1997), Raaflaub, Ober and Wallace (2007), Flemming (2004).
3. Ober (2008).

challenges which historical events presented. It is one thing to describe the powers that the Assembly had, but another to understand what would make the assembly use those powers. What were the arguments that persuaded Athenians both individually and as a group? What political values did Athenians share, or what principles were contested?

None of the questions posed in the last paragraph is a question to which the material assembled in this book – or any other material from antiquity – offers a definitive answer. The questions are interesting precisely because the evidence that we have from antiquity can be used to argue for more than one position. Modern scholars often come to hold that one interpretation of the evidence is correct, putting a lot of emphasis on one source and ignoring or denying the accuracy of another. The point of encouraging close reading of all the evidence gathered here is to make such scholarly manoeuvres explicit, to reveal the stories that particular scholars do not want to tell, as well as the stories they do want to tell – and to think about why one story might indeed be a better, more persuasive, story than the other. In weighing up evidence in this way the reader of this book will be acting like a juror in an Athenian court, or a citizen attending an assembly and voting. In the Athenian courts and in Athenian assemblies individuals heard evidence mustered in arguments and then had to decide upon the significance of that evidence for those arguments and for the issue in hand. They had to do so in circumstances which prevented serious discussion with others. If that seems a difficult task with this evidence, and if we are thankful to those who have marshalled the evidence previously, we get some impression of how hard a thing it was to run Athens under its democratic rules.

Notes on Authors and Works Quoted

Aiskhines (c.397–322). Athenian orator, politician and bitter rival of Demosthenes. Their dispute centred around Aiskhines' support for negotiation and peace with the expansionist Philip II of Macedon and eventually culminated in Demosthenes mounting a vigorous attack on Aiskhines in his speech *On the Crown* (330), after which Aiskhines was fined, his judicial powers limited, and eventually went into exile on Rhodes.

Andokides (c.440–390). Athenian orator and politician who was involved in and informed upon the plot to mutilate the Herms in 415.

Antiphon (flourished 420–411). The first Athenian to write speeches for others to deliver and almost certainly himself prominent in the oligarchic coup of 411. Six speeches substantially survive (see M. Gagarin *Antiphon: Speeches* (Cambridge, 1996) along with a collection of model speeches (*The Tetralogies*).

Aristophanes (c.445–after 375?). Comic dramatist whose earliest recorded work is the *Babylonians* of 427 and latest the *Wealth* of 389. The earlier of the eleven surviving plays all choose political targets.

Scholia on Aristophanes: line by line commentaries, sometimes deriving their information entirely from the text but on other occasions conveying the fruits of impressive Alexandrian critical scholarship.

Aristotle (384–322). His *Politics* seems to derive from lectures given by the philosopher in the 330s and is rich with allusions to particular political incidents as well as generalised claims about political behaviour.

[Aristotle] *Constitution of the Athenians* (*Athenaion Politeia*). This work, largely known from a papyrus purchased by the British Museum in 1888–9 and published in 1891, is the only one of the 158 Constitutions of Greek states compiled under Aristotle's direction substantially surviving. Written in the 330s and revised in the 320s, it consists of a history of the Athenian constitution down to the end of the fifth century, followed by a description of how the Athenian constitution worked in the later fourth century. The historical section is compiled from earlier written accounts, particularly those by the local historians of Athens known as Atthidographers. There is a magisterial commentary on the whole work by P.J. Rhodes (Oxford 1981, with addenda 1993).

Deinarkhos (c.360–290). Athenian orator and speech-writer. Originally from Corinth, and thus a metic, Deinarkhos was disbarred from political activity and speaking himself in court. Despite this, he achieved considerable success.

Demokritos (c.460–370). Pre-Socratic philosopher from Abdera in Thrace. Best known for developing, along with Leukippos, an atomic theory. He is known to have written on a wide range of topics in philosophy and natural science, but little of his work now survives.

Demosthenes (384–322). The most famous of all Athenian orators and an influential fourth-century politician. From the late 350s until the battle of Khaironeia in 337 Demosthenes urged the Athenians to resist Philip II of Macedon's expansion of his powers. One of Demosthenes' chief persuasive gambits was comparing the Athenians of the fourth-century with (a rose-tinted view of) their fifth-century ancestors.

[Demosthenes] (394–after 340) A number of speeches preserved with those of Demosthenes are not by him but by Apollodoros son of Pasion. Pasion had started life as a slave and ended up as a citizen. His son seems to have felt in consequence that he had to prove himself and he engaged in aggressive legal and political battles. See J. Trevett *Apollodoros the son of Pasion* (Oxford 1992).

Diodoros (active 60–36 BC). A native of Sicily, Diodoros wrote a *Universal History* in 40 books which attempted to give a year-by-year account of both Greek and Roman history.

Diogenes Laertios (fl. 3rd century AD). Otherwise virtually unknown author of *Lives of the Philosophers*, giving biographies and summaries of the doctrines of philosophers.

Dionysios of Halikarnassos (active 30–8 BC). Antiquarian and writer on rhetoric.

Eumelos (after 322). Peripatetic philosopher and historian, mentioned in two fragments but otherwise unknown.

Eupolis (active 429–412). Comic dramatist, older contemporary and rival of Aristophanes. His plays include one ridiculing the wealthy Kallias son of Hipponikos and the sophists, one attacking Hyperbolos, and one bringing great Athenians of the past back from the Underworld.

Euripides (c.480–406). One of the three great Athenian tragic poets. He first competed in the Great Dionysia in 455, but did not win until 441, and only three other times thereafter. His reputation as an innovator and iconoclast, self-consciously clever and interested in 'gritty' and 'realistic' themes, is memorably satirised in Aristophanes' *Frogs*.

Harpokration (late second century AD). Alexandrian lexicographer, whose Lexicon of the Ten Orators is designed as an aid to reading Attic Greek. He draws his information both from scholars of the imperial age and from direct acquaintance with classical and hellenistic works of history and scholarship, as well as from the orators themselves.

Hellenika Oxyrhynkhia An account of Greek history by an unknown author, probably written in the fourth century BC and found on two sets of papyri from Oxyrhynkhos.

Herodotos (c.480–?410). Born at Halikarnassos but from its foundation resident at

Thourioi, Herodotos seems to have been writing his *History* during the Peloponnesian War, but his allusions to events after the defeat of the Persians in 479 are few and far between, perhaps for political reasons.

Hypereides (389–322). Athenian statesman and orator, whose reputation in rhetoric was only surpassed by Demosthenes. He was bitterly opposed to Macedonian dominance over Athens and long urged resistance and revolt, before he was eventually captured and executed.

Isaios (c.420–340s). Athenian speech-writer and teacher of Demosthenes. He specialised in inheritance cases.

Isokrates (436–338). Although not himself active as a speaker in the Athenian assembly, Isokrates' written orations provide an important commentary on Athenian politics in the fourth century, and he was important enough as a teacher of rhetoric to be attacked by Plato in the *Phaidros*. Isokrates thought that Greek cities should work together against the Persians, and he finally urged Philip to lead the Greek states in a campaign against them.

Lykourgos (c.390–325/4). Athenian politician and orator, who spent a long spell in control of Athens' finances.

Lysias (459/8 or later–c.380). He spent his early life in Thourioi but returned to Athens in 412/11. As a metic Lysias could take no part in the Athenian Assembly, but many of his forensic speeches have a political slant. In his Funeral Oration he turns his skill at glossing over inconvenient facts to the service of the encomium of Athens. He too is attacked in Plato's *Phaidros*.

Menander (c.344/3–392/1). Athenian comic poet and the leading exponent of the New Comedy. His works were lost after antiquity, but many fragments have been recovered from papyri.

Old Oligarch *Constitution of the Athenians*. This short work included among the pamphlets of Xenophon is distinct from them in style. From its historical allusions it has been thought to date to the late 420s and it is thus the earliest surviving work of Attic prose. The author, who is often referred to as the 'Old Oligarch', explains, as if to oligarchs outside Athens, how it is that democracy sustains itself in Athens and cannot easily be overthrown. Although it offers little detailed historical analysis it mentions in passing much that we are not told by other literary sources. For a full edition with introduction and commentary see LACTOR 2.

Philokhoros (c.340–260). Historian and scholar, particularly celebrated for his *Atthis*, or history of Attica.

Plato (c.429–347). The works of the Athenian philosopher are frequently given a more or less specific historical setting, but other historical allusions in the *Dialogues* are rare. *The Seventh Letter*, whose genuineness is uncertain, is autobiographical.

Plutarch (before 50 AD – after 120 AD). Philosopher and biographer from Khaironeia in Boiotia who also became a priest at Delphi. He himself insists that his *Parallel Lives* of famous Greeks and Romans, of which we have 23 pairs, are not history, and he is interested in character rather than the analysis of events. He was extremely well read although given to anachronistic assumptions and not consistently critical of his own sources.

Pollux (2nd century AD). Scholar and rhetorician from Naucratis in Egypt, best known for his encyclopaedic Onomasticon which included, in book 8, a section on Athenian constitutional terms.

Solon (c.638–558). Best remembered as a law-giver, statesman and poet. His reforms classified Athenian society by wealth and seems to have ended the dependent status of *hektemoros* (sixth-parter, i.e. share-cropper).

Souda A historical encyclopaedia and lexicon compiled in the late tenth century AD.

Theopompos of Khios (378/7–c.320). Historian whose epitome of Herodotos, continuation of Thucydides, and history of Philip survive only in later quotations. His work displayed wide interests and frequent digressions, was laudatory of Philip and critical of Athens. Both his erudition and his strong invectives were famous in antiquity.

Theophrastos of Eresos (c.371–287). Successor to Aristotle as head of the Lyceum. Several works (*On Plants*, *On Stones* etc.) survive, but the work that would be most useful to historians, *On Laws*, survives only in later quotations.

Thucydides (c.455–c.400). Athenian of aristocratic background with Thracian connections whose *History of the Peloponnesian War* in 8 books, with its account in Book 1 of the years between the Persian and Peloponnesian Wars, forms the backbone of all subsequent histories of Greece during this period.

Xenophon (c.430–c.350). Athenian who wrote *Memoirs of Sokrates*, an account of a mercenary expedition into the heart of Persia (the *Anabasis*), a continuation of Thucydides down to 362 (the *Hellenika*), and a number of pamphlets. Exiled from Athens for fighting against her at Koroneia in 394, he spent some time in Sparta and on an estate in Elis before retiring to Corinth. His historical works combine accurate detail and some perceptive analysis with a certain economy with the truth. His *Ways and Means*, written in the 350s, advises Athens on how to improve her economy.

Part I How Athens Became a Democracy

Note A   On writing the history of the Athenian constitution

A book that begins by telling the history of the Athenian constitution and then gives a more or less static description of how the individual institutions worked follows exactly the plan of *The Constitution of the Athenians* (often known, after its abbreviated Greek title, as the *Ath. Pol.*) written in the 330s and revised in the 320s. This work was part of an Aristotelian research project which, according to a list given by Diogenes Laertios (*Lives of the Philosophers* 5.27) in the third century AD, produced studies of the constitutions of some 158 Greek cities (with Carthage included among them). Although later authors not infrequently quote from these works, and some 51 of them are cited by title, *The Constitution of the Athenians* is the only one of these studies to survive substantially intact. It survived not with the corpus of works of Aristotle, but on four papyrus rolls dug up in Oxyrhynkhos in Egypt and acquired by the British Museum in 1888–9 and on two leaves from a codex. The papyrus was written close to 100 AD and the codex during the second century AD.

When it came to describing the institutions of Athenian democracy at work, the Aristotelian researcher had the advantage of being able to observe the system in action. For the history of the constitution, however, the researcher was in very much the same position as modern scholars. Although no doubt much more was available to the author of the *Ath. Pol.* in the way of earlier attempts to relate the early history of Athens, the *Ath. Pol.* was constructed primarily from written sources. And for the Aristotelian researcher, as for us, that meant a mix of texts contemporary with the events they related to, such as the poetry of Solon, and stories of those events told very much later and as part of a larger story.

Modern attempts to construct the history of the Athenian constitution traditionally focus their discussions on three individuals – Solon, Kleisthenes, and Ephialtes.[4] It is traditional to talk of the 'reforms' of Solon, the 'revolution' of Kleisthenes, and either the reforms or the revolution of Ephialtes.[5] For these three episodes we have very different sorts of evidence.

Only the flimsiest of oral traditions seems to have surrounded Solon, who became reputed as one of the Seven Sages, and whose reforms are normally dated to the year in which he was the (eponymous) arkhon (chief magistrate) at Athens (594/3). Ancient writers – and Plutarch, around 100 AD, wrote a whole *Life of Solon* – attempted to flesh those out by drawing on Solon's own poetry and, to a much lesser extent, looking into the laws that he introduced. In consequence, the tradition on Solon is somewhat schizophrenic: on the one hand there is a Solon of fantasy, to whom ancient writers, from Herodotos in the fifth-century onwards, attribute all sorts of pieces of verbal and practical wisdom; on the other, there is the Solon who can be reconstructed from his laws and from what he himself says in his poetry, some of which is directly political.[6] Whether we regard Solon as the founder of Athenian democracy depends upon both what exactly we think his laws established and what we think his intentions were. In assessing the former we are hampered because whereas some of his other laws

---

4. Hignett (1952) is now seriously out-dated, but has not been replaced. Most general books about Athenian democracy start with some history of the constitution, cf. Ober (1989) ch.2, Hansen (1991) ch.3.
5. Cf. Osborne (2006).
6. On Solon's poetry see Irwin (2005), Noussia-Fantuzzi (2010).

continued in use throughout the fifth and fourth centuries, his constitutional rules were at least partly replaced by Kleisthenes.[7] In assessing the latter we are hampered by the difficulty of understanding what are often only short quotations of poetry without knowing the original context.

But if the deficiencies of the sources prevent our acquiring a definitive view of Solon, what the ancient sources say and do not say should nevertheless be taken seriously. Although the economic crisis faced by Solon has attracted much scholarly attention, the evidence for it is thin. It is clear that later writers knew very little about what the 'Sixth-parters' (*Hektēmoroi*) were or what Solon's 'shaking off of burdens' (*Seisakhtheia*) consisted in. That he did something to rescue the poor from conditions of slavery is clear on his own testimony, but it is equally clear from various of his laws that he protected rather than undermined property rights, and sought to bring order and fairness rather than to upturn society. The Solonian census classes indicate a desire to see a person's duties reflect their resources rather than a desire to abolish distinctions between rich and poor.

In the case of Kleisthenes, our primary evidence comes from the *History* of Herodotos, who told the story of Kleisthenes' reforms in order to explain how Athens moved from a minor to a major power in Greece, and so came to be in a position to play a leading rôle in the defeat of the Persian invasion. Herodotos was convinced that being a democracy made a fundamental difference to Athens, and so gave a brief account of the reforms in order to show something of the magnitude of the changes wrought. As other parts of his work – and particularly the 'constitutional debate' in book 3.80–82 – show, Herodotos had an interest in political theory. He also had an interest in day-to-day politics, and so offers us an account of how Kleisthenes got into a position to introduce the new constitution. Almost all later accounts of Kleisthenes depend upon Herodotos.

Working out what the Kleisthenic political arrangements were and exactly how the institutions he created operated depends on reading back from fifth- and fourth-century history. How far all the rules about frequency of office-holding, choice of officials by lot, etc. were in place immediately after Kleisthenes is not clear, but the limited extent of the reforms we do hear of later encourages us to think that the basic structure familiar from the later fifth and fourth century was indeed established by Kleisthenes.

That there is much we do not understand, even about the early fifth-century constitution, is undeniable. This is most obviously the case when it comes to the rôle of the Areopagos and the reforms of Ephialtes. Given that Ephialtes' reforms led to his assassination, there is little doubt that their passing was contentious. Nevertheless, Thucydides did not think they merited any attention in his account of events between the Persian and Peloponnesian Wars in book 1 of his *History*, and we rely for our knowledge on the *Ath. Pol.*, on Aristotle's *Politics*, and on quotations from fourth- and third-century historians by Plutarch in his *Life of Kimon*. Although this event was much closer in time to Aristotle and his team than Solon's reforms, the material available to them was much less adequate.

Modern historians' primary interest must be in understanding what the constitutional rules were that Solon, Kleisthenes, and Ephialtes introduced. But it is important to realize also that the stories that the Athenians in the classical period told themselves

---

7. It is a further complication that in the classical period all sorts of laws were attributed to Solon that were in fact of much more recent origin; see Thomas (1994). Moreover, not all texts of laws that appear in law-court speeches are genuine Athenian laws (see notes to **6** and **18**).

about the history of their constitution actively shaped their political expectations and attitudes. Although the selection of sources below, particularly on Solon, is largely restricted to material which sheds light on particular constitutional rules, the authority given to Solon by the often anachronistic anecdotal material that circulated in classical Athens did play a part in creating respect for Athenian democratic institutions, and particularly in promoting Athenian attachment to popular jury courts.

For all aspects of the history of the Athenian constitution discussed by the Aristotelian *Constitution of the Athenians*, P.J. Rhodes' *A Commentary on the Aristotelian* Athenaion Politeia (Oxford, 1981; revised edition 1993) remains invaluable.

I   WHAT DID SOLON DO?

What the Athenians said in the fourth century

1   This (the restoration of democracy in 403) was the eleventh in number of the changes. For the first alteration of the original arrangements was the responsibility of Ion and those who helped him found the city – for it was then that they were first divided into four 'tribes' and established the 'tribe-kings'. Second, and the first change after this relating to the order of the constitution, was the change that happened under Theseus, which moved slightly away from monarchy. After this the change under Drakon occurred in which the Athenians first wrote up laws. Third, after civil strife, came the change under Solon from which democracy took its beginning. Fourth came the tyranny under Peisistratos. Fifth was Kleisthenes', after the overthrow of the tyrants, and this was more populist than Solon's. Sixth was the change after the Persian Wars, when the Council of the Areopagos took charge. Seventh, coming after this, was the change which Aristeides pointed the way to, but Ephialtes finished when he overthrew the Council of the Areopagos. Under this constitution it came about that the city made many errors because of the demagogues because of the rule over the sea. Eighth was the establishment of the Four Hundred, and after this, ninth, democracy again. Tenth was the tyranny of the Thirty and the Ten. Eleventh was that after the return from Phyle and from Peiraieus, from which it has prevailed until now, always adding power to the people. For the people itself has made itself sovereign over everything, and it administers everything through decrees and the lawcourts, in which the people is in charge. For even the judgements of the Council are brought before the people. And this seems to be the right thing to do, since the few are more corruptible than the many, whether by money or favour.

[Aristotle] Constitution of the Athenians 41.2

This summary of constitutional changes comes at the end of the first part of the Aristotelian *Constitution of the Athenians*. This work, which dates to the 330s and 320s, depends upon research done by earlier historians of Athens. These historians traced Athens' history back into mythical times. The fluidity of what might be claimed about Athenian history is reflected here in the mention of the 'constitution of Drakon'; this is included in the list since it has been discussed in chapter 4 of the *Constitution*, but it is not a numbered change, presumably because the source for this list did not know about it. Modern scholars have suspected that the 'constitution of Drakon' in chapter 4 in fact derives from a political pamphlet written in association with the oligarchic revolutions of the late fifth century.

2   After that, there was civil strife between the nobles and the mass of the people for a long time. For the whole political arrangement was oligarchical both in every other respect and, in particular, poor men were enslaved to the rich, both themselves and their wives and their children. They were called '*Pelatai*' and '*Hektēmoroi*' (sixth-parters), for that was the rent that they paid for cultivating the land of the rich. All the land was in the hands of a few, and those who did not pay their rent could be sold into slavery, themselves and their children. For everybody loans were on the security of the body, until the time of Solon. He was the first to become a leader of the people.

[Aristotle] Constitution of the Athenians 2.1–2

This brief account of Solon's social and economic reforms has been very influential, but it appears to come from a different source from that used for the fuller account of Solon's reforms later in the Aristotelian *Constitution*. That later account makes no mention of the *hektemoroi*. The explanation of the name *hektemoroi* here has been doubted since rent of one sixth seems relatively low, rather than high, and unlikely of itself to bring on economic crisis.

3   When Solon got charge of affairs, he freed the people for the present and for the future by prohibiting loans on security of the body. He made laws and enacted a cancellation of debts both private and public, a measure which people call *seisakhtheia* ('shaking off of burdens'), since in this way they shook off their load.

[Aristotle] *Constitution of the Athenians* 6.1

Abolition of debts and redistribution of land were the rallying cry of radical politics in the fourth century, and it was natural for fourth-century writers to try to find them in the policies of earlier 'radical' figures. The prohibition on debt-slavery here is likely to have been a major factor in the development of imported chattel slavery in Athens.

4   He (Solon) divided the people into four classes by an assessment of wealth, just as they had been divided before – *pentakosiomedimnoi*, *hippeis*, zeugites and thetes. And he distributed the magistracies to men from the *pentakosiomedimnoi*, *hippeis* and zeugites – the nine arkhons, the treasurers, the *poletai*, the Eleven, and the *kolakretai* – giving to each the magistracy suitable for the size of their assessed wealth. To those assessed as thetes he gave only a share in the assembly and the courts. A man came into the *pentakosiomedimnoi* if he produced 500 bushels, counting wet and dry together, into the *hippeis* if he produced 300. But some say if those able to support horses were *hippeis*; they take the name of the class as evidence, on the grounds that the name was given from that capacity, and the dedications made by men in the past; for a statue of Diphilos is dedicated on the Akropolis on which is inscribed the following: 'Anthemion son of Diphilos dedicated this to the gods, after he had exchanged the class of thete for that of *hippeus*', and a horse is part of this dedication, as a witness that that that was what the *hippeus* meant. Still, it is more reasonable to suppose that *hippeis* were defined by measures, like *pentakosiomedimnoi*. Those who produced 200, both sorts together, were zeugites and the rest were thetes and had no part in any magistracy. So even now, whenever a man who is about to be allotted some magistracy is asked what class he come into, no one would ever say he was a thete.

[Aristotle] *Constitution of the Athenians* 7.3–4

The division of Athenians by wealth rather than birth has been thought the fundamental break between the putative 'aristocratic' Athens of before 600 and later Athens where family connections were relatively unimportant except in terms of religious cult (see below on *genē*). Whether the Aristotelian *Constitution* is correct in its description of the wealth required for each class is much debated. No dedication remotely like that claimed here for Anthemion has survived on the Athenian Acropolis. For the modern debate see van Wees (2006), and see generally van Wees (2013).

And some things they almost certainly made up…

5   Of all these, none is our discovery or new, but the ancient law, which he has broken, orders laws to be made in the following way: if anyone thinks that one of the current laws is not good he is to bring a case against it, and propose a replacement law which he would bring in if that law was repealed, and when you have heard the case you are to choose the better law. [90] For Solon, who laid down this way of making laws, did not think that it was right that the *thesmothetai*, who have been chosen by lot over the laws, should hold office only when they have been scrutinized twice, in the Council and among you in the court, but the laws themselves, which govern how they hold their magistracy and how you all live, should be made at a particular chance moment and be valid never having been scrutinised.

Demosthenes 20.89–90 (355)

The tendency to describe any existing law as Solonian was widespread among fourth-century Athenian orators, particularly when they wish to contrast what they believe to be more incompetent recent practice. In fact the procedure for scrutinizing proposed replacement laws was slightly different, according to a law included in the text of another Demosthenes speech (**6**). For the complicated question of the rules about law-making in the fourth century see Canevaro (2013b).

6   LAW: If someone who has repealed one of the existing laws proposes in its place a law that is not suitable for the Athenian people or which contradicts an existing law, a case may be brought against him according to the law which covers the bringing of an unsuitable law.

Demosthenes 24.33 (summer 353)

The texts of the laws that appear in the speeches of Athenian orators have been added at various points in the transmission of the text, and cannot be trusted automatically; their genuineness has to be established on a case-by-case basis. See Canevaro (2013a).

7   I used to wish, Athenians, that the Council of 500 and the Assemblies were correctly run by those who presided over them, and that the laws continued to be valid which Solon made about the orderly behaviour of speakers, so that it was possible, as the laws command, first for the most elderly of the citizens to come to the speaker's platform soberly, with no heckling or disturbance, and advise the city best from his experience, and second for any of the other citizens who wished to reveal their judgement by age, separately and one-by-one, as each could. That is how I think that the city would be best run and disputes would be fewest.

Aiskhines 3.2 (330)

For Aiskhines' invention of past practices to contrast to contemporary politics see Lane Fox (1996).

The evidence of Solon's poetry

8   Our city will never be destroyed through the action of Zeus and the intentions of the blessed immortal gods. For Pallas Athene, such a stout-hearted guardian, born of a mighty father, holds her hands over it. But it is the citizens themselves

who display a will to destroy a great city by their acts of thoughtlessness and through subservience to money. The mind of the leaders of the people is unjust; many painful sufferings are ready and waiting for them because of their great arrogance (*hubris*). For they do not know how to keep control of excess or to enjoy in an orderly and peaceful manner the festivities of the present feast [*A line is lost at this point*] they grow wealthy, persuaded to act unjustly [*A line is lost at this point*] They do not spare either sacred or private property, they steal and snatch, one from one source, one from another, and they do not even take notice of the august foundations of Justice, who is silently conscious of what is done now and what was done, and who in time comes to exact punishment for everything. This is now coming upon the whole city, an inescapable wound, and the city has rapidly approached evil enslavement, which arouses civil strife and slumbering war, which destroys the fair youth of many. For at the hands of cruel men the much-loved city is rapidly worn down with conspiracies dear to the unjust. These are the evils that revolve among the people, and many of the poor are arriving in a foreign land, sold, and bound in shameful fetters. [*A line is lost at this point*] And so the public evil comes home to each man and the gates of the yard are no able to withstand, but it leaps over the high fence and finds people out everywhere, even if someone hides in the innermost corner of a room. My spirit urges me to teach the Athenians that lawlessness (*dusnomia*) brings the most trouble to the city, but lawfulness (*eunomia*) shows everything to be orderly and fitting, and often puts fetters on the unjust, smoothes out what is rough, puts an end to excess, tones down arrogance, dries up the flourishing blossoms of ruin, straightens out crooked justice, makes gentle proud deeds, and puts an end to civil strife and puts an end to the anger of grievous conflict. It is through her agency that all things among men are fitting and rational.

Solon frg. 4 (quoted by Demosthenes 19.255)

Solon's poetry survives only in as far as it is quoted by later writers. Demosthenes quotes this poem to make a political point against Aiskhines. Tradition maintained that Solon put his political analysis into poetry because the political climate in Athens was such that he could not have said this in a political speech without being silenced. His is undoubtedly a critical voice, but his criticisms are extremely general.

9   I gave the people just as much privilege as is sufficient, not taking away from their worth and not giving yet more. I took thought that those who had power and were the leading men in wealth should suffer nothing unseemly. I took a stand and cast a mighty shield round both sides, allowing neither to be unjustly victorious.

Solon frg. 5 (quoted by [Aristotle] *Constitution of the Athenians* 12.1)

It is one of the virtues of the Aristotelian *Constitution* that it endeavours to support its presentation of Solon by quoting from his poetry. This leaves no doubt that Solon presented himself as the man in the middle, the man who restrained the rich while not simply transferring power to the poor.

10   In this way the people would best follow their leaders, neither let loose too much nor restrained too much. For excess breeds arrogance (*hubris*), whenever much prosperity comes to people whose mind is not fitting.

Solon frg. 6 (quoted by [Aristotle] *Constitution of the Athenians* 12.2)

11   Some came for plunder; they had hopes of wealth, that thought, each of them, that he would find much prosperity and that I, though I used gentle words, would display a harsh intentions. Empty were their thoughts then, and now, angry with me, they all look askance as upon an enemy. They should not. For I have accomplished, with the gods' help, what I said I would, and I did not do anything else, fruitlessly; it gives me no pleasure to achieve something using the violence of tyranny or that the good (rich) should have an equal share of the fatherland's rich earth with the bad (poor).

Solon frg. 34 (quoted by [Aristotle] *Constitution of the Athenians* 12.3)

The use of evaluative moral language ('good', 'bad') to refer to differences of wealth (rich, poor) is common in archaic authors and is found still in the Old Oligarch.

12   Did I stop before achieving any of the aims for which I gathered the people together? May black Earth, the greatest mother of the Olympian gods, bear witness to this in the court of time: I took up from her the boundary-stones, which were fixed in many places, and once enslaved she is now free. I brought back to Athens, their fatherland founded by the gods, many who had been sold, some unjustly, others justly, along with those who had fled through necessity and debt, men who no longer spoke the Attic tongue, as you would expect with those who had been wandering the world over. I freed those here who were in a state of unseemly slavery and feared the behaviour of their masters. I did this by the power of law, harnessing force and justice together, and I carried through my promises. I wrote laws that were the same for good (rich) and for bad (poor), making straight justice fit each. If someone other than I had taken the goad, some ill-intentioned and greedy man, he would not have controlled the people. For had I been willing to do what pleased the opposition then, or what the others devised for them, this city would have lost many men. For these reasons I made myself a stout defence all round, turning as a wolf turns when surrounded by many hounds.

Solon frg. 36 (quoted by [Aristotle] *Constitution of the Athenians* 12.4)

This poem, written in trimeters rather than elegiac couplets, offers the most detailed description of what Solon did. In antiquity the tearing up of the boundary-stones (*horoi*) was taken as a sign of abolition of debts, because in classical times the fact that a property was mortgaged was marked on such boundary-stones (see below **112**), and so tearing them up would be like ripping up a mortgage agreement. But it is more likely that these boundary-stones were just that, boundary stones, and that it is the attempt of private individuals to take over land that was not theirs (and so to 'enslave' it) that is in question. Since in **11** Solon declines to give equal shares of the rich earth to all, it is unclear what exactly happened to the earth that he 'freed'.

13   If I must come out into the open and rebuke the people, they would never have seen with their eyes, even in their dreams, what they now have. [*Some words are missing here*] And those who are greater in power and better would praise me and make me their friend.
For if someone else had obtained this office he would not have controlled the people and he would not have stopped until, having stirred up the milk, he had taken off the cream. But I stood between the opposing lines like a boundary-stone.

Solon frg. 37 (quoted by [Aristotle] *Constitution of the Athenians* 12.5)

Solon's laws and Solon's Courts:

14   Some people consider that Solon was a good lawgiver who put an end to
undiluted oligarchy, liberated the people from slavery and established the
traditional democracy with a skilful blending of the constitution: the council of
the Areopagos being an oligarchic element, the elective offices aristocratic, and
the jury courts democratic. In the case of the council and the election of officials,
Solon seems merely to have preserved existing institutions, but by his creation
of jury courts drawn from all the citizens, he does seem to have founded
democracy. Accordingly, some blame him for having ruined the rest of his work
by making the jury court, which was picked by lot, sovereign over all. For as
the jury courts grew strong, men humoured the people like a tyrant and so
converted the constitution into the existing democracy. Ephialtes and Perikles
docked the power of the Areopagos, and Perikles instituted payment for jury
service, and in this way each successive leader of the people enlarged the
democracy and advanced it to its present position.

   All this seems to have happened not in accordance with Solon's intentions
but as a result of circumstances; for because the common people had been
responsible for Athenian naval supremacy in the Persian Wars, they grew proud
and chose worthless men as their leaders when respectable people were
pursuing contrary policies. Certainly Solon himself seems to have given the
people only a necessary minimum of power – the election of officials and the
examination of their conduct; if the common people were not in control even
of this, they would be no better than slaves or foreign enemies. He provided
that all officials were to be drawn from the notable and the rich – the
pentakosiomedimnoi, and the zeugites and from a third order called *hippeis*.
The fourth order, the thetes, were excluded from office.

                                                        Aristotle *Politics* 1273b35–1274a21

The idea of the mixed constitution, with elements of monarchy, oligarchy, and democracy, was developed
in political thought in the classical period (and later famously applied to Rome by Polybios). Here Aristotle
interprets Solon's constitution in that way. Notable here are the stress which Aristotle puts both on the courts,
and on the way in which Solon may not have planned the consequences of his constitutional arrangements.

15   The following three points seem to be the most democratic features of Solon's
constitution: first and most important, the ban on loans on the security of the
person; second, permission for whoever wished to seek retribution for those
who were wronged; third, the one which is said to have contributed most to the
strength of the masses, the right to appeal to the jury court; for when the people
are masters of the vote, they are masters of the constitution. What is more,
because of the laws not having been written simply and clearly, but like the law
on inheritance and heiresses, it was inevitable that many disputes occurred and
the court ended up deciding all matters, both public and private. As a result,
some think that Solon deliberately made the laws unclear in order that the people
should have sovereign judgement. That is not in fact likely, rather it was that
he was unable to give an exhaustive definition of what was best. One should
not speculate on Solon's intention from how his laws work now, but on the basis
of the rest of his constitution.

                                                        [Aristotle] *Constitution of the Athenians* 9.1–2

What is at issue here is clarified by the following passage, as well as by Aristotle's general thoughts about law-making in **17**.

16 [The Thirty] were initially moderate towards the citizens and claimed to be running the ancestral constitution, and they took down from the Areopagos the laws of Ephialtes and Arkhestratos concerning the Areopagos and repealed all Solon's laws that gave rise to disputes, and so ended the sovereignty that rested with the courts, claiming that they were correcting the constitution and making it beyond dispute. One example: they made a man completely sovereign on the matter of bequeathing his property to whomsoever he wished, removing the additional qualifications 'unless he is mad or senile or under the influence of a woman' so that there was no way for vexatious litigants to get a foothold. They acted similarly in this case and in the case of other laws.

[Aristotle] *Constitution of the Athenians* 35.2

See below **24** for the full text of this law. The point is that without these qualifications there was no question for a court to answer, whereas with the qualifications every will could be disputed by those claiming that a man was not in his right mind (etc.) at the time he made his will.

17 It is also clear that the disputant's sole task is to show that the thing existed or did not exist, happened or did not happen; whether it was big or small or just or unjust, everything that the lawgiver did not define, it is up to the juror himself to decide and not to learn from the disputants. It is particularly the task of laws that have been properly made, in as far as it is possible, to define everything themselves and to leave as little as possible to those who judge. First because it is easier for one man or a few rather than many to form the sensible opinion and be able to pass laws and decide justice. Second, laws are made after long consideration, but court decisions happen on the spur of the moment, so that it is difficult for those passing judgement to express well what is just and expedient. But the greatest consideration of all is that the judgement of the lawgiver is not partial but about future events and universal, but the man sitting in the assembly or the court judges now about the present and particular case; in addition to this, what a man loves and hates at this moment and his own advantage often play a part preventing him sufficiently discerning the truth, but his judgement is clouded by personal pleasure and pain. So, as we say, on other matters the judge should decide as few things as possible. It is necessary to leave to the judges decisions about what happened or did not happen, what will be or will not be, what exists or does not exist: for these matters it is not possible for the lawgiver to foresee.

Aristotle *Rhetoric* 1354a26–1354b16

The multiple qualifications in Solon's inheritance law (**16** and **24**) show how hard it is in fact to achieve what Aristotle recommends. Arguably Solon had indeed decided in advance that valid wills could not be written by those who were mad or senile, etc., but rather than reducing the rôle of the court, this enlarged it since madness, senility, etc. are not simple matters to decide but are themselves subject to discussion (and all the more so when the person concerned is now dead!).

18   Solon, who made these laws... did not give just one way to those who wanted to exact justice from the offenders for each offence, but many ways. For he knew this, I think, that there was no way all those in the city would be equally clever, or bold, or moderate. So if he made the laws in such a way as to suit the moderate exacting justice then there would be many bad people about with the fear of being prosecuted. But if he made it suitable for those who are bold and able to speak, then private individuals would not be able to exact justice in the same way as these. He thought that it was right to deprive no one of obtaining justice, as each was able. So how could this come about? If he gave many ways through the laws against offenders, as for example in the case of theft. You are strong and trust yourself: make a summary arrest – you will risk a 1000 drakhma fine. You are weaker: bring in the magistrates and they will then manage the procedure. You are afraid even of that: use a *graphē*. You have no confidence in yourself and since you are poor could not pay a 1000 drakhma fine: bring a case for thefts before the arbitrator and you will run no risk.... Now none of these actions is the same. In the case of impiety in the same way, you can use summary arrest, a *graphē*, a case before the Eumolpidai, a denunciation before the Basileus. It is roughly like that for all the other offences.

Demosthenes 22.25–27 (between 357 and 354)

This rationalization of Solon's laws shows how much serious thought the Athenians gave in the fourth century to the rationale of their complicated legal system. Modern scholars dispute whether this passage should be treated as special pleading by Demosthenes or whether it reflects at least the way the law worked in the fourth century, if not Solon's own reasoning. See Osborne (1985/2010).

Solon's laws: some samples

Homicide:

19   LAW: If someone kills someone accidentally in the games, or knocking them down in the road, or having failed to recognise them in war, or having intercourse with a wife or a mother or a sister or a daughter or a concubine whom he keeps for the procreation of free children, in these cases he is not to be prosecuted for homicide.

Demosthenes 23.53 (352)

Solon included among his laws the existing laws on homicide that had been introduced a generation earlier by Drakon. Although the texts of the laws that appear in the speeches of Athenian orators have been added at various points in the transmission of the text, and cannot be trusted automatically, and their genuineness has to be established on a case-by-case basis (see Canevaro 2013a), in this case we may be confident that the law, also quoted in other places, is genuine. Not only are we otherwise told that Solon preserved Drakon's homicide laws unchanged ([Aristotle] *Constitution of the Athenians* 7.1) but we have other parts of Drakon's law preserved in its late fifth-century republication (see **113**). Other indications that this law has not been altered since the archaic period are its structure, the archaic term *damar* used for 'wife', and the concept of the 'concubine'.

Theft:

20   LAW: Whatever someone loses, if he receives it back, the thief is to receive a double fine, but if he does not receive it back, the double fine to be in addition to the additional penalty. The thief to be bound in the stocks by his feet for five days and as many nights if the Heliaia orders the additional penalty. Anyone who wants to can call for the additional penalty in the discussion of penalties.

Demosthenes 24.105 (summer 353)

This is another law cited also by others. The use of the stocks suggests it is an archaic law.

Verbal abuse:

21   If anyone speaks ill of the dead, even if he is abused by the children of the dead man, he is to be condemned to pay a fine of 500 dr., 200 to the public treasury and 300 to the individual.

Lex Cantabrig. 671.7

Laws against verbal abuse are further attested by Plutarch *Solon 21.1* and Lysias 10: 6–12, although Lysias does not call the laws Solonian. The *Lexicon Cantabrigiense*, though a late source, seems to preserve the wording of his law, but comparison with Plutarch, who cites laws about abuse of the living, suggests that its fines are a hundred times too high. See Ruschenbusch (2010) 63–7.

Water supply:

22   Since the land did not have a sufficient supply of water from perpetual streams or lakes or plentiful springs, but most people had to use dug wells, he wrote a law that where there was a public well within a *hippikon* (that is, a distance of four stades [740m]) they should use that, but where it was further away they should seek their own water. And if digging to a depth of ten fathoms (18 m) on their own land they find no water, then they could take it from a neighbour, filling a six *khous* jug of water twice a day (2 x 19.5 l).

Plutarch *Solon* 23.6

The depth to which a man is expected to dig his well his remarkable here, making it plausible that this law was as much to limit neighbours' claims to each other's water supply as to facilitate such claims.

Legitimacy:

23   If a father, or a brother sharing the same father, or a paternal grandfather betroths a girl on just conditions to be a wife, the children born from her are to be legitimate. And if none of these male relatives exists, if she is an heiress the man who has legal charge of her is to have her, if she is not, whatever man she is entrusted to is to have legal charge of her.

[Demosthenes] 46.18 (c.351)

The term for 'wife' is again here the archaic *damar*.

Wills and inheritance:

24   LAW: A man may dispose of his property by will as he wishes provided that he does not have legitimate male children and provided that he is not mad, senile, out of his mind by reason of one of the following: drugs, illness or the influence of a woman, or constrained by necessity or by a chain.

[Demosthenes] 46.14 (c.351)

This is the full law of which part is cited in the account of Solon and of the Thirty in the Aristotelian *Constitution of the Athenians* (above **15** and **16**).

25   If any man dies without having made a will, if he leaves female children the
property is to go with these, but if he does not, the following are to have legal
charge of the property: any brothers of the same father; any legitimate sons from
brothers are to obtain their father's portion; if there are no brothers or brothers'
sons (the paternal cousins and their sons) are to obtain the property in the same
way. Males and those born of males, whether they are in the same degree of
relationship or whether they are more distant relations, are to prevail. But if
there are no paternal relatives no more distant than cousins' sons, the maternal
relatives are to have legal charge of the property in the same way. If there are
no relatives on either side within the stated degree the closest paternal relative
is to get charge. There is no kinship for a bastard, either male or female, as far
as either religious or other rights and duties are concerned, from the arkhonship
of Eukleides (403/2).

Demosthenes 43.51 (date uncertain)

It appears to be the final clause regarding bastards that was added in 403/2. This is consistent with the
Athenian insistence, introduced in 451/0 but reaffirmed in 403/2 (**44** and **58** below), that all citizens should
have an Athenian mother as well as an Athenian father.

Heiresses:

26   The law seems strange and laughable which grants to the heiress that if the man
who has claimed her and has charge of her according to the law is not himself
able to be (sexually) intimate, she is to be have marital relations with his nearest
relatives. And some say that this is correct regarding those not able to have
intercourse but taking heiresses for the sake of the money and doing violence
to nature by law. For if they see the heiress having intercourse with the man she
wants they will either reject the marriage or keep it with shame, convicting
themselves of love of wealth and arrogance. And it is also a good decision that
the heiress have intercourse not with all but with whomsoever she wants of the
kin of the man, in order that the baby born should belong to the household and
be party of the family line. It further contributes to this end that bride be shut
up with the bridegroom eating up a quince together, and that the man who takes
her should have intercourse three times a month with the heiress. For even if
no children are born this produces honour and kindness from the man towards
his modest wife, taking away many of those differences which have
accumulated on each occasion and not allowing them to diverted in every way
by disagreements. In the case of other marriages, he reduced the dowries,
ordering that the woman being married bring three cloaks and equipment worth
a small amount and nothing else.

Plutarch *Solon* 20.2–4

The elaborate law about heiresses attests to the degree of detail that Solon's laws included and to Solon's
concern for property transmission and for sorting out matters that might otherwise lead to disputes. The
disregard for the woman's feelings in insisting that she marry her next of kin is combined with serious thought
about how to make the forced marriage work both at a functional level (producing the required heir to inherit
the property) and at a personal level.

Funerals:

27 The dead man must be laid out inside in whatever way he wants. The dead man is to be carried out to burial on the day after he has been laid out, before sunrise. The men are to walk in front, when the body is carried out, the women behind. No woman less than sixty years old is to enter the dead man's house, or to follow the man when he is taken to the tomb, except for those who are cousins or closer. Nor is any woman to enter the dead man's house when the corpse has been carried out except for those who are cousins or closer.

Demosthenes 43.62 (date uncertain)

28 He also established a law with regard to women going out and mourning and attending festivals that attempts to limit the disorderly and wanton: so he ordered that a woman should go out with no more than three cloaks and carrying no more than an obol's worth of food and drink, a basket no bigger than a cubit, and only by night if carried in a waggon with a light in front of it. He prohibited laceration of those mourning, composition of special laments and non-relatives wailing at burials. He did not allow sacrifice of an ox, nor putting more than three cloaks with the corpse, nor going to others' tombs apart from in the funeral procession itself.

Plutarch *Solon* 21.4–5

Funerals can be moments of high tension when rivalries get displayed and this seems to have been true in archaic Greece (see Seaford (1994), ch. 3). Solon's laws both show how much competition in material display there might be among the wealthy in archaic Athens and how central the rôle of women was in such display.

2   THE KLEISTHENIC REVOLUTION

Who was Kleisthenes?

29 So ended the affair of the suitors, and thus it was that the name of the Alkmeonids was noised abroad in Greece. One son of the marriage of Megakles and Agariste was Kleisthenes, the man who gave Athens her tribes and her democracy (*demokratia*). He was named after his maternal grandfather, the Sikyonian. Another son of Megakles was Hippokrates, father of another Megakles and another Agariste, name after Agariste the daughter of Kleisthenes. She married Xanthippos son of Ariphron. When she was pregnant, she dreamt that she had given birth to a lion. A few days later she gave birth to Perikles by Xanthippos.

Herodotos 6.131

This is the conclusion of Herodotos' account of how Kleisthenes tyrant of Sikyon found a husband for his daughter Agariste. Kleisthenes and Perikles both belonged to the same family – attesting not merely to Kleisthenes' origins among those brought up expecting to run Athens, but to the continued importance of family background, informally if not formally, through the fifth century.

30 [On]eto[rides]
[H]ippia[s]
[K]leisthen[es]
[M]iltiades

[Ka]lliades
[.....]strat[os]

A fragment of a list of Arkhons: ML 6c (c.425)

This list was only inscribed in the fifth century but seems to be a true record of the arkhons of the late sixth century. This fragment gives the arkhons for 6 years (527–6 to 522–1) during the rule of the Peisistratids in the 520s (the Hippias here is the son and successor of Peisistratos) and shows that, despite later claims that they had long been in opposition to the tyrants, the Alkmeonid family to which Kleisthenes belonged had been prepared to collaborate with the tyrants.

Political manoeuvres after the removal of the tyrants

31   After the dissolution of the tyrants they made a scrutiny (*diapsephismos*) on the grounds that there were many who shared in citizenship who did not belong.

[Aristotle] *Constitution of the Athenians* 13.5

The Aristotelian *Constitution* has a particular line about Kleisthenes' reforms being designed to mix up the people so as to obscure the origins of some dubious citizens (see **36**). It is not clear where this line came from, or how plausible a scrutiny of the citizen body, such as we know for the fifth and fourth centuries (below **46** and **75**) would have been in 510.

32   Athens had been great before, but now that she had been liberated from the tyrant, she became greater still. There were two men of influence in the city: Kleisthenes, a member of the Alkmeonid family, said to have bribed the Pythia, and Isagoras son Teisandros, a member of a distinguished family. I do not know the family's origin, but his kinsmen sacrificed to Zeus Karios. These two competed for power, and on being worsted, Kleisthenes took the people into his following. He subsequently raised the number of Athenian tribes from four to ten. They had previously been named after Geleon, Aigikores, Argades and Hoples, the four sons of Ion. Dropping these names, he selected names from those of other heroes, all of them natives apart from Aias. Though Aias was a foreigner, Kleisthenes added him as being a neighbour and ally.

Herodotos 5.66

The bribery of the Pythia (i.e. the Delphic priestess who gave utterance to oracles) referred to here is the bribery to get her to instruct all Spartans who consulted the oracle that they should remove the tyrant, Hippias, from power in Athens. The phrase Herodotos uses here for 'took the people into his following' implies the existence of political clubs (*hetaireiai*) such as we meet in the late fifth century (**48** cf. **121**). But it is likely that Herodotos is introducing language from his own time, and that nothing more than Kleisthenes' consciously deciding to seek popular support is involved. The four tribes into which the Athenians were previously ordered were found also in most cities of Ionia, which traced their origins back to Athens. Aias, identified here as a 'foreigner', was associated with the island of Salamis, which had been in Athenian control since the time of Solon. Zeus Karios is the manuscript reading here, but the amendment by Rhodes to Zeus Ikarios, that is Zeus of the deme of Ikaria, is plausible.

33   Kleisthenes of Athens was the grandson of Kleisthenes of Sikyon on his mother's side and was named after him. Out of contempt, I believe, for the Ionians, he did not wish the tribes of Athens to be the same as theirs, and so he followed his namesake's example. When he had brought over the previously despised people of Athens entirely on to his side, he renamed the tribes and increased their number. He raised the number of tribal chiefs from four to ten, and he also assigned the demes to the tribes in ten groups. Now that he had acquired the backing of the people, he was much more powerful than his opponents.

Herodotos 5.69

For Kleisthenes' family see above, **29**. It is a theme of Herodotos' *Histories* that the Ionians are despised. It was certainly the effect of changing the number and names of the tribes in Athens that Athens made herself look different from Ionian cities, but within 10 years of Kleisthenes' reforms the Athenians decided to send ships to support the Ionian cities in their revolt from Persia, leading directly thereby to the Marathon campaign and the Persian Wars. The old tribes seem not to have been formally abolished, simply to have been superceded for all but a tiny range of religious purposes (see Kearns 1985).

34   Thus did Athens grow in strength, and it is plain, not just from the instance but generally, that freedom of speech (*isegoriē*) is a good thing. Under the tyrants, the Athenians were no better fighters than any of their neighbours, but when they had been liberated from the tyrants, they became by far the best. This shows that under oppression they let themselves be beaten because they were working for a master, but once they had been freed, each man was eager to achieve something for himself.

Herodotos 5.78

Herodotos is keen throughout his work to indicate both how central Athens was to the war against Persia and how important democracy was to Athens' performance. See also Herodotos' debate on the best constitution (below **422**).

35   After the overthrow of tyranny, Isagoras son of Teisandros, a friend of the tyrants, and Kleisthenes, of the Alkmeonid family, competed for power. As he was losing the party struggle, Kleisthenes attached the people to his cause, by proposing to give power to the masses.

[Aristotle] *Constitution of the Athenians* 20.1

Much of the account in the Aristotelian *Constitution* is derived from an intelligent reading of Herodotos and this passage is entirely dependent on **32** above.

36   For these reasons people trusted Kleisthenes. Then, as champion of the masses, in the fourth year after the overthrow of the tyranny, in the arkhonship of Isagoras (508/07), he first distributed all the citizens into ten tribes instead of the existing four, wishing to mix them up, so that more could share in government. Hence the saying 'Don't judge by tribes', aimed at those wishing to examine ancestries. He then made the Council 500-strong instead of 400-strong – fifty from each new tribe, instead of a hundred from each old tribe ... He also divided the land by 'demes' into thirty parts – ten parts in the region in and around the city, ten in the coastal region, and ten in the interior – and he called these parts *trittyes* ('thirds'). He assigned three *trittyes* to each tribe by lot, in such a way that each tribe should have a share in every region. He made the men living in each deme fellow-demesmen, so that they should not refer to one another by their father's names (son of So-and-so), and thus expose the new citizens, but should refer to them by their demes (of such-and-such a deme). Hence, Athenians now refer to themselves by demes.

He also introduced 'demarkhs', with the same responsibilities as the old *naukraroi*; he had indeed replaced the old *naukrariai* with the demes. He named some of the demes after their localities and some after their founders; for not all founders of demes were still known. He allowed each *genē*, phratry and priesthood to retain its traditional privileges. To the tribes he assigned ten eponymous heroes, whom the Pythia chose from a short list of a hundred founding heroes.

[Aristotle] *Constitution of the Athenians* 21.1–6

For the Aristotelian *Constitution*'s interest in new citizens see above **31**. Here the basic information that Herodotos gives is fleshed out both with reference to the previous arrangements (e.g. the Council of 400 attributed to Solon, and the slightly mysterious *naukrariai* (perhaps local groups responsible for funding and rowing a ship?). The claim that Athenians stopped referring to individuals by their father's name does not correspond with the surviving evidence, which shows continued use of the father's name and gradual addition of the deme name. See Winters (1993) and see also below **337**. The demes seem to have been largely pre-existing villages, not new creations. Most plausibly Athenians were asked to register in whatever they considered their local village and wherever sufficient individuals clustered a 'deme' was recognized and ascribed a quota on the Council of 500 corresponding to the numbers who had registered there. The decision to have the Delphic oracle select the heroes after whom the tribes were named reflects the religious rôle of the new tribes.

37   A democracy of this (fourth) kind will also find useful such arrangements as Kleisthenes adopted at Athens when he wished to strengthen the democracy ... different tribes and phratries should be created, more in number; private cults should be reduced to a few public ones; and any device should be adopted to ensure that so far as possible everyone is mixed up together and old associations are dissolved.

Aristotle *Politics* 1319b19–27

Not all the devices listed here applied to Athens. Kleisthenes did change the tribes and increase their number, but he did not intervene with the phratries except in as far as the demes may have taken over some phratry rôles. The emphasis on mixture here is one shared with the Aristotelian *Constitution* (see above **31, 36**).

3   FIFTH-CENTURY CONSTITUTIONAL CHANGES

The Council of 500 and its powers; the introduction of ostracism

38   up to 500 dr., but not impose a larger fine...the Council in the Council chamber...The Athenian people decided at a meeting in the Lykeion...without the decision of a full assembly not declare war nor end war nor...without the decision of a full assembly not to punish with death...without a decision of a full assembly...however it wants. Not to be...within 30 days whenever it decides; the people is not to...any Athenian, not even one, neither for the Council nor...without the decision of a full assembly not to impose a fine on any Athenian not even one...or deliberation without the decision of a full assembly...however a full assembly decides...choose in the same way. The 500 are to give an account of their handling of public money in the Assembly before they cease from office...to the full assembly of the Athenian people whatever it wants...of the public money it is necessary that the Council...first sacred, then embassies, then public money...to the *prytaneis* and serve as councillor...

IG i³ 105.32–49 (c.409)

This fragmentary inscription was inscribed in the late fifth century, at the same time that the Athenians wrote up the 'Law of Drakon' (below **113**). But the law contained on this inscription is rather older, as is betrayed by some of the language ('decision of a full assembly'). Scholars debate whether it should be placed in the aftermath of Solon's reforms (and refer to the Council of 400) or in the aftermath of Kleisthenes' reforms (and refer to the Council of 500). The insistence on the limited powers of the Council and the ultimate responsibility of the Assembly arguably fits best with the period shortly after the introduction of the Council of 500 (cf. the introduction of the Councillors' oath, mentioned in the following passage).

39   When this happened, the constitution was much more democratic than that of Solon. Under the tyranny, the laws of Solon had perished through lack of use, and Kleisthenes, who was aiming for the support of the masses, introduced other new ones, including the law about ostracism. First, in the eighth year after this settlement, in the arkhonship of Hermokreon (501/00), they introduced the oath for the Council of 500 which they still swear. Then they began to elect the generals by tribes, one from each tribe, but the commander of the whole army was still the polemarkh. In the twelfth year after this, in the arkhonship of Phainippos (490/89), they won the battle of Marathon. Letting two years pass, now that the people were confident after their victory, they then, for the first time, used the law about ostracism. It had been passed out of suspicion of men in positions of power, because Peisistratos had become tyrant as popular leader and general.

The first man to be ostracised was a kinsman of his, Hipparkhos son of Kharmos, of Kollytos. It was because of him in particular that Kleisthenes had carried the law, since he wanted to drive him out. Exercising the people's customary mildness, the Athenians had allowed those of the tyrants' friends who were not implicated in their misdeeds during the disturbances to go on living in the city, and Hipparkhos was their leader and champion. In the very next year, in the arkhonship of Telesinos (487/86), for the first time since the tyranny, the nine arkhons were picked by lot on a tribal basis from a short list of 500 elected by the members of the demes: before this all the arkhons had been elected. They also ostracised Megakles son of Hippokrates, of Alopeke. For three years they continued to ostracise friends of the tyrants, on whose account the law had been carried; but after that, in the fourth year (485/84), they started to remove anyone else who seemed too powerful, and the first of those not involved in the tyranny to be ostracised was Xanthippos son of Ariphron.

[Aristotle] *Constitution of the Athenians* 22.1–6

For the Council oath see **139**. The gap between the supposed introduction of ostracism by Kleisthenes and its first use almost 20 years later has surprised scholars, who sometimes suggest that ostracism was invented only at the time that it was first used. See Forsdyke (2005) 281–4.

40   The procedure was, in outline, like this. Each voter took a potsherd (*ostrakon*) and after writing on it the name of whichever citizen he wished to remove, he took it to a place in the Agora which was fenced round with barriers. The arkhon first counted the total number of ostraka cast; for if there were fewer than 6,000 voters, the ostracism was invalid. Then they sorted the *ostraka* by names, and the one whose name had been written by the greatest number of voters was sent into exile for ten years, though he retained the income from his property.

Plutarch *Aristeides* 7.4–5

It is a crucial part of ostracism that it did not involve loss of property. A man who was ostracized could live off the proceeds of his property while in exile and then return 10 years later to enjoy full political rights and re-enter political life. On the eve of the Persian wars the Athenians did recall those who had been ostracized, and they played a major part in Athenian success in the war. For later ostracisms see **188, 295, 406**.

The Council of the Areopagos and its powers

41   So then the city made progress up to this point, strengthening itself little by little along with the democracy. But after the Persian Wars the council of the Areopagos gained power again and administered the city, having taken the leadership not through any public decision but because it had been responsible for the sea-battle at Salamis. For when the generals were at a loss what to do and had made an announcement that every man should save himself, it was the council of the Areopagos that provided eight drakhmas to every man and handed it over and embarked them on the ships. This is the reason why they took second place to it in esteem, and the Athenians were well ruled at that time.

[Aristotle] *Constitution of the Athenians* 23.1–2

42   One example is the council of the Areopagos which, after it had distinguished itself in the Persian Wars, seemed to have tightened up the constitution, another, the naval crowd which, after it was responsible for the victory off Salamis and so for the city's predominance resulting from its naval power, made the democracy stronger.

Aristotle *Politics* 1304a20–24

As these two passages show, by the late fourth century there was speculation about how democracy changed after the Persian Wars and why. The story about the Areopagos, first found in these texts, seems likely to be a 'back-projection' from Ephialtes' reforms. Those reforms demanded that the Areopagos was significant, and so a story had to be invented to explain how it came to be significant. But this story about how the Areopagos increased its reputation by putting the Athenians onto the ships to win the sea battle at Salamis had to fight against another story current in the fourth century which held that it was precisely the people's rôle in Salamis that made the Assembly, and thus democracy, stronger.

43   For some seventeen years after the Persian Wars the constitution in which the Areopagos was dominant survived, though it gradually declined. As the masses increased, Ephialtes son of Sophonides became the champion of the people. He appeared to be both incorrupt and loyal to the constitution. He attacked the Council of the Areopagos. First of all, he removed many of its members, prosecuting them for their conduct in office. Then in the arkhonship of Konon (462/1) he took away all the accretions which had made possible their guardianship of the constitution, giving some to the Council of 500 and some to the people and jury courts.

[Aristotle] *Constitution of the Athenians* 25.1–2

This is the most detailed surviving ancient account of Ephialtes' reforms. The Aristotelian *Constitution* later

(27.1) mentions attacks on the Council of the Areopagos by Perikles, and Aristotle in *Politics* (**14**) and other ancient sources describe a joint attack by Ephialtes and Perikles. The Aristotelian *Constitution* elsewhere (**16**) implies a joint attach by Ephialtes and Arkhestratos, and this chapter itself goes on to make chronologically impossible claims about Themistokles. All of this strongly implies that there was little certain knowledge in the fourth century about who had done what exactly to the powers of the Areopagos. What is undisputed is that the only serious powers left to the Areopagos were as a homicide court. It is these powers that are celebrated in Aiskhylos' *Eumenides* which was produced less than four years after the reforms, in 458. For a full discussion of the Areopagos see Wallace (1985). See also **1, 230, 446**.

Eligibility of office and for citizenship

44   In other respects the Athenians did not conduct their affairs with the same attention to the laws as before, but they did not at first tamper with the appointment of the nine arkhons. However, in the sixth year after the death of Ephialtes they decided that zeugites should be admitted to the short list from which the nine arkhons were picked by lot, and Mnesithides was the first zeugite arkhon (457/6). All arkhons before that had been *hippeis* or *pentakosiomedimnoi*, and the zeugites had held only routine offices, except when some aspect of the law was ignored. In the fifth year after this, in the arkhonship of Lysikrates (453/2), the thirty so-called deme justices were instituted again. In the third year after that, under Antidotos (451/0), the number of citizens caused them to decide, on the proposal of Perikles, that a man should not be a member of the citizen body unless both his parents were citizens.

[Aristotle] *Constitution of the Athenians* 26.2–4

The various reforms detailed in this passage seem mainly to be fall-out from Ephialtes reform of the Areopagos. The Areopagos Council was formed of ex-arkhons and the inclusion of zeugites, that is men of the second lowest Solonian census class (see **4**), to the arkhonship follows the decision in 487/6 to choose arkhons by lot rather than election (**39**). Reducing the status of the members of the Areopagos Council and docking the Council's powers were both moves to lessen its prestige. The introduction of deme judges can be seen as a way to eliminate minor matters from the popular jury-courts to which business from the Areopagos Council had been transferred. The introduction of pay for the courts (below **45**) in these years similarly reflects the increased load on the court. The one change mentioned here that seems quite different is Perikles' citizenship law. The decision to impose strict birth criteria on Athenian citizens contrasts with the Aristotelian view that the introduction of democracy had allowed ill-qualified people to become citizens (**36**). The explanation given here, that numbers of Athenian citizens had become too great, seems plausible on the basis of what we know of Athenian population in the fifth century: there does indeed seem to have been an increase in citizen numbers between the Persian and Peloponnesian Wars that cannot be accounted for plausibly by natural increase (see Patterson (1981), Watson (2010)). For the consequences of the law for the status of women see Osborne (1997/2010).

Pay for jurors and magistrates

45   SOKRATES: But tell me this as well: are the Athenians said to have been improved by Perikles or, quite the reverse, corrupted by him? What I hear is that by being the first to introduce pay, Perikles has made the Athenians lazy, cowardly, talkative and money-loving.

Plato *Gorgias* 515e

The pay that we know Perikles to have introduced is pay for service as a juror (**14, 237–42**), introduced in the 450s.

Scrutiny of the citizen body?

46   But when, after the King of Egypt had sent gifts to the people, it was necessary to divide 40,000 *medimnoi* of wheat among the citizens, many court cases grew up against those who those who were bastards according to that decree (Perikles' citizenship law) but had been unnoticed and overlooked, and many fell victim to attacks by informers. Slightly fewer than 5,000 men were convicted and removed from the register, and those who remained Athenian citizens and were judged Athenian on examination were 14,040.

Plutarch *Perikles* 37.4

It is not easy to find a context for this gift from the King of Egypt (the Athenians had been fighting in Egypt in support of an Egyptian rebellion from Persia in the 450s but had lost). Even if there is some truth in the story, the numbers given here, both for those disenfranchised and those left, are implausible although consistent with those given in other sources (Philokhoros *FGrH* 328 F 119). I have followed Ziegler's text here which removes the claim that those found not to be citizens were sold into slavery.

The invention of a committee of elders (*probouloi*)

47   Nevertheless they resolved, with such means as they had, to keep fighting... and to manage the affairs of the city more economically, and to elect a board of elders to advise on the situation as occasion should arise. In the panic of the moment they were ready to order everything aright; such is the way of the masses.

Thucydides 8.1.3–4

Defeat in the Sicilian expedition caused massive shock-waves in Athens. Democracy had been protected from its critics not least by its success, as the Old Oligarch acknowledges. When the force sent to Sicily was defeated so that 'out of many, few returned home', as Thucydides notes (7.87.6), those opposed to oligarchy seized their chance. The Athenians had no doubt invented new boards of magistrates at various points in the fifth century, not least in connection with ruling the empire (see below **273** for the total number of officials in fifth-century Athens), but the invention of the *probouloi* was different. The significance of the *probouloi* lay in their intended rôle in giving advice to the Assembly: to put elderly men in this position was certainly a move to expose democratic decision-making to moderating influence. We know Sophokles, the tragedian, and Hagnon, the founder of the Athenian colony at Amphipolis and father of Theramenes, to have been among the *probouloi*. See further **439**.

The oligarchic coup of 411

48   [65] As Peisandros and his colleagues sailed alongshore they abolished, as had been agreed, the democracies in the cities, and they also took some heavy infantry from certain places as their allies, and so reached Athens. There they found that most of their job had already been done by the members of the secret societies. Some of the younger men had combined to assassinate one Androkles secretly. He was the leader of the people and had been mainly responsible for the exiling of Alkibiades. They had got rid of him for two reasons: partly because of his leadership of the people, but mainly because they wanted to gratify Alkibiades who was, they supposed, going to be recalled and make

Tissaphernes their friend. In the same way they secretly disposed of some other objectionable people. Their public proclamation that only those on active service should be paid and that no more than five thousand should have a share in government, and they should be those most able to benefit the city financially and physically.

[66] But this was mere window-dressing for the masses, since only the revolutionaries were going to govern. All the same the Assembly and the lot-selected Council continued to meet, but they discussed only what the conspirators approved: the conspirators supplied the speakers and vetted their speeches. Fear and the sight of the number of the conspirators ensured that nobody else now spoke in opposition; or if anyone did so speak, he was at once put to death in some convenient way. There was no search for the murderers, nor, if they were suspected, was punishment inflicted. The people kept quiet. They were so cowed that they counted it gain if they were spared violence even when they said nothing. They misjudged and thought that the conspiracy was much larger than it really was because of the size of the city and because they did not know one another. For the same reason it was impossible for anyone to voice his distress to another and so to concert retaliatory measures; for he would have had to speak either to someone he did not know or to someone he did know but could not trust. All democrats approached each other with suspicion, each thinking that the other was involved in what was going on. The conspiracy did include some whom no one would ever have believed would turn oligarchic. It was they who created the greatest distrust of others and who did most to make the few safe by establishing mutual distrust among the masses.

[67] It was at this point that Peisandros and his colleagues arrived, and they immediately set about the rest of the job. First they assembled the people and proposed the election of ten commissioners with full powers to draft a constitution and then on an appointed day to introduce to the people their proposals for the best way of governing the city. Afterwards, when the day came, the conspirators enclosed the Assembly at Kolonos – there is a temple of Poseidon a little under two kilometres (just over a mile) from the city – and the commissioners introduced just this one measure, that any Athenian should be free to propose any motion he pleased with immunity. They imposed severe penalties on anyone who prosecuted for unconstitutionality or otherwise harmed anyone for so doing.

Now at last it was plainly stated that all tenure of office under the existing order and all receipt of pay were at an end, and that five men were to be elected as presidents, who would in turn elect a hundred men, and that each of them would elect three men; and the resulting four hundred would enter the Council-house with full powers and govern as they judged best, and would convene the five thousand whenever they saw fit.

[68] It was Peisandros who moved this resolution, and all along he had seemed most eager to overthrow democracy; but the man who had shaped the whole enterprise to turn out as it had and who had been longest in charge was Antiphon, one of the ablest Athenians of his day. He proved exceptionally good at devising policies and expounding them. He did not willingly come forward to address the Assembly or any other such gathering: his reputation for cleverness made him the object of popular suspicion. He was, however, the one man best able

to help those who had to address a jury court or the Assembly and who consulted him on any point...

Phrynikhos also showed himself exceptionally eager for oligarchy. Afraid of Alkibiades and well aware that Alkibiades knew of his intrigues at Samos with Astyokhos (the Spartan admiral), he thought that it was unlikely that an oligarchy would ever recall Alkibiades. Once committed to the cause, he proved much the most resolute in the face of danger. Prominent also among the subverters of democracy was Theramenes son of Hagnon, an able speaker and analyst of situations.

Since it was the work of so many gifted men, the enterprise naturally prospered, great though it was. It was no easy matter to deprive the Athenian people of their freedom in about the hundredth year since the overthrow of the tyrants, seeing that throughout that period they had been subject to none, and that for more than half of it they had been accustomed to rule others as their subjects.

[69] Nobody opposed Peisandros. The Assembly ratified his proposals and was dissolved. They subsequently brought the Four Hundred to the Council-house in the following way. Because of the enemy at Dekeleia, all Athenians were constantly under arms, either on the wall or in the ranks. On the day those not in the know were allowed to go home as usual; those in the conspiracy were under orders to hang about unobtrusively at some distance from their arms. In the event of opposition to what was happening, they were to seize their arms and suppress it... When these dispositions had been made, the Four Hundred went, each with a dagger concealed about his person, accompanied by 120 young men, whom they employed whenever physical force was needed, and confronted the lot-selected Council who were in the Council-house. They told them to take their pay and go. They had brought them pay for the rest of their term and gave it to them as they left.

[70] When the Council left like this without a protest and the rest of the citizens stayed silent and made no move, the Four Hundred entered the Council-house. To begin with, they drew lots for a presiding committee of their own and merely offered prayers and sacrifices to the gods as they entered office. Later, however, they departed widely from the democratic system – except that, on account of Alkibiades, they did not recall the exiles – and governed the city by force. Some few men whom they thought better out of the way they put to death; others they imprisoned or exiled. They sent word to the Spartan king, Agis, at Dekeleia, saying that they wished to make peace and that he might well prefer to come to terms with them, now that they were in power, than with the unreliable masses.

Thucydides 8.65–70

This long account of the acts that led to the abolition of democracy in Athens in 411 and its replacement by the regime of the 400 is highly revealing both about the areas where democracy was vulnerable (e.g. suspicion of popular politicians; a belief that limiting voters to those who served as hoplites would be a good thing; hostility to those receiving public pay for 'doing nothing'; desperation to win the war and to avoid military mistakes; weakness in the face of the appeal of a charismatic leadership) and about the mechanics of politics (the importance of small groups; the problems of information-flow; the importance of personal contacts). One particularly striking feature is that many of those involved had earlier been very active within the democracy (most of all Peisandros himself).

Oligarchic success was, however, short-lived, partly because the Athenian troops on Samos had not been convinced and partly because the 400 did not manage to maintain unity (see below **438–45**). Democracy was restored and Athens fought on for another six years until the Athenian fleet was defeated in the Hellespont in 405 (at the Battle of Aigospotamoi) and the Spartans, controlling the sea, effectively starved Athens out. Spartan influence saw to the installing of an oligarchic régime (the Thirty, see **16**, **149**, **310–12**), but it too was short-lived, again in part because not united. In 403, democracy was restored.

4   THE CREATION OF FOURTH-CENTURY DEMOCRACY

The restoration of democracy in 403/2

49   The Athenians seem to have handled the disasters that happened to them both privately and publicly in the most admirable and politically wise way. Not only did they wipe out blame over what had happened before, but they even all paid back together to the Spartans the money which the Thirty had received for the war – even though the agreements only stipulated that each of the groups, those from the city and those from the Peiraieus, should pay back separately – considering that it was a good idea to make this first step towards concord...
In the arkhonship of Pythodoros (404/3) the people took charge of affairs and set up the current constitution, and they seemed justifiably to take charge of the constitution since it was the people who had made the return of its own initiative.

[Aristotle] Constitution of the Athenians 40.3–41.1

The amnesty agreement which the Athenians made 'not to remember past wrongs' was much praised in antiquity – even though a number of notorious breaches occurred, including effectively the condemnation and execution of Sokrates where the issue of his political views and the political actions of some of his pupils lurks in the background (see below p. 33). There is a problem with the date given here: the arrangements for the restored democracy are repeatedly dated elsewhere to the arkhonship of Eukleides (403/2) (see below **51**, **52**, **53**), not that of Pythodoros. See generally Wolpert (2002).

50   When you returned from the Peiraieus, you saw that some of the citizens were starting to make vexatious prosecutions and trying to break the agreements. Because you wanted to stop them and to show others that you had not made the agreement under compulsion but thinking that it was in the city's interest, you made the law, on Arkhinos' proposal, that if anyone brought a case in violation of the oaths, the defendant could put in a special plea and the arkhons would hold a case about that first, and the special pleader was to speak first, and whoever lost the case be subject to a fine of one sixth in order that those who dared to break the amnesty might not only be convicted of oath-breaking and endure divine punishment for that, but also suffer immediate punishment.

Isokrates 18.2–3 (400–399)

As commonly, Isokrates here assumes an identity between the Athenians who are gathered in the court and the Athenians who had made decisions on new laws. The 'special plea' invented in 403/2 to protect the amnesty came to be used generally to claim that a case was inadmissible. Demosthenes *Speeches* 32–38 are all special pleas of this sort. Arkhinos was responsible for a number of measures designed to prevent the Athenians reacting too strongly to the Thirty and receives special praise from the Aristotelian *Constitution* 40.2 for this (see also **53**).

The revision of the laws

51   When you returned from the Peiraieus, and you could have taken vengeance, you decided to pass over what had happened and you put saving the city before private revenge, and you decided not to remember what you had done to each other in the past. When you had decided this you chose twenty men, to look after the city until other laws had been made, and until that time to use the laws of Solon and of Drakon. [82] When you elected a Council by lot and chose law-makers (*nomothetai*), they found that there were many laws of Solon and Drakon to which many citizens were liable because of what had happened earlier. So you held an Assembly and deliberated about them and decided that when you had examined all the laws you would then write up in the stoa those laws that had been tested. Read out the decree:

[83] The people decided, on the proposal of Teisamenos, that the Athenians should keep their traditional constitutional arrangements, and use the laws, weights, and measures of Solon, and use the laws of Drakon which we used in past time. However many additions are needed, the lawmakers chosen by the Council are to put on display written up on boards by the Eponymous Heroes for anyone who wishes to consider, and are to hand over to the magistrates during this month. [84] The Council and the five hundred law-makers (*nomothetai*) whom the demesmen chose, are first to examine the laws that have been handed over once they have taken the oath. Any individual who wishes to may come to the Council and give any good advice that he has concerning the laws. Whenever the laws are passed, the Council of the Areopagos is to take care of the law in order that the magistrates use the laws that have been made. And write up those of the laws that are validated on the wall where they were formerly written up for anyone who wishes to consider.

[85] The laws were therefore examined, gentlemen, in accordance with this decree, and they wrote up those that were validated in the stoa. When they were written up we made the law which you all employ: read the law for me:

Magistrates are not, even on a single matter, to use an unwritten law... No decree, either of the Council or of the people is to prevail over the law. Nor is it possible to make a law about an individual unless the same law applies to all Athenians, unless six thousand voting secretly decide this... All the court cases and arbitrations that occurred in the democratic city are to be valid. The laws are to be employed from the arkhonship of Eukleides.

                                         Andokides 1.81–5 (399) and laws quoted in 1.87

Again here the speaker identifies the Athenians in the court with the Athenians who had made decisions in the Assembly. There is no reason to disbelieve Andokides' claim, made at his trial in 400 BC, that in 403 a commission was appointed to review the laws. Whether the texts of the decree of Teisamenos or the law quoted in chapter 87 are genuine, or invented on the basis of the surrounding text at some point in the transmission of the speech, is disputed. The case against genuineness is made by Canevaro and Harris (2012) 110–19 but some of their arguments are weak: given the exceptional circumstances, unique phraseology is not an argument against genuineness, and the identity between the text of the decree or law and what Andokides says can as well be caused by Andokides quoting the law as by the law being invented on the basis of what Andokides said about it. Nevertheless the differences, particularly in procedure, between what Andokides says and what the decree of Teisamenos lays down, and the incoherence of Teisamenos' decree, do not encourage the view that it is genuine. By contrast all the provisions of the law in chapter 87 appear to be genuine except possibly the provision that a law could be aimed at a single individual provided that 6,000 people voted for it. Other references to this law omit the exception. Fragments of the law-code inscribed as a result of the decision recorded in this passage survive. For the remaking of Athenian law in these years see **348** and Rhodes (1991).

52   LAW: Diokles said: The laws made before Eukleides in the democracy, and all the laws made under Eukleides that have been written up, are to be valid. The laws made after Eukleides and being made in the future are to be valid from the day on which each was made, except if some period is specified for a law to be in force. The secretary of the Council is to add the new law to the now existing laws within thirty days. For the future, let whoever happens to be the Secretary write in that the law is to be immediately valid from the day on which it was made.

Demosthenes 24.42 (summer 353)

This law is good evidence for the extent to which the Athenian considered Eukleides' arkhonship to be a new start.

A new alphabet

53   Arkhinos persuaded the Athenians to use Ionian letters in the arkhonship of Eukleides.

Theopompos *FGrH* 115 F155 (= Photius and Souda s.v. *Samion ho dēmos*)

Until this date most official inscriptions in Athens had used the 'Attic' alphabet, which had no letters eta, xi, phi, psi and omega, and represented various diphthongs by single vowels. The Ionic alphabet had all these letters and could be reckoned to represent the sounds of Greek more fully and less ambiguously. The Ionic alphabet had appeared in a number of inscriptions over the last quarter of the fifth century, and to some extent what happened in 403/2 was merely the official confirmation of what was in any case becoming regular practice. Nevertheless, there are reasons for thinking that this change was not simply the change to a functionally better-suited alphabet. Both the timing (immediately on the restoration of democracy), and the proposer (Arkhinos, for whom see above **50**) urge that this was a politically charged gesture. Arkhinos' proposal seems to have been motivated by a desire to ensure that in rejecting oligarchy the Athenians did not turn their back on a wider world. The Ionic alphabet was a symbol of cosmopolitanism. See D'Angour (1999).

The question of who should be a citizen

54   I think that the only salvation for the city is this, that all Athenians should share civic rights, since even when we were in possession of walls and the navy and the money and the allies we did not put our minds to how to expel some Athenian from civic rights but even gave the Euboians rights of intermarriage. And now are we now going to get rid of the existing citizens? We will not, if you obey me, raze ourselves along with the walls, large numbers of hoplites and knights and archers. If you keep hold of them, you will secure your democracy, get more power over your enemies, and be in a better position to benefit your allies.

Lysias 34.3–4 (403)

This is an extract from a speech opposing the proposal to limit Athenian citizenship to those who owned land. That such a proposal was moved is a sign of the depth of the debate in 403 BC about what was the right sort of constitution for Athens.

The introduction of pay for the assembly

55   At first they decided against giving pay to the Assembly, but when the people did not go to the Assembly and the *prytaneis* were coming up with many schemes in order that the masses should be present when it was necessary to decide things by vote, Agyrrhios first made provision for payment of an obol, and after this Herakleides of Klazomenai, nicknamed 'The King' set it at two obols, and Agyrrhios again at three obols.

[Aristotle] *Constitution of the Athenians* 41.3

The exact date at which pay for attending the Assembly was introduced is not clear. Since the rate of 3 obols was reached by the time of Aristophanes' *Women at the Assembly* of c.392 it is plausible that the 1-obol rate was introduced shortly after 403/2. For earlier attempts to use the stick, rather than the carrot, to get citizens to attend the Assembly, see **198**. Agyrrhios is variously connected to money-matters. He had combined with Arkhinos at some point before 405 to reduce the payment for comic poets at the Dionysia (scholiast to Aristophanes' *Frogs* 367), he was himself involved in farming the import and export tax in the years down to 401 (Andokides 1.133–6), he was imprisoned for embezzlement (Dem. 24.134–5), and on his release he proposed a law about collecting tax on Imbros, Lemnos and Skyros in grain (RO 26).

Part II: Athenian Democratic Institutions

Note B: on rules and their interpretation

Whereas the first part of the Aristotelian *Constitution of the Athenians* is a chronological history of constitutional changes (**1**), the second part is a description of the institutions of Athenian democracy as they worked at the time the *Constitution* itself was written in the 330s and 320s BC. This is invaluable, not only because it is the only systematic discussion of the institutions of Athenian democracy, but because it shows how someone resident in Athens thought that the constitution hung together as a whole. Nevertheless, it is in many ways an ideal construct, describing how the constitution should work rather than illustrating the constitution in action. In fact there are very few allusions in the second half of the *Constitution of the Athenians* to particular historical events.

The passages in the following section attempt to illustrate both what the formal institutional arrangements were and how those institutions worked in practice. For the latter we rely variously on Aristophanic comedy, the orators, and, for certain sorts of practice, inscriptions. Between them these forms of evidence cover roughly a hundred years, with comedy illuminating practice in the late fifth century and oratory practice during the fourth century. But we should beware of thinking that just because the institution was unchanged the way in which the institution worked was also unchanged. This is particularly a danger in the case of the lawcourts, where the vivid evidence of Aristophanes (particularly in *Wasps*) cannot safely be applied to the courts of the fourth century, and where fourth-century evidence may not apply to the fifth century.

In a number of areas there is reason to think that Athenian attitudes changed quite dramatically, even if the formal rules did not change. One of these is attitudes towards individuals who are active in public life. In the fifth century the award of public maintenance and a front seat in the theatre to Kleon after the victory at Pylos is one of very few exceptions to the rule that the Athenians never gave honours to citizens during their life-times for political services, but only to non-Athenians. During the fourth century the Athenians, both in the Assembly and in the demes and other sub-groups of the city, came to honour both individuals and groups for the ways in which they have performed their duties, and the issue of whether or not an individual or group ought to be rewarded became a major one. Together with this changed practice came a changed attitude to the ambitious man. In the fifth century open ambition led to suspicion, from the middle of the fourth century onward the Athenians publicly encouraged displays of ambition (*philotimia*, love of honour).

A perhaps related set of changes of attitude surrounds relations between Athenians and individuals in other Greek cities. Perikles' citizenship law of 451/0 (**57**) required that an Athenian had both an Athenian father and an Athenian mother to be a citizen. This already problematized the sort of international marriage that was a feature of wealthy Athenian families in the sixth century (see **29**). In the fourth century the possibility that one's children would not be citizens was thought insufficient deterrent to foreign marriages, and marrying a foreigner was itself made illegal.

The possibility of very significant changes in attitude, like these, complicates our interpretation of the 'rules' that governed Athenian civic life. For all that the great tragedies of the fifth century were repeatedly re-performed in the fourth century and the speeches over the war dead given annually repeated the sentiments pioneered by

Perikles and others in the fifth century, there is good reason to think that the Athenian outlook on the world was quite different. The philosophical schools of Plato (the Academy) and Aristotle (the Lyceum [*Lykeion*]) were different both in form and in content from the virtuoso charismatic teaching from visiting sophists found in the houses of rich Athenians in the fifth century. A cultural revolution had taken place which the continuity of institution significantly hides (see Osborne ed. (2007).

Note C: The civic and the religious in Athenian democracy

What areas of life is it appropriate for the state to intervene in? We are used to state intervention in education, in matters of health and safety, in the age at which individuals can have sexual relations, in who is fit to drive different sorts of vehicles, and so on. But we are also used to the thought that there are aspects of individuals' lives that should not be determined by the state, and in particular freedom of religious belief. Indeed, the 1948 United Nations Universal Declaration of Human Rights, article 18, declares:

> *Everyone has the right to freedom of thought, conscience and religion; this right includes freedom to change his religion or belief, and freedom, either alone or in community with others and in public or private, to manifest his religion or belief in teaching, practice, worship and observance.*

In many western countries 'church' and 'state' are today effectively separate, and even where the Church is 'established', intervention by the state to favour the established religion over other religions is, at the least, controversial. In general the state keeps out of matters religious, and states and religious bodies clash mainly when the religion demands a behaviour that the state would otherwise prefer to discourage (as with Muslim veiling of women) or with behaviours that the state would like to encourage (as with the clash between Sikh turbans and motor-cycle helmets).

The Athenian democratic state took no concern for many of the matters where we take state intervention for-granted. There were essentially no health and safety regulations, though those guilty of negligence could be tried for its consequences under the law about 'harm', and there were no laws about education except those that concerned the military training of 18 year-olds (**277–83**). By contrast a great many of the decrees and laws passed in Athens had to do with the conduct of religious cult, a high proportion of public expenditure was on religious festivals (second only to expense on the navy during war) and some of the most striking episodes of Athenian domestic history concern crises resulting from behaviour held to be irreligious (above all the affair of the mutilation of the Herms and the profanation of the Mysteries. below **173, 374–7**).

The justification in a modern state for state intervention is that it is required for the greater good of the civic community as a whole. Health and safety legislation is meant to prevent employers from placing their workers in danger; insistence on qualifications (in terms of age, fitness, or possession of certified skills) prevents individuals harming others by incompetence in driving a vehicle, acting as a doctor or whatever; insisting on a minimum age for consensual sexual relations prevents those who might not be in a position to understand the full consequences from being placed under pressure to engage in sexual acts. Governments who object to the veiling of Muslim women do so because they believe that others feel threatened by people who are veiled because veils can conceal who individuals truly are. Governments do not intervene in what individuals believe about god or gods, or in individual religious worship, because in a world where most people think that it is not possible objectively to demonstrate the truth of any particular religion there are no grounds for thinking any particular religious practice either desirable or harmful.

The justification in classical Athens for state intervention was effectively identical to the justification in the modern world. What was different was ancient views about the gods. Atheism, that is denial that gods exist, was rare in antiquity, and although there was plenty of criticism of the picture of the Olympian gods derived from Homer and Hesiod, and of particular cult practices, both on stage in Greek tragedy (cf. Euripides' *Hippolytos* or the fragments of a tragedy about Sisyphus often ascribed to the Athenian oligarch Kritias) and in the works of philosophers such as Herakleitos and Xenophanes, these did not lead to the rejection of belief that there were supernatural powers. But given the very wide acceptance that the gods existed, it was clearly important for the greater good of the civic community that the gods were pleased, rather than annoyed.

Pleasing the gods took a number of different forms. Most obviously it meant worship – the offering of goods, of superlative human achievements (as manifested both in expensive temples and in what was done in competitive festivals, whether athletic or 'musical' – where the musical included drama and recitation of epic), and above all of sacrifices, normally involving the killing and eating of a farm animal. The state therefore laid down a calendar of festivals and sacrifices, and when this was changed the man responsible was put on trial for missing some traditional festivals off the new calendar, and so threatening the security of the state by risking offending gods (**348**). The state also took care to prescribe more precisely what happened at these festivals so as to ensure that behaviour was appropriate and that income was sufficient to sustain the worship.

But pleasing the gods also meant not offending them. This meant not stealing their money, not acting offensively towards sacred officials, not taking religious actions in jest, and not causing physical harm to images of the gods. Should any such thing happen, the state took action. In the normal course of events there were no state prosecutions in Athens – the state relied on the injured party taking action or, in cases where the injured party was not in a position to take action because of the nature of the offence, on another individual prosecuting on his behalf. But in the case of offences against the gods, where the gods, as the injured party, were not in a position to avail themselves of the remedy of the Athenian courts, and where the possibility that they would take action of their own was to be dreaded, the Athenians from time to time appointed special investigators and prosecutors – as they did in the affair of the Herms and the Mysteries (**173**). Similarly, whereas normally slaves were not encouraged to tell on their masters, in the case of offences against the gods they were (see Osborne (2000)).

In the past scholars have sometimes talked as if the evidence for extensive state involvement in matters religious was evidence that the state 'took over' previously independent cults. This is to misconstrue what is happening. Although individual families (*genē* below **115**) seem to have had responsibility for maintaining particular cults, the adequate worship of all the gods must have been a concern of the whole community from the beginning. In a polytheistic world it could never be enough to ensure that one god was happy; all the gods had to be kept happy, and whatever the form of government in a state, seeing that all the gods were happy was so important that, in the end, the government had to see that it happened.

What makes democratic Athens different is not the fact of state interference in religion, but its visibility. Because officials were short-term and needed not just to see that the right things were done, but to show that they had done the right things, decisions that were taken about the gods got written up. And because many decisions about the gods were decisions about doing something regularly in future, rather than decisions about one-off action, those decisions got displayed very publicly and kept visible over long periods of time – indeed sometimes being re-inscribed, as was the whole Athenian law-code, including its calendar of sacrifices (**51**, cf. **92**). New priesthoods instituted from the middle of the fifth century were appointed from all eligible Athenians, not from the members of a particular *genos*, were appointed not for life but annually. It was therefore important that the regulations establishing these priesthoods were displayed. The decree concerning the priestess of Athene Nike (**161**) is particularly interesting in that regard, although that priesthood does seem to have been held for life.

On one level, then, good relations with the gods were just a matter of national security, like good relations with other Greek states and foreign neighbours or making sure there was enough food. Just as matters to do with the grain supply had to be discussed once every prytany in the Assembly, so too space was reserved for the Assembly to discuss three matters of sacred business each prytany (**190**). But on another level, the gods were different, since while what other Greeks and foreigners were intending to do could, at least in principle, be discovered with some confidence, as could the amount of grain available in Attica or on the market, the gods were always inscrutable. And whereas foreign powers would only exceptionally take action because of something done by an individual acting without a mandate from his city, and would never take action just because of what an individual thought, in principle the gods might visit a whole community with revenge for the action, or the impious thoughts, of one of its members.

The inscrutability of the gods, and their capacity to know even individuals' unspoken attitudes, meant that ensuring that the gods were happy was extremely difficult. The city could take exceptional measures to elicit from all its residents their knowledge of potentially impious acts, but there was no objective way of knowing what the limits were of what the gods might be offended by. Theophrastos in his *Characters* includes the *Deisidaimon*, the 'Superstitious man', who finds in everything that he finds out of place or untoward a sign that the gods are offended, and so takes action to restore divine favour. Readers are intended to find this man, like the other Theophrastan Characters, excessive and amusing – but his problem was everyone's problem – and it was the state's problem too.

One way of dealing with divine inscrutability was to employ the traditional mechanisms for discovering the gods' preferences. One of these was the examination of divine signs in general and of the entrails of sacrificial animals in particular. Knowing what abnormalities in the entrails, and above all in the liver, might signify was a science passed on between *manteis*, seers, who were often members of a particular family. The Athenians used seers in particular at moments of crisis – when a new settlement was founded, or to accompany the army on campaign. Lampon was used by the Athenians when they founded the settlement at Thourioi in south Italy in the 440s, and he acquired sufficient renown to get himself listened to in the Assembly on religious matters (**362**). A second way of discovering what the gods wanted was to ask an oracle, and in particular the oracle at Delphi. Oracles in principle might be – and were – asked about almost anything; consultation of the oracle at Dodona was by submitting a question inscribed on a strip of metal, and enough strips survive to show the very large range of questions, about past, present and future, that individuals asked. During the classical period the Athenians consulted the Delphic oracle on a number of different occasions – but always about matters which obviously directly concerned the gods themselves (cf. **362**), not about matters that the Assembly could have decided itself by rational argument.

The problem that the gods might react to individuals' actions and thoughts, and not just to the visible actions of the community as a whole, or at least or a substantial group within the community, was harder to deal with. When things were going well in Athens the Athenians seem to have concluded that there were sufficient signs of the gods' good-will towards them that they could be as relaxed about what individuals were doing as is Perikles' ideal Athens of the Funeral Oration. It was when things were tense and not everyone was sure that they were going well that there were problems. So it was at the moment when the Athenians were undertaking a risky and unprecedented foreign expedition against Syracuse that the mutilation of the Herms (**173**) occasioned a public witch-hunt that then brought out allegations of private parodies of the Eleusinian Mysteries and turned these into offences that led to death sentences and property confiscation. And it was in the tense years after the end of the Peloponnesian War and the bloody rule of the Thirty Tyrants that what gods Sokrates did or did not worship, and whether his teaching of the young pleased or displeased the gods became an issue for an Athenian court (**250**) and led to his judicial execution.

Sokrates' death has often been seen as one of the signs of how badly governed Athens was. It would be foolish to deny that Athenian politics played a major part in bringing him to trial and having him condemned, but the major problem here was theological. Given that everyone thought that the world was full of gods, and that those gods took a keen interest in mankind and could and did intervene directly in the affairs and prosperity of a city, how could a city be confident that its most outspoken members were acceptable to the gods? It is because they lived with this theological problem that the Athenians spent so much of their time in cult activities and so much of their time in Council and Assembly overseeing the cult practices that they had resolved upon at some point in the past, and revising those cult practices for the future.

6　Citizenship

The criteria for citizenship

56　A citizen pure and simple is not better defined in any other way than by his
sharing the right to decide legal cases and to hold public office. Some offices
are limited tenure, so that some of them may never be held twice by the same
man, or only after a stated interval of time. Other offices, like membership of a
jury or an assembly, enjoy unlimited tenure.

Aristotle Politics 3 1275a22–26

At the beginning of book 3 of *Politics* Aristotle ponders at length how the citizen is best defined. He is
interested in the citizen as person who has particular rights in the city, and seeks to define what the irreducible
minimum of civic rights should be. He concludes, as in this passage, that citizens should be those who
actually or potentially hold political and juridical office in a city. But he then recognizes that in many cities
not all citizens are in such a position. His description fits well the situation in classical Athens, however.

57　For practical purposes they define a citizen as the one born from parents who
are both citizens and not only one, a mother for instance or a father; and some
demand more than this – such as there being citizen ancestors over two or three
or more generations.

Aristotle Politics 3 1275b22–4

Athens moved from being at one end of the spectrum, demanding only one citizen parent, before 451/0, to
the middle, with its demand that both mother and father (but not grandparents or great grandparents) be
Athenian. Since the mother or father being Athenian came over time to require that their mother and father
were Athenian, the Athenian requirement became effectively, if not formally, more restrictive as time passed.

Insistence on Athenian parents on both sides

58　Eumelos the Peripatetic in the third book of his *On Old Comedy* says that a
certain Nikomenes passed a decree that none of those born after the arkhonship
of Eukleides should share civic rights unless he could demonstrate that both his
parents were citizens, but those born before Eukleides' arkhonship should not
be subject to scrutiny.

Eumelos FGrH 77 F2 (Scholiast on Aiskhines 1.39)

This re-enactment of Perikles' citizenship law follows the precedent of that law in not being retrospective.
Other sources too imply that during the Peloponnesian War the Athenians had allowed both marriage to
foreigners and indeed bigamy (Diogenes Laertios 2.26 [of Sokrates]).

The procedure for enrolment

59　The present form of the constitution is as follows. Those share civic rights both
of whose parents are citizens, and they are enrolled as members of their deme
at the age of eighteen. When they are enrolled, the members of the deme vote
on them under oath to decide, first, whether they have reached the legal age –
if the decision goes against them, they return to the status of boys – and,
secondly, if they are free and born as the law requires. Then if they vote that he

is not freeborn, he appeals to the court and the demesmen choose five men from their own number as accusers; and if he seems not to have been enrolled properly the city sells him, but if he wins the demesmen are compelled to enrol him. After this, the Council vets those who have been enrolled, and if anyone proves to be less than eighteen, it punishes the demesmen who enrolled him. When the ephebes have been examined, their fathers are got together by tribe, and, under oath, choose the three members of the tribe over 40 years old whom they think best and most suitable to look after the ephebes, and from these the people elects one per tribe as *sophronistes* and elects a *kosmetes* from the rest of the Athenians with charge over all.

[Aristotle] *Constitution of the Athenians* 42.1–2

This is how the description of the constitution in the second half of the Aristotelian *Constitution of the Athenians* begins. Presumably deme involvement in recognizing who was and who was not a citizen had been necessary from the start, though demes were sufficiently small institutions that suspicion could arise that they had been bribed to give the 'right' answer. The description of the choices before the demesmen is here incomplete: they decide not simply whether or not a man is freeborn, but whether his parents were citizens. It is not clear what procedure applied when a deme decided that a man was free but that one of his parents was (say) a Corinthian, but Athenian procedure more generally implies that in this case too he could appeal to a court (see further **61**). The question of whether the Athenian parents had to be married to one another is difficult to resolve. No text concerning the citizenship law mentions marriage, but we do hear that being the son of married parents was essential for inheritance (see above **25**) and for phratry membership. Those granted citizenship as an honour (below **65–6**) are regularly enrolled also in a phratry, but nothing ever says that Athenians *had* to be members of a phratry. See Ogden 1996.

60   As soon as someone has been enrolled in the deme register, and knows the laws of the city, and can now tell the difference between right and wrong...

Aiskhines 1.18 (345)

61   BDELYKLEON: Give me an example of the good things that come from the exercise of your powers in ruling Greece.
PHILOKLEON: Well, when the boys are scrutinised there's a jolly good view of their genitals.

Aristophanes *Wasps* 577–78 (422)

The implication of this passage is that in the fifth century the courts played some part in the scrutiny of new citizens. But this only requires the possibility of appeal to the courts by those rejected. See above **59**. The implication is that at least a major part of the judgement as to the age of a youth was made on the basis of his physical maturity.

The special status of those granted citizenship

62   All those to whom the Athenian people makes grants of citizenship the law explicitly bars from the possibility becoming one of the nine arkhons or sharing in any priesthood. But the people gave a share of everything to their children, adding 'provided they are born from a citizen wife betrothed according to the law'.

[Demosthenes] 59.92 (343–40)

Apollodoros, the author and speaker of sections 16 to 116 of the speech *Against Neaira*, who was himself the son of a man who had been granted citizenship, is keen to emphasise Athenian care at ensuring that Athenian religious rituals are in true Athenian hands in order to emphasise the enormity of having such rituals performed by a women like Neaira, whom he claims to be no Athenian. The claims made here slightly over-simplify the situation, as the later quotation of the law about the Plataians reveals (**66**). It is worth noting how much of our evidence (passages **62–66** here) about the laws governing citizenship and citizen marriage derive from this single speech in which Apollodoros is arguing a particular case.

Laws against marriage to a foreigner

63   If a foreign man lives with a citizen woman by any manner or means, let anyone who wants to, bring a written indictment against him before the *thesmothetai*. If he is convicted, let him be sold, together with his property, and let the third part be given to the prosecutor. And if a foreign woman lives with a citizen man let it be in the same way, and let the man living with the foreign woman who has been convicted be fined 1000 drakhmas.

[Demosthenes] 59.16 (343–40)

This law is one of the pieces of evidence for hardening attitudes to cohabitation between Athenians and non-Athenians in the fourth century. It is particularly notable that the Athenians feel free to enslave a foreign man when they only impose a (heavy) fine on the citizen man – an extreme instance of the general rule that non-Athenians can be treated more harshly than Athenians. One reason for this may be that the children of a foreign woman can far less easily be passed off as Athenian than the children of an Athenian woman born to a non-Athenian father. As in English, so in Greek 'live with' is a euphemism for a sexual partnership. The reward for the prosecutor here seems to have been standard in cases of denunciation (*phasis*).

64   If someone gives away a foreign woman in marriage to an Athenian man, on the basis that she is related to him, let him lose his civic rights and let his property be confiscated and the third part belong to the successful prosecutor. Let those who are able to do so bring a written indictment before the *thesmothetai* as in the case of a foreigner claiming to be a citizen.

[Demosthenes] 59.52 (343–40)

The loose wording here ('If anyone' for 'If any citizen', 'as belonging to himself') does not necessarily mean that this is not a genuine Athenian law. If genuine this was presumably a law made together with or subsequent to the law in **63**.

Grants of citizenship

65   First, the people have made a law that it is not possible to make someone an Athenian who does not deserve to become a citizen because of his manly goodness toward the Athenian people. Second, when the people is persuaded and makes the grant, the law does not allow the grant to become valid unless in a vote at the following meeting of the Assembly more than 6000 Athenians voting secretly vote for it. [90] The law orders the *prytaneis* to place the urns and give out the voting pebbles to the people as they come in, before the foreigners enter and they take away the wicker hurdles, in order that every individual knowing his own mind should consider for himself whom it is that he is about to make a citizen, and whether the man who will receive the grant is worthy of it. Then after this the law offers an indictment against illegal proposals brought against the new citizen by any Athenian who wants to, and entering the law-court he can try to prove the man unworthy of the grant, and that it has occurred contrary to Athenian law. [91] In some cases, when the people had given a grant deceived by the argument of those proposing it, when an indictment against an illegal proposal was brought to a court, the man who had received the grant has been convicted of being unworthy of it and the court took it away. It would be a labour to go through the many instances long ago, but you all remember cases like Peitholas the Thessalian and Apollonides the Olynthian, who were made citizens by the people but the court took the grant away.

[Demosthenes] 59.89–91 (343–40)

The cardinal virtues named in honorific decrees are discussed by Whitehead (1994). The voting procedure used here is standard on matters that involve individuals, and since such votes can be shown to have taken place at Assemblies at various different points in the year and in the prytany they are good evidence that the Assembly in the fourth century, whatever the problems earlier (see **55** and **177**), was regularly attended by 6000 people (Hansen 1983, 1–23). We know nothing of the particular cases referred to here, but the keen debates over the worthiness of those offered citizenship serve to emphasise the degree to which the spare language of the decrees which record the grants glosses over significant political debate (cf. Osborne 1999/2010). The evidence for grants of citizenship at Athens is collected by M.J. Osborne (1981–3).

66 Hippokrates proposed: that the Plataians be Athenians from this day, with full rights just as the other Athenians, and have a share in all that the Athenians share, both civil and religious, except if there is a priesthood or religious rôle drawn from a particular family, and that they shall not be the nine arkhons; but their descendants may be. And to distribute the Plataians among the demes and the tribes; and once they have been distributed, no Plataian may become Athenian unless he wins the grant from the Athenian people.

[Demosthenes] 59.104 (343–40)

Although slightly edited, this may well be the genuine text of a fifth-century grant to the Plataians after they were up-rooted from their city by the Spartans in 427 (for an earlier grant, made perhaps after their fighting at Marathon, see Thuc. 3. 55.3, 63.2), despite Canevaro (2010) who argues that it is a forgery. Apart from the explicit exception of priesthoods attached to a particular family, all the clauses here are paralleled elsewhere. The distribution among demes and tribes, without mention of phratries, is paralleled by the grant of citizenship to the Samians (RO 2).

The privileges of the citizen

67 When therefore Phormio leased the working of the bank and the deposits, seeing that, since he was not yet a citizen among you, he would not be able to recover what Pasion had lent on land and tenement houses, he chose to have Pasion himself as the debtor for these moneys rather than the other debtors to whom he had made loans.

[Demosthenes] 36.6 (uncertain date)

This is a nice example of the practical difference made by having the right to own real estate in Attica, a right restricted to citizens and those to whom a specific grant (known as a grant of *enktesis*) was made. Phormio, while he is a metic, is free to lend money on landed security, but would never be able to take over the land if the debtor defaulted.

68   It was called the theoric fund because, when the Dionysia was about to happen,
Euboulos distributed the money for the sacrifice in order that everyone might
be able to join in with the feast and no citizen be deprived of the opportunity to
join in the spectacle because of shortage of his own means; and then later the
money was defined as for spectacles and sacrifices and feasts as is clear in the
first Philippic of Demosthenes...

Harpokration s.v. *Theorikon*

Although some other sources claim that Perikles or Agyrrhios initiated the theoric fund, there is no allusion
to it in fifth century literature and this attribution to Euboulos (in the middle of the fourth century) is the
most plausible. Set up to fund citizen attendance at festivals, the theoric fund received surplus revenue at
the end of the financial year and politicians frequently tried to divert it for other uses.

69   [Leostratos] got together just a few members of the deme Otryne and persuaded
the demarkh, when the record-book was opened, to write in his name. And after
this, when the Great Panathenaia was on, he came along at the distribution of
the *theorikon* and when the other demesmen took it, he claimed that it should
be given to him and that he should be written into the book under the name of
Arkhiades. When we demurred, and others also asserted that what was
happening was terrible, he went away neither having been written into the book
nor having got the *theorikon*.

Demosthenes 44.37 (uncertain date)

This is the best evidence for how the distribution of the *theorikon* worked, with demesmen coming to claim
it, and their names being recorded as they took it.

70   Let them distribute the meat to the Athenian people in [the Kerameikos] just as
in the case of the other distributions of meat. They are to distribute the portions
to each deme in accordance with the number of men each deme provides.

RO 81 (*IG* ii^2 334) 24–7 (mid 330s)

This distribution at the Little Panathenaia suggests that a head-count was done before meat was distributed,
but that then it was the job of the deme to ensure that only its members claimed a share.

71   After this [Perikles] went to the Khersonese and made the territory into a
kleroukhy for one thousand citizens. At the same time that this was being done,
Tolmides, the other general, crossed to Euboia with another thousand citizens
and divided this land and the land of the Naxians.

Diodoros 11.88.3

Distribution of land taken from rebellious allies to Athenian citizens was one significant cause of dislike of
the Athenians in the fifth century.

72   The colonists to Brea are to go from the thetes and the zeugites.

ML 49 (Fornara 100) 39–42 (430s)

Those who formed a colony – a new and self-governing city – ceased to be citizens, unlike those who simply
took a share of confiscated land abroad as kleroukhs. The colonists here are taken from the two lowest
property classes in Athens, perhaps because for the poor the exchange of citizenship for land abroad was a
more attractive exchange. See also **437**.

73 The Laws of Athens: By granting our permission we give public notice that once he has been vetted and seen the workings of the city and its laws, any Athenian who does not care for us may take his property and leave for wherever he likes.

Plato *Kriton* 51d

Plato has Sokrates imagine the Laws speaking to him and persuading him that he should not flee from prison since he has voluntarily agreed to abide by their rule through deciding to live in Athens rather than leave.

7 DEMES

The mechanics and politics of deme membership

74 Scrutinies have taken place in the demes, and each of you has given your vote about the individual, as to who is truly an Athenian and who is not. And I, whenever I come to the court and hear those who are disputing, see that the same consideration always prevails with you. For when the prosecutor says 'Gentlemen of the jury, the demesmen condemned this man after they had taken the oath, although no one had either made an accusation or borne witness against him, because on the basis of their own knowledge', then immediately, I think, you cry out that the man being judged has no share in the city. For what someone clearly himself knows does not, I think, seem to you to need argument or witness statements.

Aiskhines 1.77–8 (345)

The procedure for becoming a member of a deme was the same as that for becoming a citizen – see **59** above. Both the virtue and the problem of the small community is that so much knowledge is implicit. Although demes varied greatly in size, in all but the largest people would expect to know the personal lives of all the residents. It was more of a problem, however, that a man remained registered in the deme where his ancestor had registered at the time of Kleisthenes, even if he or his parents had never lived there. In those cases no one would securely know who was and who was not properly qualified for deme membership.

75 He (Euboulides) was a member of the Council, gentlemen of the jury, and he was master of the oath and of the documents in virtue of which he convened the demesmen. So what does he do? In the first place, when the demesmen had assembled, he wasted the whole day in speechifying and drawing up resolutions. This did not happen by accident: he was plotting against me, to ensure that the vote about my standing should take place as late as possible, and he achieved his purpose. The demesmen who took the oath numbered seventy-three, and we began voting late in the evening, with the result that when my name was called, it was already dark. My name was about the sixtieth, and I was the last of those called on that day, when the older demesmen had gone back to their farms; for, gentlemen of the jury, our deme lies some thirty-five stades (about four miles) from the city and most of the demesmen live there; so most of them had gone home.

Demosthenes 57.8–10 (c.345)

Euxitheos of Halimous had been voted off the list of members of Halimous in the scrutiny that was held in the middle of the fourth century. He appeals to the court, and describes here how Euboulides manipulated the deme meeting to ensure the result he wanted. We do not have to believe every word Euxitheos says in order to see how the community life of a small deme could be manipulated by a determined man. One surprising feature of this account is that the deme meeting was held not in the deme itself but in the city. Euxitheos' failure to remark on this as odd may imply that in cases where many deme members had moved temporarily or permanently to the city the deme meeting might be held in the city too.

The deme as a community

76   Migration proved hard for them because most of them had always been used to living in the country.

Thucydides 2.14.2

This and the next extract come from the context of the first invasion of Attica by the Spartans in the Peloponnesian War. Part of Periklean strategy was that people should come within the long walls of Athens from outside for protection when the Spartans invaded.

77   They took it hard and resented having to leave their homes and the ancestral temples which had always been theirs since the earliest days of their constitution. They were about to change their way of life, and each of them really felt that he was leaving his native city.

Thucydides 2.16.2

Both the facilities in demes (theatres, sanctuaries etc.) and the fact that demes held their own meetings in which they decided local matters, encouraged the thought that the deme was a city. Thucydides implies that many were quite unused to the life of the city proper.

78   After this, when the city was now flourishing and a great deal of money had been gathered [from tribute, Aristeides] advised them to assert their leadership and coming in from the fields to live in the town. For there would be food for all – for those on campaign, for those in the garrison posts, for those looking after the city's business, and in this way they would get a firm grip on leadership. The Athenians were persuaded...

[Aristotle] *Constitution of the Athenians* 24.1

This fourth-century reconstruction should not be preferred to Thucydides' evidence, but it does show how Athenians came to associate the fifth-century empire strongly with life centred on the town of Athens – despite the investment in rural sanctuaries (e.g. at Sounion, Rhamnous, Brauron, Thorikos and Pallene) attested by archaeology.

79   ...until they reached Akharnai, the largest of the areas of Attica called 'demes'.

Thucydides 2.19.2

80   The Akharnians thought of themselves as a sizeable part of the citizen body, and since it was their land that was being ravaged, they pressed most eagerly for the sally.

Thucydides 2.21.3

There is no doubt that Akharnai was an unusual deme, at least in the early years of the Peloponnesian War; its exceptional size (in the fourth century it returned 22 Councillors to the Council of 500 when the next largest deme, Aphidna, returned 16) combined with its position (directly in the path of invading

Peloponnesian armies) to create an unusual pressure-group out of its inhabitants. This is reflected both in Thucydides' account and in Aristophanes' decision in 425 to present Akharnians as the chorus of his play about belligerence and peace at Athens. See Kellogg (2013).

81   DIKAIOPOLIS: ...looking out into the countryside, longing for peace, hating the city, yearning for my own deme...

Aristophanes *Akharnians* 32–3 (425)

The Peloponnesian invasions of the early years of the Peloponnesian war caused Athenians to leave the countryside and gather within the long walls of Athens, which ran down from Athens itself to the harbour town of Peiraieus. The density of the population temporarily gathered there (the longest Spartan invasion was 42 days) was an important factor in bringing about the outbreak of plague which seems to have killed around a third of the Athenian population. Modern scholars have debated how much of a town-country split there was between town-based and country-based Athenians (Osborne 1985, 2010: 62–3, 167, Whitehead 1986, minimizing the gap, versus Jones 2004).

82   STUDENT: And this [area] really is Attica.
STREPSIADES: Then where are the Kikynnians, my fellow-demesmen?

Aristophanes *Clouds* 209–10 (419/8, in this version)

The joke here is presumably about scale – on a map where one can just distinguish Attica one will not be able to see an individual rural deme – but it is a joke based on the expectation that a man will place himself among his fellow demesmen and will think of his deme as a geographical location. Kikynna was in the tribe Akamantis, and perhaps located between modern Koropi and Paiania on the east slopes of Hymettos.

83   STREPSIADES: 'Blessed are you, Strepsiades, for your native wit and for the splendid son you are raising' is what my friends and fellow-demesmen will sing in envy when by your speeches you win our cases.

Aristophanes *Clouds* 1206–11 (419/8, in this version)

When an Athenian comes to placing himself in a group larger than his immediate family it is among his fellow-demesmen that he places himself.

84   FIRST CREDITOR: To recover my money, I have now to drag you in as a witness, and, what is more, make an enemy of a fellow-demesman.

Aristophanes *Clouds* 1217–19 (419/8, in this version)

Strepsiades is being presented as an ordinary man who is now applying the new wisdom learned from Sokrates to his life. That he has been lent money by a fellow-demesman (who is now about to try to recover that money) is something that one would not be surprised to discover of any Athenian.

85   STREPSIADES: Help! Help! Neighbours, relatives, fellow-demesmen, do all you can to protect me from this battering.

Aristophanes *Clouds* 1321–23 (419/8, in this version)

Strepsiades is presented as a man who lives in his deme – and indeed deme self-government presupposed that most demesmen continued to reside in their ancestral deme. For the complex reality see Osborne 1991/2010.

86 DEMOSTHENES: Good heavens, he (Paphlagon) did just the same thing to me, with the result that I became a complete laughing-stock to my fellow-demesmen and my friends.

Aristophanes *Knights* 319–20 (424)

The deme as religious community

87 He took thought for me as a father reasonably would about his son, and I in the same way as for a parent looked after him as my own father and felt shame before him, I and my wife likewise, so that he praised us to all the demesmen… and when he died I buried him in a way worthy of him and of myself, and I put up a fine tombstone, and I carried out all the ninth-day and other rituals at his tomb as well as I could, so that all the demesmen praised me.

Isaios 2.18, 36 (c.355)

The speaker is making the case for his inheritance from the man who adopted him, and is keen to draw attention to the way that the demesmen had recognised his actions as appropriate.

88 NIKIAS: My dear Lysimakhos, you really seem to me to know Sokrates only from what you knew of his father and never to have had anything to do with him personally, except maybe when he was a boy. Perhaps, while escorting his father among the demesmen, he met you at a temple or at some other gathering of demesmen.

Plato *Lakhes* 187de

This incidental reference indicates how the son of a citizen might become known to his fellow demesmen. Sokrates' deme was Alopeke, just outside the walls of Athens.

89 When he gives a feast for the demesmen he cuts the meat small before he serves it up.

Theophrastos *Characters* 10 (Penny-pincher) 11

Given that the man is mean, he is presumably feasting the demesmen only because obliged to do so.

90 AN ELEUSINIAN: I had come from town to meet the demesman who was going to serve up a skinny bullock, and got to hear all the insults those who had shared a cut produced. I myself was one of them!

Menander *Sikyonian* 183–6

As well as more evidence for meanness among demesmen, this is also good evidence for men moving back and forth between their deme, in this case Eleusis, and Athens.

91 And in the deme, once he had inherited a household worth three talents, if he had married he would have been compelled on behalf of his wedded wife to feast the women at the Thesmophoria and bear all the other liturgies that there are in a deme on behalf of a wife if you have so much property. Well, it is apparent that none of these ever happened.

Isaios 3.80 (uncertain date)

The focus here on the deme liturgies that are incurred through having a wife is a consequence of this being a speech about inheritance that depends on claims concerning a wife.

92   During Boedromion. The Prerosia. To Zeus Polieus, a selected sheep, a selected piglet. To Automenai, a bought piglet, burnt whole. The priest is to provide breakfast for the attendant. For Kephalos a selected sheep, for Prokris an offering-table.

For Thorikos a selected sheep, for the Heroines of Thorikos an offering-table. To Sounion for Poseidon, a selected lamb.

For Apollo a selected kid.

For Korotrophos a selected piglet, for Demeter a full-grown victim, for Zeus of the Courtyard a full-grown victim.

For Korotrophos a piglet, for Athene a sheep, to be sold at the salt-works.

For Poseidon a full-grown victim.

For Apollo a piglet.

IG i^3 256*bis*13–24

This extract from the late fifth-century deme calendar from Thorikos gives the sacrifices happening during just one month, Boedromion (September). A number of calendars of sacrifices survive from different demes, all of them slightly differently organized and giving different sorts of details depending on the purpose. This is a rather minimal list, indicating the god or hero to whom the sacrifice is made, the victim, the location of the sacrifice, if that is not in Thorikos, and occasional oddities of ritual (here that one of the victims is to be burnt whole – with the nice note that this means that the priest has himself to provide a meal for the attendant!). Notable here are the frequency with which a deme holds sacrifices and the mix of local heroes and city-wide festivals that are marked. So the Prerosia here is a festival celebrated generally across Attica, but Kephalos and Prokris, as well as Thorikos and the Heroines of Thorikos, are local figures. For discussion see Parker (1987).

93   When Onetor was demarkh, in the arkhonship of Arkhippos, the Eleusinians and the Athenians on garrison duty decided: With good fortune. [*Name lost*] son of Euthydemos of Eleusis said, since the law orders that the man who receives the grant be added to the decree as a benefactor of the city, and Xenokles, elected in charge of the temple of the two goddesses and the Mysteries has done his duty in the magistracies piously and with enthusiasm, and, in order that the sacred things and the festal gathering of the Greeks arriving at Eleusis and at the sanctuary might move safely and well and those who live in the suburb and the farmers might be safe, is preparing a stone bridge by an expenditure of his own money, and after handling public moneys, both formerly and now, is crowned for his justice and for his liturgies... [*text breaks off*]

IG ii^2 1191 (321/20)

Demes governed themselves in ways that paralleled the way in which the city governed itself. Although their structure of magistrates and officials was, naturally, much simpler, consisting primarily of a 'demarkh', appointed by lot, and treasurers, they too made decisions at public meetings. Eleusis, with its major sanctuary of Demeter and Persephone and with its military garrison (because close to the border with Megara) is hardly a 'typical' deme, and in this decree the deme associates with itself the Athenians on garrison duty at Eleusis, but this decree does show well how officials in a deme ended up engaging widely with religious and civic officials. The physical provision for the initiates at the Mysteries concerned both the officials of the cult, the officials of the city, and the officials of the deme. See further below (**358–66**) for the city's oversight of the sanctuary at Eleusis.

Deme finances and administration

94 Euthemon said: in order that the common funds be safe for the demesmen and that the demarkhs and the treasurers submit to scrutiny, the demesmen have resolved that the demarkhs and the treasurers should deposit the account of their receipts and expenditure in the chest each month, since also those serving in the arkhonship of Nausigenes (367/6) have voluntarily deposited the account each month. They are to undergo scrutiny in the following year before the month Metageitnion on the basis of the accounts in the chest and not of any others. And to stand the stele in the agora, having inscribed this decree. Let the demarkh exact the oath from the scrutineer and the assistants to conduct the scrutiny according to the decree written up in the agora. But if…and do not complete the scrutiny according to the decree… [*text breaks off*]

IG ii^2 1174 (367/6)

Deme decrees are most frequently concerned with honouring individuals, but they are also capable of being as interested in their own procedures as was the city itself. Like city officials, deme officials had to give an account at the end of their year of office. Here the rules are changed to oblige the deme officials to submit their accounts monthly during their time in office, rather than producing accounts after the event. Whether the decision of the demarkh of 367/6 to do this voluntarily followed suspicion of earlier malpractice, or was simply the adoption of exemplary procedures, is unclear. The deme involved here is Halai Aixonides, a deme at the south-west tip of Hymettos, close to Cape Zoster, which is now quite well known archaeologically (see Osborne 1985 24–6 and Goette 1993 186–90).

95 In past time some of the magistracies drawn by lot were allotted from the whole tribe along with the nine arkhons, others – those allotted in the Theseion – were divided between the demes. But after the demes were found to be selling the positions, they allot these too from the whole tribe, apart from the Councillors and the guards, who are still assigned to the demes.

[Aristotle] *Constitution of the Athenians* 62.1

It is likely that this change happened about 370 BC when bronze allotment plates, which had earlier been introduced for jurors, were introduced for the allotment of other officers too (see Kroll (1972)).

8   OTHER SUBDIVISIONS OF THE *DEMOS*

96 It is not possible to form a polis without a process of division and distribution – partly into associations for common meals and partly into phratries and tribes.

Aristotle *Politics* 1264a6–8

Aristotle is thinking here both of the need for social groups within the city, but also of the need for organisations at the sub-polis level to facilitate both civic/military and religious activity.

97 A city is a community of households and *genē* in living well, for the sake of a perfect and self-sufficient life.

Aristotle *Politics* 1280b30–35

Aristotle's 'households' recognise that people are linked by living together, his *genē* recognise that people are linked by descent and shared religious life.

98   If a deme or members of a phratry or *orgeones*, or *gennetai*, or messmates (*sussitoi*), or funerary associates (*homotaphoi*), or *thiasotai*, or those away for booty or trade, make arrangements with each other in these matters they shall be valid unless forbidden by the laws.

Digest 47.22.4

This law, the date of which is uncertain, seems to be intended to indicate that no agreement within a group was exempt from the laws of the city. The absence of the tribe from this list may suggest that close ties among tribe members were relatively unusual. We know of this law from a dgest of Roman law where it is suggested that an early Roman law was taken from Solon. For *orgeones* see below **106** and **116–7**.

99   As for the so-called nine arkhons, the method of appointing them from the beginning has already been described; nowadays six *thesmothetai* and their secretary, the arkhon, the Basileus and the polemarkh are appointed by lot from each tribe in turn. They are vetted first in the Council of 500... When the arkhons are vetted, they are asked first 'Who is your father and from which deme? Who is your father's father? Who is your mother? Who is your mother's father, and from which deme?' Then they are asked if they have a cult of the Ancestral Apollo and of Zeus of the Courtyard, and where these sanctuaries are; whether they have family tombs and where they are; whether they treat their parents well; whether they pay their taxes; whether they have done military service.

[Aristotle] *Constitution of the Athenians* 55.1–3

These questions asked of candidates for the arkhonship at Athens recognise the links that people have through family and deme, and the way in which such links get expressed through cult activity.

Tribes

100   Gods. Resolved by the Pandionid tribe on the proposal of Kallikrates: to praise Nikias son of Epigenes of Kydathenaion for his manly goodness towards the tribe, in that he was a good and keen *khoregos* for the boys and was victorious at the Dionysia, and at the Thargelia for the men, and to crown him. The *epimeletai* are to inscribe this decree on a stone stele in the sanctuary of Pandion. And inscribe also anyone else who is victorious after the arkhonship of Eukleides with the boys or the men at the Dionysia, Thargelia, Promethia or Hephaistia. And the *epimeletai* are to inscribe in the future anyone who is victorious in any of these and the contest in which he is victorious on this same stele.

IG ii^2 1138 (c.403/2)

Dionysia:	Thargelia	
Boys	Men	Boys
Nikias son of Epigenes of Kydathenaion	Nikias son of Epigenes of Kydathenaion	Apemon son of Pheidippos of Myrrhinous
Andokides son of Leiogoros of Kydathenaion	Demon son of Demoteles of Paiania	Xenopeithes son of Nausimakhos of Paiania
Euripides son of Adeimantos of Myrrhinous	Kharmantides son of Khairestratos of Paiania	Antisthenes son of Antiphatos of Kytherros
	Philomelos son of Philippides of Paiania	

Although the main function of the Kleisthenic tribes, the formation of which is described in **36**, was arguably military (cf. **39** and LACTOR 1⁴ **42**), they were used to organize the Athenians into groups for other purposes too. On occasions when demes were either too small or simply too inconsistent in size, the city called upon tribes, and the tribes had to organize themselves to fund the activities in question, not merely to supply teams. So here the tribe Pandionis celebrates those *khoregoi* who have funded its teams on occasions when they have performed successfully in the state festivals which required team competition – the Dionysia, the Thargelia, the Promethia and the Hephaistia. Victorious *khoregoi* in the fourth century came frequently to erect monuments to celebrate their victories (cf. the famous 'Khoregic monument of Lysikrates'), but this decree of, or shortly after, 403/2 stands at the head of the surviving commemorations. It is notable that Pandionis should organize itself so quickly after the restoration of democracy to display its festal prowess, but celebration of the return of democracy and the old festival order may be one of the factors that encouraged them to do so. The term 'manly goodness' seems to be a coinage of this time to avoid the overtones which some other terms had acquired through their use by the oligarchs. For more detail see Wilson (2000) esp. 171.

101 One of the *nomothetai* made a law…concerning those who, without your having decreed it, were being crowned by their tribesmen and demesmen and concerning those who were freeing slaves, and concerning crowns given abroad, and he clearly forbids either freeing a slave in the theatre or announcing a crown given by a tribe or deme, or by anyone else, on pain of the herald losing his civic rights.

Aiskhines 3.44 (330)

Aiskhines claims that the theatre had become disrupted by everyone using it to make announcements of honours and acts of manumission, and so this law had to be brought to prevent such proclamations.

102 And he moved a decree in order that the Erekhtheids might all know their own property and the *epimeletai* customarily established each year, walking over the property twice during the year, might consider whether the lands were being farmed according to the agreements and if the boundaries were established in the same places, and he did this neither putting obligations even to a single person above the interests of the tribe nor as a result of bribery, even by a single person, but always speaking and doing continuously what was best for the tribe, he was never complained about by any of his fellow tribesmen. So, with good fortune, the Erekhtheid tribe has decided to praise Antisthenes son of Nikander of Lamptrai and crown him with a gold crown according to the law because of his virtue and justice which he continually showed to the Erekhtheid tribe. And since it happens that the daughter of Antisthenes has become an heiress according to the laws, the *epimeletai* who are customarily appointed each year are to look after Aristomakhe the daughter of Antisthenes, and if she needs anything to mention it to the tribe when it holds its meeting in order that she be not wronged even by a single individual. Goodwill belongs to the daughter of Antisthenes, Aristomakhe, from each of the tribesmen both individually and as a body because of the good qualities which her father continuously showed towards the Erekhtheid tribe.

IG ii^2 1165.17–38 (early 3rd century)

The beginning of this tribal decree, which dates to the first half of the third century BC, is unfortunately poorly preserved, but it seems to have described at length Antisthenes' good services to the tribe in managing their finances, seeing to their sacrifices etc. The part that survives indicates that the tribe had lands which it rented out, and about whose value it was concerned. Uniquely, it also establishes the rôle the tribe might play as a benevolent institution, here in looking after the daughter following her father's death.

Trittyes

103   At this point the *trittys* of the Diakrians ends and the *trittys* of Phrearrhioi begins.

IG i^3 1121 (mid fifth century)

104   At this point the tribe Akamantis and the *trittys* of the Thorikians ends and the tribe Hippothontis begins.

IG i^3 1122 (later fifth century)

These two stones were found in the Athenian Agora. Since the demes of Thorikos and Phrearrhioi were miles from the Agora these cannot be conventional boundary stone, but must instead be muster stones: when the Athenians gathered in tribal and *trittys* order they were expected to line up according to these stones. A number of these stones have been found in the Athenian Agora and others in the Peiraieus. It is most likely that the purpose of mustering in this way was military, but one similar stone has been found on the Pnyx, and some think that the Athenian assembly sat in tribe and *trittys* order (but contrast **184**), just as others have suggested that the theatre seating was so distributed. See Traill (1986), Winkler (1990a).

Phratries

105   Thrasyboulos shall be made an Athenian and be inscribed as a member of whatever tribe and phratry he chooses...

IG i^3 102 15–17 (later fifth century)

Phratry membership is regularly, but not always, included in grants of citizenship. Whether all citizens had to be members of phratries is disputed, see above on **59**. For a study of the phratry see Lambert (1993).

106   The phrateres must accept both the *orgeones* and the *homogalaktes* whom we call *gennētai*.

Philokhoros *Atthis FGrH* 328 F35

What phratries did about their membership will have mattered only in as far as phratry membership was required for, or at least strengthened the argument for, membership of other bodies, most obviously membership of the citizen body itself. This law therefore strengthens the case for membership of a phratry being necessary to citizenship. For *orgeones* see below **116–7**.

107   Our father, when we were born, introduced us to the *phrateres* and swore by the laws that are laid down that he was introducing children who were born from a wife who was a citizen and properly married, and none of the *phrateres* opposed him or expressed doubt that this was true, although many were present and these things were closely considered.

Isaios 8.19 (between 383 and 363)

This statement is made during an inheritance case by a man keen to demonstrate his unimpeachable claim to belong to a particular family, and in particular the status of his mother.

108   Well, these kinsmen of my father who are still alive, from the male and from the female side, have given witness statements that he was an Athenian on both sides and justly had a share in the city. Summon now for me the *phrateres* and then the *gennetai*: WITNESS STATEMENTS. Take also the witness statements of the demesmen and those of the kinsmen about the *phrateres*, how they chose me phratriarkh: WITNESS STATEMENTS.

Demosthenes 57.23 (c.345)

The members of the phratry are here called upon to support the claims of kin, and the kin and demesmen to testify to what phratry members had done. We do not know the procedure for being appointed phratriarkh, nor exactly what the duties of a phratriarkh were (but see below **111**). Both demes and phratries were descent groups, and phratries are likely to have been originally based in a single location; it is therefore likely that there would be quite an overlap between members of a phratry and members of a deme. We do not know certainly how many phratries there were, and therefore whether phratries were generally larger or smaller than demes.

109   For when Phrastor was sick he introduced the son born from the daughter of Neaira to the *phrateres*, and to the Brytidai of whom Phrastor is himself a *gennetes*. The *gennetai* knowing, I think, who the woman was that Phrastor had first married, the daughter of Neaira, and his divorcing the woman, and that because of his sickness he had been persuaded to take up the child again, voted against the child and did not enrol him among their own number. [60] When Phrastor then brought a case against them because they did not enrol his son, the *gennetai* challenged him to swear an oath over perfect victims before the arbitrator that he did indeed consider that this was his son born from citizen woman properly married according to the law. But when the *gennetai* challenged Phrastor before the arbitrator about this, Phrastor abandoned the oath and did not swear.

[Demosthenes] 59.59–60 (343–340)

The implication of this story is that the introduction to the *genos* (here the Brytidai) and to the phratry was effectively the same, but that the smaller group, the *genos*, took the lead (with the phratry obliged to follow that lead, see **106** above). Divorce (for which the Greek term is literally 'sending away') was both easy to effect and easy to reverse. Apollodoros wants to persuade us that the issue here is not primarily the divorce, nor doubts about the paternity of the child, but whether Neaira's daughter was indeed herself an Athenian citizen (cf. **62** above).

110   Why did he have so clearly to rub his relatives up the wrong way when, if he
was properly married to the sister of Nikodemos he could have introduced the
daughter born from her to the *phrateres* as his legitimate offspring and left her
as heiress to the whole estate?

Isaios 3.73 (uncertain date)

111   Of Zeus Phratrios. The priest, Theodoros son of Euphantides, inscribed and
set up the stele. The following are to be given as priestly dues to the priest: from
the *meion* a thigh, a rib, an ear, 3 obols of money; from the *koureion* a thigh, a
rib, an ear, a cake weighing one *khoinix*, half a *khous* of wine; 1 drakhma of
silver.

The following was resolved by the *phrateres* when Phormion was arkhon
among the Athenians (396/5), and when Pantakles of Oion was phratriarkh.
Hierokles proposed: those who have not yet undergone adjudication in
accordance with the law of the Demotionidai, the *phrateres* are to adjudicate
about them immediately, after swearing by Zeus Phratrios, taking their ballot
from the altar. Whoever is judged to have been introduced, not being a *phrater*,
the priest and the phratriarkh shall delete his name from the register in the
keeping of the Demotionidai and from the copy. The man who introduced the
rejected person shall owe 100 drakhmas sacred to Zeus Phratrios: this sum of
money shall be exacted by the priest and the phratriarkh, or they themselves
shall owe it. The adjudication is to take place in future in the year after that in
which the *koureion* is sacrificed, on the Koureotis day of the Apatouria. They
shall take their ballot from the altar. If any of those who are voted out wishes
to appeal to the Demotionidai, that shall be permitted to him: the *oikos* of the
Dekeleians shall elect as advocates in their cases five men over thirty years old,
and the phratriarkh and the priest shall administer the oath to them to perform
their advocacy most justly and not to allow anybody who is not a *phrater* to be
a member of the phratry. Whomever the Demotionidai vote out after he has
appealed shall owe 1,000 drakhmas sacred to Zeus Phratrios: this sum of money
shall be exacted by the priest of the *oikos* of the Dekeleians, or he himself shall
owe it; it shall also be permitted to any other of the *phrateres* who wishes to
exact it for the common treasury. This shall apply from the arkhonship of
Phormion. The phratriarkh is to take the vote each year on those who have to
undergo adjudication: if he does not take the vote he shall owe 500 drakhmas
sacred to Zeus Phratrios; the priest and any other who wishes shall exact this
sum of money for the common treasury. In future the *meia* and the *koureia* shall
be taken to Dekeleia to the altar. If he (the phratriarkh) does not sacrifice at the
altar, he shall owe 50 drakhmas sacred to Zeus Phratrios: this sum of money
shall be exacted by the priest, or he himself shall owe it.

RO 5 (*IG* ii² 1237) A 1–58 (396/5)

This inscription, dating to 396/5, provides the most detailed evidence we have for the life of a phratry. It
poses some very complicated problems of interpretation – scholars have long debated whether the
Demotionidai or the Dekeleians are the phratry here, for instance – but it makes clear that the issue of phratry
membership bulked very large in phratry life and was thought to be a big deal. The procedure outlined here
was further amended by a subsequent decree recorded on the other side of the stone and not translated here.

Comparison of the procedure for admission to the phratry with the procedure for admission to a deme (**59**) – note in particular the use by the phratry of five advocates (*sunegoroi*), who have a rôle parallel to the five accusers (*kategoroi*) in **59** – is enlightening. For although the demesmen act under oath, there is no sign that admission to the deme is part of a religious occasion; but admission to a phratry takes place at the big phratry festival, the Apatouria, and is accompanied by sacrifices. The phratry has records (referred to later in the inscription as 'common records') but it appears to be run entirely by the phratriarkh and the phratry priest. The complicated relationship between Demotionidai and *oikos* of the Dekeleans here has no parallel in demes, where there are no sub-groups with special rôles, but can be compared to the relationship between the phratry and the Brytidai in **109**. The *meion* ('Lesser') and the *koureion* ('Hair-cutting') were two sacrifices, possibly corresponding to two points at which children were introduced when small to the *phrateres* and then registered when adolescents (perhaps at 16, perhaps at 18). See further Lambert (1993), Hedrick (1990).

112   Boundary-stone of land sold upon redemption to Kephisodoros of Leukonoion for 1500 drakhmas and to the *phrateres* with Eratostratos of Anaphlystos for 200 drakhmas and to the Glaukidai for 600 drakhmas and to the Epikleidai for 150 drakhmas and the *phrateres* with Nikon of Anaphlystos for 100 drakhmas.
Finley (1951/1985) no.41

This fourth-century boundary stone (*horos*), the findspot of which is unknown, is one of a number of such stones that have survived. Placed on the boundary of property, these served as notices to anyone who might buy the land that the land had been used as security for some sort of loan (which is what 'sold upon redemption' here means). These stones are interesting both for the evidence that they give for widespread borrowing among the propertied in classical Athens, and because of the social groups who are revealed to be willing to offer credit. What is notable in this case is that the same property is separately used to secure five different loans, two from groups of *phrateres* (presumably belonging to the same phratry with a local focus at Anaphlystos in SW Attica) and two from two different patrilineal groups, presumably *genē*.

113   Even if someone kills someone else unintentionally, he is to go into exile. The Basileis are to pass judgement of guilt on the one who killed or who planned the killing. The *Ephetai* are to decide. Pardon may be granted if the father or brother or sons all agree, otherwise the objector to prevail. If none of these relatives exists, then the relatives to the degree of first cousins once-removed and first cousins, if all are willing to pardon, if not the objector is to prevail. If none of these exists, and the killing was unintentional, and the fifty-one *Ephetai* decide that he killed unintentionally, let ten *phrateres* admit him [to Attica], if they are willing, and let the fifty-one choose these by rank.
ML 86.11–19 (409/8)

Although the inscription of this law of Drakon dates to 409–8, this is certainly an archaic law, and it shows the formal involvement of the phratry in the judicial arrangements of archaic Athens. The phratry stands here as the wider kin-group, empowered to act when there are no closer family who might do so. The Athenians regarded homicide as an offence against the family – it was actually a crime which only members of the family could prosecute. The provisions of this law are given also in Demosthenes 43.57, although the orator has there re-ordered some of the clauses. See above **19**. For the *ephetai* see **229**.

114   When he hosts a feast for the *phrateres* he asks for food from the common table for his slaves, and he lists the bits of radish left on the table so that the slaves serving do not take them.
Theophrastos *Characters* 30 (The Shabby Profiteer) 16

Compare this miserliness at the feast for the members of the phratry to that displayed in giving a feast for members of the deme at **89, 90**.

Genē

For *genē* and citizenship see above **106, 108, 109**.
For *genē* and the phratry see above **109, 111, 112**.

115   Gods. In the arkhonship of Kharikleides (363/2) at Athens the arbitrators, Stephanos of Myrrhinous, Kleagoras of Akharnai, Aristogeiton of Myrrhinous, Euthykrates of Lamptrai and Kephisodotos of Aithalidai, settled the disputes between the Salaminioi of the Heptaphylai (Seven Tribes) and the Salaminioi from Sounion on the following terms, both parties being mutually in agreement that the decision of the arbitrators was good: the priesthoods shall be common to both for all time, namely those of Athene Skiras, Herakles at Porthmos, Eurysakes, Aglauros and Pandrosos and Kourotrophos. When one of the priestesses or priests dies a successor shall be chosen by lot from both groups taken together. Those thus chosen by lot shall serve as priests on the same terms as those who held the priesthoods previously. The land at the Herakleion at Porthmos and the Saltpan and Agora in Koile shall be divided into two equal parts for each party, and each party shall set up boundary-markers of its own land. They shall sacrifice to the gods and heroes as follows: such victims as the city provides at public expense or as the Salaminioi happen to receive from the Oskhophoroi or the Deipnophoroi, these both parties shall sacrifice in common and each shall receive half the meat raw. Such victims, on the other hand, as the Salaminioi usually sacrificed from rental income, they shall sacrifice from their own funds according to ancestral custom, each party contributing half for all the sacrifices.

RO 37 (*SEG* 21.527) 1–27 (363/2)

Ironically, but not unusually, our richest source of evidence comes from a rather peculiar example of a *genos*. The Salaminioi, a *genos* whose link to the island of Salamis is mysterious, fell into two branches, the Salaminioi 'of the Seven Tribes' and the Salaminioi 'from Sounion'. These two branches came into dispute, and this is the record of the resolution of that dispute. Since that resolution involved recognizing the split in the *genos* it also involved listing all the resources of the *genos* and all the duties of the *genos*. We therefore get a picture of this *genos* as owning various tracts of land and other resources (notably a salt-pan) from which it derives rental income which it uses to fund its activities, which are entirely religious, involving the celebration of various festivals. Details of these sacrifices and of the rental arrangements are given later in the document. The Oskophoroi ('vine-branch carriers') and Deipnophoroi ('supper-carriers') were chosen by the *genos* to take partiular rôles in the festival. Presumably in return for the honour of having been chosen these men might provide additional sacrificial animals.

Although the origins, and perhaps the size, of this *genos* may be unusual, the pattern of *genos* property and sacrifices is probably relatively typical. It would presumably be on the basis of accumulated rental income that a *genos* would be in a position to lend money (cf. above **112**).

Orgeones

116   ...Seleukos in his commentary on Solon's *Axones* says that those who hold
meetings about some god or hero are called *orgeones*...

Souda s.v. *Orgeones*

Orgeones were members of cult groups officially recognized as having close knowledge of their members
(see above **106**). Unlike *genē*, however, *orgeones* did not all belong to the same family, and indeed we know
of the Thracian *orgeones* of the goddess Bendis (cf. **117**), so not all *orgeones* were Athenian citizens. See
further Jones (1999).

117   ...or as many as have been inscribed on the stele or their children. If any of those
orgeones who belong to the shrine sacrifice to the goddess they shall sacrifice
free of charge, but if some individual sacrifices to the goddess he is to give to
the priestess, in the case of a sucking animal 11/2 obols and the skin and
complete right thigh, and in the case of a full-grown animal 3 obols and the skin
and thigh in the same way, and in the case of an ox 11/2 obols. and the skin. In
the case of female victims the priestly portion is to be given to the priestess, and
in the case of male victims to the priest. No one is to sacrifice *parabomia* or
else owe 50 dr. In order to equip the building and the shrine the rent of the
building and the water, whatever it is sold for, is to be spent on the equipment
of the shrine and of the building and for nothing else, until the temple and the
building are equipped, unless the *orgeones* vote something else in the way of
expenditure on the shrine. Water to be reserved for the person renting. If anyone
speaks or puts something to the vote contrary to this law, let him who has spoken
or put it to the vote owe 50 dr. to the goddess, and let him cease to be a member
of the association. Those in charge are to record him as owing this money to
the goddess on the stele. The *epimeletai* and *hieropoioi* are to hold an agora and
meeting in the shrine concerning the affairs of the association on the second of
each month. Each of the *orgeones* who belong to the shrine is to give 2 dr. to
the *hieropoioi* for the sacrifice before the 16th of Thargelion, and whoever is in
Athens and well and does not pay shall owe 2 dr. sacred to the goddess. In order
that the *orgeones* might be as numerous as possible, it shall be possible for
anyone who wants to bring [*figure missing*] drakhmas and become a member
of the shrine and be inscribed on the stele, and the *orgeones* are to scrutinise
those inscribed on the stele and hand over the names of those who have been
scrutinized to the secretary during Thargelion.

IG ii^2 1361 (later 4th century)

This decree, which was found in Peiraieus and dates to the third quarter of the fourth century seems to belong
to the Athenian *orgeones* for Bendis – something deduced from the fact that the central annual event for this
thiasos is a sacrifice on 16th Thargelion, which we know to be the date of the festival of Bendis. The
administrative structure of the group includes *epimeletai*, *hieropoioi*, and a secretary, as well as a priestess.
The seriousness with which the group takes its own rules, with fines for those proposing anything that
contravenes them, is notable. The phrase 'sacrifice *parabomia*' occurs only in this insription and we do not
know what *parabomia* are.

Thiasoi

118 A group gathering for the rites and honour of a god. Thus Demosthenes and
Xenophon. But Ion uses the name for any gathering. Those who take part in
thiasoi are called *thiasotai*. So Isaios.

Souda s.v. *Thiasos*

Any group of revellers might be called a *thiasos*, and the word is also used for the entourage of a god. But
in Athens it acquired a semi-technical meaning as an association of individuals devoted to a particular cult.
The term occurs mainly in later classical and Hellenistic inscriptions.

119   In the arkhonship of Nikokles (302/1) the members of the *thiasos* decided:
since Stephanos the maker of breastplates, elected the official in charge of all
the association's affairs cared for the curatorial duties which he had to care for,
and in other respects was constantly diligent in the interests of the association,
and particularly sent out the procession for the Adonia in the ancestral way,
with good fortune, the members of the *thiasos* have decided to praise Stephanos,
the official in charge, for his diligence and goodness toward the association of
the members of the *thiasos* and to crown him with an olive crown and give him
10 drakhmas. Having been crowned by the association he made a dedication to
Demeter for the unity of the association. The members of the *thiasos* of
Aphrodite: Stephanos son of Mulothros.
      In the arkhonship of Klearkhos (301/300) the members of the *thiasos* decided:
since Stephanos formerly elected official in charge, and now chosen by lot to
be *hieropoios* with the other fellow *hieropoioi*, has been a good man and made
the sacrifices to the gods which are traditionaly theirs and has looked after all
the other things that he should have looked after, with good fortune the members
of the *thiasos* have decided to praise Stephanos the *hieropoios* for his goodness
and diligence towards the association of the *thiasotai* and to crown him with
an olive crown and give him 10 drakhmas. The members of the *thiasos* of
Aphrodite: Stephanos son of Mulothros.
      In the arkhonship of Hegemakhos (300/299), with good fortune Sokles
proposed: since Stephanos, elected *hieropoios*, looked after the sacrifice of
Aphrodite well, the members of the *thiasos* decided to praise Stephanos son of
Mulothros and to crown him with a crown of olive and give him 20 dr. from
the association funds, and he having taken it made a dedication in the sanctuary
with this decree written on it in order that those who are keen on the cult might
be many in the knowledge that the members of the *thiasos* know how to return
thanks.

IG ii^2 1261 (c.299)

In this and the next text, the *thiasos* conducts itself as if it were a formal sub-group of the city, not only
holding official meetings and electing (and scrutinizing) its own officials (an *epimeletes*, a secretary, and a
treasurer, who perhaps serve only once and for one year, and *hieropoioi* who can evidently be re-elected),
but passing honours for them in exactly the language that is used by the city itself and by demes and other
sub-groups (cf. Osborne 1989/2010). The man honoured has no demotic, and his father's name is the word
for a 'miller' and not otherwise attested as a personal name – which suggests that we may be dealing here
with a freedman whose father was, and perhaps died as, a slave.

120   In the arkhonship of Hegemakhos (300/299), on the 16th of Pyanopsion. A chief
meeting (*agora kuria*) of the members of the *thiasos*. The members of the
thiasos decided: Kleon son of Leokratos of Salamis said: since Demetrios,
having been chosen secretary by the members of the *thiasos* in the arkhonship
of Klearkhos (301/0), has looked after all the affairs of the members of the
thiasos well and justly and has given accounts correctly and has stood scrutiny
(*euthunē*) for the things he was responsible for, and did the audit for all the
others who handle the associations affairs, and now continues to do and to say
what is advantageous for the members of the *thiasos* as a group and for each
individual, and when the members of the *thiasos* voted to pay him from the
common funds he gave this pay to the members of the thiasos, with good
fortune, the members of the *thiasos* decided to praise Demetrios son of
Sosandros of Olynthos for his excellence and justice, which he continually
displays towards the association of the members of the *thiasos*, and to crown
him with a dedication worth 50 dr. The dedication is to be dedicated wherever
he wants in the sanctuary, provided he first asks the members of the *thiasos*, in
order that others may show keenness towards the members of the *thiasos*
knowing that they will receive thanks from the members of the *thiasos* for their
benefactions. The treasurer in the arkhonship of Hegemakhos is to give the
money for the dedication and to see that the dedication is completed as soon as
possible. And crown him with a crown of olive now, and the *hieropoioi*,
whoever are selected by lot to be *hieropoioi*, announce this crown after the
libations, that the association crowns Demetrios with this crown because of his
excellence and goodwill which he continually displays to the members of the
thiasos. If they fail to announce it they are to pay 50 dr. to the association. This
inscription is to be written on the dedication. The *thiasotai*: Demetrios of
Olynthos.

IG ii² 1263 (c.299)

Note that the man praised here is not an Athenian but a metic, and could not have been a member of a phratry
or deme. *Thiasoi* offered social opportunities for those excluded from official Athenian social life.

Other associations

121   Peisandros approached all the sworn groups which had sprung up earlier in the
city for the sake of law suits and magistracies.

Thucydides 8.54.4

It is not clear exactly what these 'sworn groups' (*synomosiai*) did, but presumably they offered to appear as
witnesses for each other in court, support each other in elections and perhaps persuade others not to put their
names forward for allotment when one of their number wished to be elected. These 'sworn groups' were
just one of a number of more or less directly political 'clubs' (*hetaireiai*), such as appear in the next passage.
For the context more generally see **48**.

122   I gather, gentlemen of the jury, that that Bakhion, who was executed by you,
and the Aristokrates who has bad eyes, and other such people, together with
Konon here were companions (*hetairoi*) when they were lads, and gave
themselves the name 'Triballians'. When they gathered together on any
occasion they made their supper from offerings left to Hekate and the pigs'

testicles with which people purify themselves before entering the assembly, and readily swore for or against anything.

Demosthenes 54.39 (uncertain date)

This is one of a number of occasions when casual groups of youths who form a 'club' or 'gang' are mentioned in speeches in court. The Triballians were a Thracian tribe, so the Athenian youths were declaring themselves to be barbarians.

9   THE COUNCIL OF 500

123   A council is a popular body; for there must be some such body whose concern is the preparation of business for the people so that they can be effective... The power of the council is weakened in democracies in which people come together and deal with everything themselves.

Aristotle *Politics* 1299b32–1300a1

124   Beside all these boards of officials is the board that that is most nearly supreme over all matters; for the same board often both executes business and introduces it as it presides over the masses, where the people is sovereign; for there must be a body to convene the sovereign body.

Aristotle *Politics* 1322b12–15

Aristotle's views in these two passages were no doubt influenced by Athenian practice although *probouleusis* in some form was widespread though (it seems) not quite universal. The Athenian Council did indeed both prepare business for the Assembly and see that the Assembly's decisions were carried out, but its own powers of decision were rather limited.

The importance of the Council of 500

125   The Council has to take many decisions on matters of the war, many on finance, many on legislation, many to do with what is happening at any time in the city, and many to do with the allies, and to receive tribute and administer the dockyards and sanctuaries?

Old Oligarch 3.2

Proposals made by the Council to the Assembly may have been proposed to it by individuals, but they may also have emerged from the discussions of the Council itself through its regular reviews of all the major areas of state activity. Almost all decrees ended up attributed to an individual proposer, but this may simply have been the man who formulated the plan for action arising from the Council discussion.

126   On only one street in the city was he to be seen walking – the one to the Agora and the Council-house.

Plutarch *Perikles* 7.4

This anecdote, even if untrue, nicely illustrates the way in which political power depended in important ways on getting matters discussed by the Council – even if an individual could serve on the Council only twice in a lifetime. For Perikles as a politician see below **384–90**.

The 'standing committee' of *prytaneis*

127   The Council of 500 is chosen by lot, 50 from each tribe. Each tribal contingent
in turn, as determined by lot, serves as the Council's *prytaneis* (presiding
committee), the first four for thirty-six days each and the remaining six for
thirty-five days each – the year is a lunar year. In the first place, the *prytaneis*
eat together in the Roundhouse (*Tholos*), at the city's expense. Secondly, it
convenes meetings of the Council and of the people – of the Council every day
that is not a day of exemption, of the people four times each prytany (the 36 or
35 days served by the *prytaneis*). They lay down what business the Council is
to deal with, what business on each particular day, and where it is to meet. They
also lay down the business of the Assembly. In each prytany there is a principal
meeting at which there is a vote of confidence to decide whether the officials
are performing their duties properly...Heralds and embassies report first to the
prytaneis, and bearers of letters deliver them to the *prytaneis*.

[Aristotle] *Constitution of the Athenians* 43.2–4, 6

These arrangements current in the 330s and 320s differ in detail from those that applied in the fifth century,
but the essential structure of meetings, with a standing committee of *prytaneis*, a Council meeting daily, and
an Assembly meeting about 40 times a year, goes back at least to the Ephialtic reforms of 462.

128   There is a single chairman of the *prytaneis*, appointed by lot: he is in charge for
a night and a day, and the same man is not allowed to serve for longer than that
or for a second time. This man keeps the keys of the temples in which the public
funds and records and the public seal are stored, and he and a third of the
prytaneis, chosen by himself, must remain in the Roundhouse. Whenever the
prytaneis bring together the Council or the Assembly, this is the man who
chooses by lot nine *proedroi*, one from each tribe except the tribe whose prytany
it is, and also out of these one president, and he hands over the order of
proceeding to them.

[Aristotle] *Constitution of the Athenians* 44.1–2

Modern scholars dispute whether this passage means a man could serve as chairman of the *prytaneis* once
during each year of his service on the Council or just once in a lifetime. Either way, the Athenian decision
to prevent any individual building up power by holding such an office repeatedly is remarkable. The degree
of engagement and expertise that was demanded of this temporary chairman was considerable. See below
145 for Sokrates as chairman. The *proedroi* were an invention of the early fourth century.

129   For sure, he arranges with the *prytaneis*, so that he can announce the sacred rites
to the people, and having got himself kitted out in a splendid cloak and put on
a crown goes and says 'O men of Athenians, we *prytaneis* have sacrificed the
Galaxia to the Mother of the Gods, and the sacrifices were good and you receive
the blessings.' When he has made this announcement, he goes away home and
tells his wife how this was an excessively good day.

Theophrastos *Characters* 21 ('Petty Ambition') 11

This little vignette is a useful reminder of how special it will have been for many Athenians to serve on the
Council. The Galaxia ('Milk-feast') seems to have been a festival at which the Athenians consumed barley
porridge cooked in milk.

130   I know that all the *prytaneis* sacrifice as a group on each occasion and dine together with each other and pour libations together. But that does not mean that the good men mimic the bad; rather, if they find one of their number doing wrong they report it the Council and to the people. The Council likewise sacrifices at the beginning of its term, and feasts together. The generals share libations and sacred rites. So do practically all other magistrates. But does that mean that they turn a blind eye to members who do wrong? Far from it.

Demosthenes 19.190 (343)

The idea that one member of the Council or the *prytaneis* should tell on another was part of the theory of having large boards of magistrates. 500, or even 50, was a large enough group to ensure that group solidarity did not overrule the desire not to be implicated in another's wrongdoing. For Council sacrifices see also **354**.

Councillors' conditions of service

131   'In order', Sokrates said, 'that there might be no doubt, define for me the age up until which one must consider people young'. And Kharikles said, 'For as long as they are not allowed to serve on the Council, on the grounds that they are not wise; so you too are not to converse with those younger than 30.'

Xenophon *Memorabilia* 1.2.35

This comment, in the context of the accusation that Sokrates corrupted the young, is the only explicit evidence we have that those on the Council had to be 30. Despite recent claims to the contrary (cf. Davidson 2007), Greek age terminology seems to have been quite fluid.

132   When these dispositions had been made, the Four Hundred went, each with a dagger concealed about his person, accompanied by 120 young men, whom they employed whenever physical force was needed, and confronted the lot-selected Council who were in the Council-house. They told them to take their pay and go. They had brought them pay for the rest of their term and gave it to them as they left.

Thucydides 8.69.4

This is the only evidence for the fifth-century Council having been paid. We do not know when pay began, but it is likely that it happened following the reforms of Ephialtes (cf. **127** on the *prytaneis*).

133   The Council receives 5 obols a day. For the *prytaneis* an extra obol is added to this for maintenance.

[Aristotle] *Constitution of the Athenians* 62.2

The Councillors met daily, except on holidays, but on many days the meeting may have been brief. The *prytaneis* were on constant duty.

Council procedure

Summoning the Council

134   Peisandros and Kharikles, who in those days were regarded as devoted to the democracy, were members of the commission of enquiry. They maintained that what had happened was not the work of a few men but a step towards the overthrow of the democracy; consequently, enquiries should still be pursued as vigorously as ever. The state of the city was such that when the herald summoned the Council to the Council-house by lowering the flag, not only did the Council go to the Council-house, but those in the Agora fled from it, each in terror of arrest.

Andokides 1.36 (400)

The implication of this claim, describing state action following the mutilation of the Hermai, is that Councillors were expected to be within sight of this flag, which is only ever mentioned here.

The Council's religious rituals

135   The prosecution ... could see that I was serving on the Council and using the Council-house. In that very building there stands a shrine of Zeus the Councillor and Athene the Councillor, and the Councillors offer prayers as they enter. I was one of them and did likewise. Together with them I entered all the other holy places, sacrificing and praying on behalf of the city, and in addition to that I was a *prytaneus* for all but two days of the first prytany and acted as *hieropoios* and sacrificed on behalf of democracy and put matters to the vote and spoke opinions about matters of the greatest moment and it was clear to everyone that I was an important citizen.

Antiphon 6.45 (between 422 and 411)

Debates in the Council

136   DEMOSTHENES: Look over there [at the audience]. Can you see the host assembled there, row upon row?
       SAUSAGE-SELLER: Yes, I can.
       DEMOSTHENES: Of all of them shall you be the lord, and of the Agora and of the harbour and of Pnyx. You will trample on the Council and trim the generals...

Aristophanes *Knights* 162–6 (424)

One of the notable features of *Knights* is that Aristophanes chooses to make the body who are persuaded by rhetoric, and for whose support Paphlagon and the Sausage-Seller compete, not the Assembly, despite the appearance of the personified People at the end of the play, but the Council. See further below **397–400**.

137   SAUSAGE-SELLER: The Council looked expectantly at me again. When he (Paphlagon) heard it, he was dumbfounded and started babbling. Thereupon the *prytaneis* and the archers began to drag him out.

Aristophanes *Knights* 663–6 (424)

The Athenians maintained a body of Scythian archers to act as a sort of riot police (cf. **429**). They saw to the preservation of public order but had no investigative rôle or rôle in bringing cases to court. See Bäbler (2005).

138   PAPHLAGON: How could there be a citizen more devoted to you, Mr. Demos, than I? In the first place, when I served on the Council, I raised enormous sums for the treasury on your behalf: some men I racked, some I throttled, and from

some I demanded a percentage. I cared nothing for any individual if only I could gratify you.

Aristophanes *Knights* 773–6 (424)

The rôle of the Council as a court is strongly emphasized here, perhaps with the overtone that it was, as a court, all too easily persuaded to take decisions that would be profitable for the city. For the Councils as court see also **155, 163, 167, 170–3**.

The Council's oath

139   I will serve as a Councillor in accordance with the laws.

I will give the best counsel I can to the Athenian people.

I will not bind any Athenian who puts forward three sureties from his own census class, except in cases when someone is caught conspiring to betray the city or to end democracy, or who has bought a tax or gone surety or made a contribution and not paid.

I will not exile or bind or execute anyone without trial.

I will declare it if I know that any of those selected by lot is unsuitable to be a Councillor.

[*added when ML 45 was passed*] If anyone strikes a silver coin in the cities and does not use the coins of the Athenians or their weights or their measures, but uses foreign coins and weights and measures, I will punish and penalise him according to the former decree which Klearkhos proposed.

[*added in 410/9*] I will sit in the seat allotted to me.

[*added in 403/2*] I will not hear any prosecution or action upon summary arrest brought over what has occurred prior to the arkhonship of Eukleides except in the case of those in exile.

Various sources, gathered by Rhodes (1972) 194

For the introduction of the Council's oath see above **39**.

The Council sets the agenda for the Assembly

140   The Council presents preliminary resolutions to the people, and the people are not allowed to decide anything which is not the subject of a preliminary resolution and placed on the agenda by the presiding committee.

[Aristotle] *Constitution of the Athenians* 45.4

Politically the most important thing that the Council did was to discuss in advance all business due to be conducted at the Assembly and to draft possible resolutions for the Assembly to agree to.

141   In those constitutions (oligarchies and tyrannies) everything happens by order, rapidly, but in your case first the Council has to hear about everything and make a proposal, and do this whenever notice is given for heralds and embassies, not on any old occasion. Then there has to be a meeting of the Assembly, and that at times laid down by law. Then those who give the best advice have to conquer and overcome those who speak against them either out of ignorance or out of bloody-mindedness.

Demosthenes 19.185 (343)

The inability of a democracy to decide fast, or in secret, was from time to time a problem for the Athenians.

142   There arrived in haste ambassadors from Sparta who were reputed friendly
to Athens...They said their piece to the Council, adding that they had come with
full powers to resolve all differences. Alkibiades was afraid that if they said the
same things to the people, they might carry the masses with them and the
alliance with Argos might be rejected.

Accordingly, he devised the following stratagem against them. By giving
them a solemn assurance, he persuaded the Spartans that if they concealed from
the Assembly that they had come with full powers, he would restore Pylos to
them – he, the current opponent of restitution, would so persuade the Athenians
– and would resolve the other points at issue. He did this because he wanted to
detach them from Nikias, and also so that he could denounce them to the people
as quite insincere about their intentions and completely inconsistent in their
utterances, and thereby make allies of the Argives, Eleans and Mantineians.
And so it turned out. When they appeared before the people, they said, under
questioning, that they had not, as they had told the Council, come with full
powers. The Athenians lost patience.

Thucydides 5.44.3–45.4

This incident (summer 420) illustrates how a skilful and dishonest individual could exploit the decision-
making structures at Athens in order to produce a particular outcome.

143   It was evening when someone arrived and announced to the *prytaneis* that
Elateia had been captured. On hearing this, some immediately got up in the
middle of supper, cleared people from the stalls in the market-place and burnt
the wicker screens, while others sent for the generals and summoned the
trumpeter. The whole city was full of noise. On the next day, at dawn the
prytaneis summoned the Council to the Council-chamber while you all made
your way to the Assembly; before the Council could proceed to business or
propose a motion the whole body of citizens had taken their places.
Subsequently, when the Council arrived and the *prytaneis* had reported what
had been announced to them, the messenger was introduced and told his tale;
the herald then put the question 'Who wishes to speak?' No one came forward.
Although he asked frequently, but there was still no response, though all the
generals were there and all the active politicians, and though our fatherland was
calling for someone to speak for her safety.

Demosthenes 18.169–71 (330)

This famous scene relating the Athenians' reaction to news of Philip of Macedon's capture of Elateia in
Phokis in 338, indicates the responsibility that might rest on the *prytaneis* in time of war, and the extent to
which the Athenians relied on individuals with public spirit to make the democratic system work.

144   When this decree had been presented by us in the Council and again in the
Assembly, the people approved our actions and the whole city chose to fulfil
its religious obligations. Demosthenes then spoke in opposition in accordance
with the money pledged to him from Amphissa and I clearly refuted him before
you. Then, since the man could not openly trick the city, he entered the Council

chamber and cleared the private individuals and brought a proposal to the Assembly which took advantage of the inexperience of the man drafting the proposal. He managed to get this same proposal voted through in the Assembly and become a decree of the people just as the Assembly was adjourning after I had gone away – for I would never have advised it to agree – and many had left.

Aiskhines 3.125–6 (330)

The truth of Aiskhines' charges against Demosthenes is less important than the procedure which Aiskhines outlines. Demosthenes seems to have been a member of the Council in this year, but gets another to put forward the proposal, presumably because it was more effective for him to be able to support another's proposal in the Assembly than simply speak on behalf of his own proposal.

Members of the Council take charge of Assembly meetings

145   SOKRATES: Gentlemen of Athens, I never held any other office in the city, but I did serve on the Council. It so happened that our tribe, Antiokhis, was presiding when you wanted to try *en bloc* the ten generals who had failed to pick up the casualties from the sea battle – unconstitutionally, as you all later realised. At the time, however, I alone of the *prytaneis* opposed your doing anything contrary to the law, and I voted against the proposal.

Plato *Apology* 32ab

It is an extraordinary co-incidence that Sokrates should have been the man picked by lot to be president of the *prytaneis* on the day when the proposal to put the generals at Arginousai on trial was made (see further **213, 215**). It is worth nothing that Sokrates was 65 years old at the time, and also that although he was so well known in the city, and although some people thought him exceptional for his wisdom, he failed to persuade the Athenians that what they were doing was illegal. The influence of officials was evidently very small.

The duties of the Council recited to justify honouring them

146   The Council under Pythodotos, arkhon (343/2), made this dedication to Hephaistos, having been crowned by the people for its excellence and justice. Deinostratos son of Deiniades of Ankyle proposed: since the Council under Pythodotos, arkhon, voted to pass judgement on those speaking in the Council in the ninth prytany and to honour whoever seems to it to have continued during the year to speak and act best, and without being bribed, on behalf of the Council and people of the Athenians, and judged, after a vote on this matter in favour of Phanodemos son of Diyllos of Thymaitadai, the Council has decided, with good fortune of the Athenian people and of the Council, to praise Phanodemos son of Diyllos of Thymaitadai for his excellence and justice toward the Council and Athenian people, and crown him with a crown from 500 drakhmas, the money for the crown to be from the decreed expense account for the Council. Those chosen to make the dedication are to inscribe on the dedication this decree of the Council. In order that the people, knowing what the Council has voted about Phanodemos, will honour him itself and crown him, if the people decides as the Council has, whichever *proedroi* obtain the lot to be *proedroi* at the first assembly should bring up the matter of Phanodemos, and the secretary shall read this decree to the people, and add the resolution of the Council to the people that the Council thinks, since Phanodemos son of Diyllos of Thymaitadai has served the Council well and justly, and without being bribed, saying and doing what is best on behalf of the Council and Athenian people and their allies, that they should praise him for his excellence and justice towards the Council and Athenian people and the allies and crown him with a gold crown from 1000 drakhmas whenever he submits to scrutiny and the money for this to come from whichever fund the people decides. In order that all the others might know that the people and Council is minded to thank those who continually say and do what is best on behalf of the Council and the people, the prytany secretary is to write this decree on a stone stele and stand it on the Akropolis, and the treasurer of the people is to give...drakhmas from the decreed expenses for the inscription of the stele...

IG ii^2 223A (343/2)

This decree, passed in 343/2 serves nicely to illustrate the procedure, whereby the Council made a resolution and this was then introduced to the Assembly by the *proedroi* (see above **128**). But it is a decree of interest in its own right since Phanodemos is someone who, as well as his political involvement, was one of the local historians of Athens writing in the middle of the fourth century. Only a handful of fragments of Phanodemos' history of Athens remain, but they are sufficient to show that he spent much time on the mythical period, and that he gave Athens a starring rôle at every possible opportunity (having the Greeks sail to Troy from Brauron in Attica rather than from Aulis in Boiotia, for instance).

The Council leaving it to the Assembly

147   Gods. In the arkhonship of Nikokrates (333/2), in the prytany of Aigeis being the first prytany, the *proedros* who put matters to the vote being Theophilos of Phegous, the Council resolved. Antidotos son of Apollodoros of Sypalettos proposed: concerning the matter about which the Kitians speak concerning the foundation of the sanctuary to Aphrodite, the Council decided that the *proedroi* who are allotted to be *proedroi* at the first assembly should introduce them and deal with the matter and contribute the opinion of the Council to the people that the Council resolves that the people shall listen to the Kitians about the foundation of the sanctuary and to any other Athenian who wants, and decide as seems to it to be best. In the arkhonship of Nikokrates, in the prytany of Pandionis being the second prytany, the *proedros* who put matters to the vote being Phanostratos of Philaidai, the people decided. Lykourgos son of Lykophron of Boutadai proposed: concerning the matter about which the Kitian merchants thought it lawful to be suppliant, requesting from the people right to own land on which they would found a sanctuary of Aphrodite, the people decided to give the Kitian merchants the right to own land on which to found a sanctuary of Aphrodite, just as the Egyptians founded the sanctuary of Isis.

RO 91 (*IG* ii^2 337) (333/2)

Although usually the Council brought a specific proposal to the people, it could simply put a matter on the agenda of the Assembly and leave the Assembly to decide what to do. Why it did that in this case is not clear. But it is notable that when the matter is brought to the Assembly it is the prominent politician Lykourgos who takes the lead and makes the proposal.

The Council oversees magistrates

148 The Council vets the next year's Councillors and the nine arkhons. It used in
past times to have power to reject someone at their examination but now there
is opportunity to appeal to a court.

[Aristotle] *Constitution of the Athenians* 45.3

Perhaps the most important rôle of the Council after that of preparing business for the Assembly was to vet
officials. It oversaw much of the state's administration (cf. **152**, below), and vetting may be considered a
part of that.

149 I think I deserve, Council, that no more trouble comes my way, provided I can
just prove to you that I am well-disposed towards the status quo and that I have
been compelled to share in the same dangers as you. If I appear otherwise to
have lived a life of moderation and very contrary to the opinion and claims of
my enemies, I beg you to pass me at my examination. First of all I will show
that I was not a member of the cavalry, and was not even in Attica, under the
Thirty and that I had no part in that constitution.

Lysias 16.3 (393–89)

The implication here is that the Council when examining candidates for office took their past political action
into account – even despite the amnesty (above **49**).

150 I would never have thought, Council, that Philon would become so brazen as
to be willing to come to you to be examined. But since he is daring not in just
one respect but in many, and since I entered the Council chamber having sworn
to advise the city as best I can, and it is in the oath that one should reveal if one
knows any of those who have been selected by lot to be unsuitable to serve as
a Councillor, I will make an accusation against Philon here, not because I am
bringing any private hostility towards him, nor encouraged by being able and
accustomed to speaking among you, but trusting in the number of his offences
and believing that I should abide by the oaths that I have sworn.

Lysias 31.1–2 (shortly after 403)

151 In addition to this, the Council interrogates all who intend to serve in some
public office, asking what sort of a person he is, if he does good to his parents,
if he has served campaigns on behalf of the city, if he has ancestral cults, if he
pays his taxes. Aristogeiton could not show any of these in regard to himself:
for instead of doing good to his parents, he had harmed his father; when you
all campaigned, he was in prison; he is so far from having a memorial to his
father to show off, Athenians, that when his father died in Eretria he did not
even carry out the usual burial rites for him there; and when other Athenians
pay contributions from their private funds he has not even paid all the public
debts that he owes!

Deinarkhos 2.17–18 (323)

152 In general the Council co-operates in the administrative work of the other
officials.

[Aristotle] *Constitution of the Athenians* 47.1

153   The Council has jurisdiction over most officials, especially those who handle
money.

[Aristotle] *Constitution of the Athenians* 45.2

154   There are ten *poletai,* one appointed by lot from each tribe. They are responsible
for all leases, and let out the contracts for the mines and taxes, together with the
treasurer of the stratiotic fund and those chosen to be in charge of the theoric
fund, in the presence of the Council. The vote of the Council makes the
transactions valid... And the property of those convicted in the Areopagos and
the others they sell in the presence of the Council, but the nine arkhons validate
these. They record the taxes which are sold annually on whitened boards,
recording both the purchaser and the price paid, and then hand over the boards
to the Council.

[Aristotle] *Constitution of the Athenians* 47.2

'Whitened boards' were used for listing things when the information on the list was only needed for, or only
true for, a short while. For the theoric fund and the stratiotic fund see **68**, p.132 and **415**.

155   [The *apodektai*] receive all (the instalment payments) on the first of two
successive days, and apportion the money among the magistrates; and on the
second day they bring the record of the apportionment, written on a wooden
tablet, and read it in the Council chamber. They place before the Council the
questions of whether anyone knows of any person, public official or private
individual, who is guilty of wrongdoing in regard to the apportionment, and
they put it to the vote for a decision if someone seems to have done wrong.

[Aristotle] *Constitution of the Athenians* 48.2

As with issues concerned with the navy, so with these financial issues the Council acts as a court of immediate
judgement. The 'apportionment' here is effectively the Athenian budget procedure; we first meet this in 386
BC (and the theory is discussed at Aristotle *Politics* 1321b31–3). In the fifth century everything was simply
paid out of a single central fund with no decisions in advance about how much should be spent on each area
– the mark of a city that always had enough money for everything.

156   The Council used to judge the models and the *peplos*, but now a lawcourt chosen
by lot does so. For the Council seemed to show favouritism in its judgement.
The Council helps the treasurer of the stratiotic fund take care of the making of
Victories and the Panathenaic games.

[Aristotle] *Constitution of the Athenians* 49.3

Presumably the disadvantage with the Council is that everyone knew who the members were, and so could
soften them up in advance. The models in question seem to be architectural models. The *peplos* is the garment
presented to Athene at the Panathenaia. All the things mentioned in this passage are linked by being
connected to the worship of the gods.

157   Gla]ukos proposed...appoint a priestess for Athene Nike...she is to be appointed
from all Athenian women, and to put a door on the sanctuary according to the
specifications of Kallikrates. The *poletai* are to put this out to tender in the
prytany of Leontis. The priestess is to receive 50 drakhmas and the legs and
hides from the public sacrifices. And build a temple according to the

specifications of Kallikrates and a stone altar. Hestiaios said: choose three men
from the Council who will help Kallikrates draw up the specifications and will
show the Council how it should be put out to tender.

ML 44 (440s or 430s)

What in the fourth-century were standing arrangements seem to have been rather less fixed in the fifth. The
Council does indeed end up here closely involved in the building of a temple, but only as an afterthought
introduced by an amendment to a decree which may have been proposed in the Assembly itself to replace
a Council proposal or because the Council proposal had simply introduced a discussion (as above **147**). This
is in fact a fine example of the way in which Athenian decrees might reflect a series of not very well structured
proposals, because that is how those proposals came up in a speech. Here proposals about the creation of a
priesthood are mixed up with proposals about doing building work in a sanctuary. In the fourth century such
a mixture would not have been possible since the proposals about the priesthood were to set up a permanent
arrangement, and this would have had to have been a matter of law and to have gone through the hands of
the *nomothetai*, whereas the building works were a matter of a one-off decision and remained with the
Assembly. Here the amendment rescues the Athenians from giving *carte blanche* to Kallikrates, one of the
architects associated with the Parthenon project, to build anything he would like. The decision that the
priestess should be drawn from all Athenian women is a democratic feature and in line with other priests
established in the fifth century who were chosen from the Athenians at large rather than from particular
families (*genē*; contrast **115**).

158   Let the Council choose heralds and send them out to the cities to announce what
the people have decided... Once they have recorded on a tablet the amount of
grain from the demarkhs, deme by deme, and the amount from the cities, city
by city, they are to deposit a copy in the Eleusinion at Eleusis and another in
the Council chamber.

ML 73.22–3, 26–30 (430s)

We see much less of the Council as the executive power in Athens, carrying through the instructions of the
Assembly, than we see of it as a body preparing the business (for the politics of this see below Note D). This
is a product of the lack of interest of our literary sources in how decisions got executed, and the fact that it
is the decision by the Assembly that inscribed decrees publish. Nevertheless a number of decrees write into
their text the precise responsibilities of the Council for carrying out the people's intentions. Here the Council
is responsible for overseeing the collection and handling of the grain that Athens has decided to ask other
Greeks to bring as an offering to Demeter and Persephone at Eleusis.

159   Kleinias proposed: The Council and the magistrates in the cities and the
Inspectors are to take care that the tribute be collected each year and brought
to Athens.

ML 46.5–11 (420s)

In the Athenian Empire it was the Council that had final oversight of everything to do with tribute payments.

160   The [*thesmo*]*thetai* are to set up a new [court of 1,000 jurors].
[As to the tribute, since] it has become less, let [this court], together with the
Council, hold an assessment during the month of Poseideion (January/
February), [just as in the last] term of office, of [all the assessments]
proportionately. They shall deal with the matter every day from the beginning
of the month [to ensure that] the tribute [is assessed] in Poseideion. [The full
Council] [20] is also to deal with the matter [continuously, to ensure that] the

assessment happens, provided [that there is no contrary decree of the people. They must not [assess less] tribute for any [city] than the tribute that city [has brought in before now], unless there [seems to be such shortage of resources that] that territory cannot [bring in more]. The Secretary [of the Council is to] write up this decision and this [decree and this] tribute that is assessed [for each city on two] stelai and [place one in the] Council Chamber [25] and one [on the Akropolis]. The *poletai* [are to put this out to contract] and the *kolakretai* [are to provide the money].

ML 69 (= LACTOR 1⁴ 138) 16–26 (425/4)

This tribute re-assessment decree from 425–4 nicely reveals the central rôle of the Council in overseeing tribute collection and tribute assessment. In this year the Athenians, who had recently taken various measures to tighten up tribute repayment (LACTOR 1⁴ **136**, **190**) decided to have an exceptional review of tribute payments and increased many of them very substantially so that the total of the assessment was recorded as something over 1460T. For the rôle of *thesmothetai* see **246**.

161   Let the Treasurers selected by lot count up, weigh and receive the money from those currently holding office as Treasurers, Overseers and *hieropoioi* in the temples, on the Akropolis in the presence of the Council, and let them write up everything on one stele, listing for every god how much money each has, and the total of all together, keeping gold and silver separate.

ML 58.18–22 (late 430s)

The Athenians on the eve of the Peloponnesian War (this decree may date to 434/3 or 431) decided to bring in the monies from sanctuaries in Attica to a consolidated treasury on the Akropolis, and this exercise too was one that the Council oversaw. For the earlier part of this decree see **357**.

162   Phanostratos of Thorai: 250 dr. having been Treasurer of the Trieropoiic fund in the arkhonship of Kharikleides (363/2), and the amount that he gave as an instalment in the Council chamber: 180 dr.

IG ii² 1622.564–72 (342/1)

163   The Council which is in power whenever it has funds sufficient for managing the city does nothing wrong, but when it is short it is compelled to accept impeachments and confiscate citizens' property and obey those politicians who give the worst possible advice.

Lysias 30.22 (399)

This claim reveals both the suspicions about the Council which it was possible for Athenians to voice in court (in 399 BC in this case), and the stress under which the Council was put in its attempts to keep control of Athenian finances. See above **138**. On similar tendencies in other courts see **271**.

164   The Council examines also the disabled. For there is a law that orders the Council to examine those who have less than 3 minas worth of property and who have some physical disability so as not to be able to do any work, and give them maintenance of two obols a day, and a Treasurer is appointed by lot for them.

[Aristotle] *Constitution of the Athenians* 49.4

Since a property of 300 dr. (= 3 minas) capital value is unlikely to yield even 40 dr. a year, this disability pension is hardly generous. Lysias 24 is a speech to the Council justifying the need for a disability allowance by someone who has been attacked as not coming within the rules.

165 SOKRATES: Where have you come from, Menexenos? The Agora?

MENEXENOS: Yes, Sokrates, from the Council-house.

SOKRATES: What took you there in particular? No doubt you think you've finished with education and philosophy and believe that you are now ready to turn to greater things. And, young as you are, do you intend to rule over us your elders, so that your house may never cease to provide someone to watch over us?

MENEXENOS: If you, Sokrates, allow and advise me to hold office, I shall do so eagerly; otherwise, not. Actually, though, I went to the Council-house because I had heard that the Council was about to choose the funeral orator. They are about to perform the rites, you know.

SOKRATES: Of course. Who did they choose?

MENEXENOS: They didn't. They put it off till tomorrow.

Plato *Menexenos* 234ab

Although the giver of the annual Funeral Oration over the war dead is not usually thought of as an office, it is notable that the process of choice involved not allotment but election, and election by the Council after discussion.

The Council overseas the navy

166 The Council takes care of the triremes that have been built and the equipment and the shipsheds, and it builds new triremes or quadriremes, whichever the people vote for, and the equipment for these and sheds. The people elect by vote masterbuilders for the ships. If the Council fails to hand these over completed to the new Council, the Councillors cannot receive the donation; in that case they take it under the later Council. The Council makes the triremes, having chosen ten men of its own number as trireme-builders.

[Aristotle] *Constitution of the Athenians* 46.1–2

167 When I was deprived of my pledges by Theophemos and was beaten up, I went to the Council and showed the marks of the blows and told what I had suffered and that I was trying to extract the equipment for the city. The Council, angry at what I had suffered and seeing the state I was in, came to the conclusion that it was not me that was the victim of violence but itself and the people that had voted and the law which compelled extraction of equipment. It ordered me to bring an impeachment, and the *prytaneis* to give him notice of the judgement in two days' time on the grounds that he was a wrong-doer and preventing the expedition, because he did not give back the equipment and deprived me of the pledges and beat me up when I was extracting the equipment and helping the city. Well, when the judgement came round for Theophemos in the Council according to the impeachment which I brought, we had a chance to give accounts. The Councillors voted secretly, and he was convicted in the Council chamber and found guilty of wrongdoing. And when the Council had to vote whether to hand him over to a court, or fine him 500 dr., the amount it can itself fine according to the laws...

                                                          Demosthenes 47.41–43 (after 356)

Financing the fleet in the fourth century was something that the Athenians found burdensome, and the attempt to minimize expenditure led to various conflicts which are likely to have made the rôle of the Council in overseeing the arrangements for the navy particularly fraught.

168   The Council of 500 is to look after the dispatch of the colony, punishing those trierarkhs who are disorderly, in accordance with the laws. The *prytaneis* are to call a session of the Council continuously at the Jetty on the matter of the dispatch, until the dispatch happens. The people are to choose 10 men from the whole citizen body to be Dispatchers, and those chosen are to look after the dispatch according to the orders of the Council. The Council and the *prytaneis* who have looked after the dispatch may be crowned with a gold crown worth 1000 dr. If this decree needs anything on the matter of the dispatch the Council shall have powers to vote it as long as it does not annul anything that has been voted by the people.

                                                                  RO 100.242–69 (325/4)

The Council overseas the cavalry

169   The Council examines the cavalry horses, and if anyone has a fine horse but seems to look after it badly, it stops his fodder allowance. They brand with a wheel mark on the jaw any horse unable to take part or unwilling to remain in line but inclined to run away, and the horse that suffers this is rejected at examination. It also examines the scouts, as many as it decides are suitable to be scouts, and if it votes against any, that one leaves the ranks. It examines also the *hamippoi*, and if it votes against one he ceases to receive pay. The Cataloguers, ten men that the people elects, catalogue the cavalry. They hand over those they enter into catalogue to the hipparkhs and phylarkhs, and these take them and bring the catalogue to the Council, and open the tablet in which the names of the cavalry are sealed. They erase the names of those formerly recorded, who have sworn that they are physically unfit to be in the cavalry, and summon those who have been catalogued; and if someone swears that he is physically unfit or has insufficient property to serve in the cavalry they release him, and if an individual has not sworn himself off they vote about whether he is able to be a member of the cavalry or not. And if they vote positively they inscribe his name onto the tablet, and if not they also let this man go.

                                        [Aristotle] *Constitution of the Athenians* 49.1–2

Being a member of the cavalry was an honour but also a burden, both financially and in terms of military service.

The Council hears impeachments

170   According to the law governing impeachment...which covers cases...where there is no law and some magistrate or orator is caught doing wrong, impeachment is given against him to the Council, and if he seems to have done a not very serious wrong the Council imposes a fine, but if a greater wrong then they hand him over to a court. And the assessment is made of what he must suffer or pay. Impeachment is available against orators who subvert democracy, or advise things that are not best for the city, or who have deserted to the enemy without having been sent, or have betrayed a guardpost or an army or ships, as Theophrastos says in his book *On Laws*.

Pollux 8.51

On the procedure for impeachment see Rhodes (1979); see also above **163, 167**.

171　So why do you think that we have to have impeachments available? You have specified this in detail in the law to prevent anyone being ignorant: 'If someone,' the law says, 'brings down the people of Athens'. That, jurors, is reasonable, for such a reason precludes pleas or delaying oaths and must be brought to the court as quickly as possible; 'or conspires in any way to bring down the people or forms a faction or if anyone betrays a city or ships or fleet or army, or, being a public speaker gives advice to the Athenian people which is not of the best because he has taken money'.

Hypereides *Defence of Euxenippos* 7–8 (330–24)

The term translated 'faction' here (*hetaireia*) lies behind the language which Herodotos uses to describe Kleisthenes' revolution, but otherwise is not met, except in much later sources (cf. **187**) till the context of the oligarchic coup of 411 (**48**). Forming a group with some political objective was clearly not against the law, and we should be wary of the amount of interpolation Hypereides had engaged in here.

172　I was about to prosecute Aristion, Philinos and Ampelinos and also the secretary to the *thesmothetai*, with whose embezzlements they had been involved, on charges which I had brought before the Council in the form of an impeachment.

Antiphon 6.35 (422–411)

173　A second act of informing took place. Teukros, a metic here, who had gone off secretly to Megara, sent a message to the Council from there that if they gave him immunity, he would give information about the Mysteries, since he had been a participant, and about his fellow-participants, and tell what he knew about the mutilation of the Herms. The Council took the vote (it had full powers for this), and went to Megara after him. Brought back to Athens and receiving immunity he listed his fellow-participants.

Andokides 1.15 (400)

The mutilation of the Herms in 415 caused a major panic in Athens because it was seen as an action offensive to the gods (see above Note C). Very unusually a state enquiry was launched, and it was that enquiry that turned up evidence for the parodying of the Mysteries. The investigative work was then overseen by the Council, whose powers in that capacity we see in action here. See also **134, 373–7**.

10   THE ASSEMBLY

The range of the Assembly's powers

174   Now we may say that the most important subjects about which all men deliberate and on which political orators give advice are five in number: revenue, war and peace, the defence of the realm, imports and exports, and legislation.

Aristotle *Rhetoric* 1359b19–23

175   As for you (the assembled people), there is no one else by whom you could be accused. It is rightly in your power to order what is yours – well or, if you so wish, ill.

Andokides 2.19–20 (perhaps 409/8)

The irresponsibility of the Assembly

176   DIODOTOS: Considering the gravity of the matter, we speakers ought, even in these circumstances, to make some claim to look further ahead than you, who have only a moment for consideration, especially as we are accountable for the advice we give, whereas you who listen are accountable to no one. If those who gave the advice and those who took it suffered equally, you would judge more sensibly.

Thucydides 3.43.4

The Assembly had no power set over it – although proposals passed by it could be subject to court action – and the people could not be called to account for anything that they had decided to do.

Attendance at the Assembly

177   Because of their military expeditions and overseas activity, the Athenians had never yet assembled to discuss a question important enough to bring 5,000 of them together.

Thucydides 8.72.1

This is our only direct evidence for numbers attending the Assembly in the fifth century, but see also **55**, **198**. But it is a statement put into the mouths of envoys arguing a case in 411, not one endorsed by Thucydides, and it is unlikely to be true. The Assembly-place on the Pnyx could hold 6000 people even in the fifth century.

Assembly pay

178   The people are paid one drakhma for the other meetings of the Assembly, but 9 obols for the main meeting.

[Aristotle] *Constitution of the Athenians* 62.2

For the introduction of pay for the Assembly see above **55**.

Assembly meetings other than on the Pnyx

179   On the 27th of the month, you were holding an assembly in the Peiraieus about
the situation in the dockyards, and Derkylos came from Khalkis and told you
that Philip had completely manhandled the Thebans and he reckoned that this
was the fifth day since they had made a truce.

Demosthenes 19.60 (343)

The Assembly normally met on the Pnyx hill in Athens, but it is also recorded meeting in the Peiraieus,
when naval affairs were at issue, and in the Theatre of Dionysos after the dramatic festival (see next passage).

180   ...and to Athene Hephaistia. Inscribe this decree and the Councillors by father's
name and deme, and the fact that they sacrificed for the health and safety of the
Council and of the Athenian people. And inscribe the decree according to which
the Council was crowned by the people in the Assembly in the theatre of
Dionysos because they seemed to have looked after the good order of the
festival of Dionysos well...

IG ii^2 223B.4–6 (343/2)

It is a measure of the importance to the people of their festivals, and of the Dionysia in particular, that of all
their duties it is their oversight of this festival that causes the Council to be publicly crowned.

181   Afterwards, when the day came, the conspirators enclosed the Assembly at
Kolonos (there is a temple of Poseidon a little under two kilometres [just over
a mile] from the city), and the commissioners introduced just this one measure,
than any Athenian should be free to propose any motion he pleased with
immunity. They imposed severe penalties on anyone who prosecuted for
unconstitutionality or otherwise harmed anyone for doing so.

Thucydides 8.67.2

It was highly irregular to hold an assembly meeting at Kolonos. Kolonos had a sanctuary of Poseidon Hippios
which we know from Aristophanes' *Knights* to have been associated with the Athenian cavalry and their
values. A meeting held there was a meeting whose conclusions were foregone.

The Assembly place on the Pnyx

182   And so later the Thirty turned the speaker's platform on the Pnyx, which had
been made so as to look out towards the sea, towards the land, because they
thought that rule over the sea was the origin of democracy and that the farmers
were less unhappy with oligarchy.

Plutarch *Themistokles* 19.4

The reversal of the meeting place on the Pnyx is clear archaeologically. That the Thirty made this one of
their priorities is a sign of the seriousness with which they had thought about how to break the Athenians
out of their democratic habits (compare **16** above on the repeal of some of Solon's laws).

People coming in from the country for Assembly meetings

183   DIKAIOPOLIS: I know the ways of the country-folk. They're highly delighted
if some humbugging speaker praises them and the city, right or wrong. That's
how they're sold down the river without knowing it.

Aristophanes *Akharnians* 370–374 (425)

Whether it was quite so easy to distinguish country residents from town residents in the Assembly is disputed
by scholars (see above on **81**), but this is good evidence for the attribution of rusticity to certain types of
behaviour in the Assembly.

184   He is ashamed in the Assembly when a skinny and unoiled man sits beside him.

Theophrastos *Characters* 26 (Oligarchic man) 4

The shame of the oligarchic man is at the evident sign that men who cannot afford sufficient food or oil are
allowed the same politial powers as he is. This not only provides evidence for all social classes involving
themselves in the Assembly but suggests that there was no fixed seating plan (cf. **186** but contrast **104**).

Craftsmen in the Assembly

185   SOKRATES: You (Kharmides) are ashamed to address an audience of dunces
and weaklings. Which of them are you ashamed to address? The fullers or the
cobblers or the carpenters or the smiths or the farmers or the merchants or the
traders in the Agora who think only of what they can buy cheap and sell dear?
These are the people who make up the Assembly.

Xenophon *Memorabilia* 3.7.6

Compare the implications of Plato's discussion of the topics on which the Assembly respected expert opinion
and the topics on which anyone might speak, below **429**.

Factions in the Assembly

186   The aristocrats were aware even before this that Perikles had already become
the greatest citizen, but they wished nevertheless to have someone in the city
who could stand up to him and blunt his power, so that it should not a be a
complete monarchy. To oppose him, they put up Thoukydides of Alopeke, a
man of good sense and a relative by marriage of Kimon. He was less of a warrior
than Kimon but more of a speaker and politician. By keeping watch in the city
and grappling with Perikles at the speakers' platform, he quickly brought the
city into equipoise. He would not allow the so-called 'fine and good' to be
scattered and mingled with the common people as hitherto, their standing
obscured by superior numbers. He set them apart and gathered them together...

Plutarch *Perikles* 11.1–2

This, and the following two passages illustrate something of the practical opposition politics of mid-century
Athens, involving manipulating institutions and exploiting the political potential of the empire, cf. **391–2**.

187 SOKRATES: You are not going to tell me that Thoukydides was a man of no consequence and did not have numerous friends in Athens and among the allies? He came from a great family and had great influence in the city and in Greece generally.

Plato *Menon* 94d

188 In the end, when Perikles ventured to face Thoukydides in the ordeal of ostracism, he secured his banishment and dissolved the faction that had opposed him.

Plutarch *Perikles* 14.2

For Thoukydides' ostracism see further **295, 406**.

189 You made a new law after the fine all-in wrestling in which this man engaged in the Assembly because you were ashamed at what had happened: to select by lot at every meeting of the assembly a tribe to sit at the front by the speaker's platform. What was it that the lawmaker was making provision for? He ordered the members of the tribe sit there and assist the laws and the democracy, on the grounds that, if we did not send help from some quarter against men who behave like this, we would not be able to take counsel about very serious matters.

Aiskhines 1.33–4 (345)

The meetings of the assembly could be both noisy and violent occasions, and preventing disruption was problematic. No evidence for the police force of Scythian archers (see above **137**) survives from after the early fourth century (Bäbler 2005), and it may be that the rôle given to the (*prytaneis* of one) tribe here was required because the Scythians were no longer available.

The standing agenda of the Assembly

190 The *prytaneis* give notice of meetings of the Assembly: one main meeting (each prytany) in which they have to: vote on the magistracies, whether they seem to do their duties well; deal with the corn supply and the defence of the country; in the case of those who want to, bring impeachments on this day; they read out the lists of confiscated property and legal claims for inheritances and heiresses, in order that nothing falling unclaimed escapes anyone's notice. In the sixth prytany, in addition to those stated items, they hold a vote on ostracism, whether to hold one or not, and hear accusations against Athenians and metics who make vexatious prosecutions, up to three of each, and if anyone has failed to do what they promised for the people. The second meeting (each prytany) is for suppliant pleas, at which anyone who wants can place a suppliant branch and then discuss with the people anything private or public. The other two (meetings each prytany) are reserved for other matters, and the law requires three matters of sacred business are dealt with, three relating to heralds and embassies, and three relating to breaches of other norms. They sometimes deal with things without a preliminary vote. Heralds and ambassadors first approach the *prytaneis* and those who bring letters hand these over to them.

[Aristotle] *Constitution of the Athenians* 43.4–6

Not all of this description of the business of the Assembly is easy to understand. The principle that certain important matters have to be considered every prytany is clear and comprehensible, but the prescribed numbers of matters of sacred business to be dealt with and the (equal) number of cases of citizen and metic vexatious litigants (*sykophantai*, see **259**) is puzzling: presumably in both cases at some stage the Assembly was worried about being overwhelmed with relatively trivial matters.

The special authority of generals over the Assembly

191   The generals and *prytaneis* are to call a meeting of the Assembly ...

Thucydides 4.118.14

How far generals had political influence because of formal powers and how far simply because they commanded informal authority is not clear (see **193**), but it is notable that all the suggestions that they have non-military powers of this sort comes from the Peloponnesian War – precisely when the military situation is likely to have increased their informal authority.

192   When the Athenians saw the enemy army at Akharnai barely eleven kilometres (seven miles) away from the city, they no longer thought the situation tolerable. Now that their land was being ravaged before their very eyes, which the young had never seen before and the old not since the Persian Wars, they were understandably outraged, and there was a determination, especially on the part of the young, to sally forth and not just watch. Bitterly divided groups formed, with some calling for a sally and a smaller number opposing the idea. Oracle-mongers chanted oracles of all sorts, which they were eager to hear, each according to his own preference. The Akharnians thought of themselves as a sizeable part of the citizen body, and, since it was their land that was being ravaged, they pressed most eagerly for the sally. The citizens were altogether in a turmoil. They were angry with Perikles and remembered none of his previous advice. They called him a coward because, general though he was, he was not leading them out, and they held him responsible for all their misfortunes.

Perikles saw that they were angry about the situation and not thinking soundly, and was confident that he was right about not marching out. He therefore called no Assembly or other meeting, for fear that if they came together swayed by anger rather than good sense, they would blunder.

Thucydides 2.21.2–22.1

Thucydides here provides us with a vivid picture of the way in which a particular mood might arise among the people, in this case in exceptional circumstances which turned the largest of all deme communities, Akharnai, into a pressure group (cf. above **80**). For the possibility of public meetings other than Assemblies see Hansen (1989) 195–211.

193   Perikles called a meeting of the Assembly, being still general.

Thucydides 2.59.3

Whether generals had formal powers or simply made their wish for an Assembly meeting known to the presiding committee is not clear, but a Hellenistic inscription (*SEG* 21.440) may suggest formal powers (the phrase used there can be translated either 'on the orders of the generals' or 'on the advice of the generals').

194   The Assembly is to sit in continuous session until this business is managed, and
to deal with nothing else before unless the generals make some request.

ML 65.54–6 (423)

The context here is Athenian relations with Methone and Macedon at the beginning of the Peloponnesian
War (430). The idea of 'continuous sessions' of the Assembly is a remarkable one, and nicely illustrates the
way in which the Assembly's assumption of control might in some circumstances lead it to have to work
very hard and in great detail.

The Assembly decides what to debate and what simply to agree without debate

195   At Athens the following seems to have happened when the Council had
formulated a preliminary proposal and the decision was brought to the
Assembly. First, a vote was taken in the Assembly as to whether the people
should consider the preliminary proposal or whether the preliminary proposal
was sufficient in its own right. This is mentioned in Lysias' speech against the
prosecution of Meixodemos.

Harpokration *s.v. Prokheirotonia*

We would like to know how often the Assembly agreed to a proposal by the Council without any debate.
Some scholars have thought that Harpokration's claim here is simply incredible and that everything must
have been debated. The evidence of amendments suggests that even issues of honouring individuals were
regularly debated. It is possible that the preliminary vote determined what items were debated, and what
left for another occasion, when more items were offered for debate than the law allowed (cf. **190**) – which
would explain why sometimes, as the Aristotelian *Constitution of the Athenians* 43.6 tells us, there was no
preliminary vote.

The Assembly meeting begins with prayers and curses

196   Whenever the purifying sacrifice has been carried round and the herald prays
the ancestral prayers, the law enjoins the *proedroi* to hold a preliminary vote
about ancestral sacred matters and for sacred matters involving heralds and
embassies and about breaches of other norms, and after this the herald asks
'Who of those over fifty wants to speak?' And when all these have spoken it is
at that point that he orders any other Athenian to speak who wants to and is
permitted.

Aiskhines 1.23 (345)

The first part of this description is uncontroversial and guaranteed by **190**, but the priority for the over-50s
is almost certainly an invention by Aiskhines (see Lane Fox 1996).

197   Athenians, just as the first lawgivers made laws for your ancestors about those
who spoke in the Assembly, in the same way you should seek to pay attention
to them, in order that you might improve those who come before you. So how
did they legislate about these things? First of all they made curses publicly at
every assembly against bad men, that if someone takes gifts, and then speaks
and tries to influence decisions about matters, he should be utterly destroyed.

Deinarkhos 2.16 (323)

The trope here – a claim that things had been done better in the past – is common in fourth-century oratory, but that there were public curses at the start of the Assembly is certain (Aristophanes parodies them in *Thesmophoriazousai*).

A comic account of Assembly procedure

198   DIKAIOPOLIS: The main meeting of the Assembly has been fixed for dawn, and here's the Pnyx empty; the people are chattering in the Agora and avoiding the ruddled rope. Even the *prytaneis* have not come. When they have come in late, then just imagine how they will jostle one another for front seats, pouring in all at once.

Aristophanes *Akharnians* 19–26 (425)

Aristophanes' *Akharnians* opens with Dikaiopolis on the Pnyx waiting for the Assembly to happen. His description provides us with our best fifth-century evidence for procedure at the Assembly. The 'ruddled rope' mentioned here is said by ancient scholiasts on this passage to have been a rope reddened with red clay which was used to sweep people out of the Agora, with a fine for anyone found with a red mark on their clothing, but the scholiasts may simply be guessing on the basis of what Aristophanes writes here.

199   HERALD: Move forward! Move, so as to be inside the purified area.
AMPHITHEOS (arriving late): Has anyone spoken yet?
HERALD: Who wishes to speak?
AMPHITHEOS: I do.

Aristophanes *Akharnians* 43–46 (425)

The purified area is the area around which the purificatory sacrifice of a piglet has been carried (**194**).

200   AMPHITHEOS: To me alone the gods have entrusted making peace with Sparta. But, gentlemen, immortal though I am, I have no journey-money: the *prytaneis* won't supply it.
HERALD: Archers!
AMPHITHEOS: Triptolemos and Keleus, are you going to ignore what they are doing to me?
DIKAIOPOLIS: Gentlemen *prytaneis*, you are wronging the assembly in arresting this man who wants to make peace for us and hang up the shields.
HERALD: Sit down and keep quiet!
DIKAIOPOLIS: By Apollo I will not unless you do your prytanic duty and put peace on the agenda.

Aristophanes *Akharnians* 51–60 (425)

For the issue of keeping order in the Assembly see above **189**; here in the fifth century the Scythian archers (**137**) are on hand.

201 DIKAIOPOLIS: *Prytaneis*, do you allow me to suffer this in my own country, and, what is more, at the hands of barbarians? I forbid you to go on holding the meeting on the subject of pay for the Thracians. I tell you that there is a sign from Zeus and a raindrop has struck me.

HERALD: The Thracians will withdraw now and be in attendance the day after tomorrow. The *prytaneis* hereby dissolve the Assembly.

Aristophanes *Akharnians* 167–73 (425)

An historical example of an Assembly being adjourned because of a divine sign is the adjournment of the assembly at Thucydides 5.45.4 because of an earth tremor.

An Assembly exceptionally reconsiders

202 The next day brought a sudden change of heart and a recognition that the decree was savage and excessive in destroying a whole city rather than the guilty few. As soon as they realised this, the Mytilenean ambassadors in Athens and their Athenian supporters induced the authorities to hold another debate. They were the more easily persuaded because they realised that most Athenians wished to be given a chance to reconsider the matter. A meeting of the Assembly was summoned forthwith...

Thucydides 3.36.4–6

This is a remarkable example of the recalling of the Assembly to discuss again a matter concluded on the previous day. It is possible that the Assembly had simply been adjourned because there was further business that it had to do, so that the meeting the next day was already expected. The practicalities of summoning an Assembly at short notice are not easy. This passage is continued in **393**.

Rare for a matter to be voted on twice

203 'And you, chairman, if you think it your business to care for the city and you wish to prove a good citizen, put the question to the vote and let the citizens debate it again. If you are afraid to put the question to the vote again, remember that with so many witnesses you could not be accused of breach of precedent, that you would prove physician to our ill-advised city, and that he performs his office well who benefits his country as much as he can or at least does it no deliberate harm.' So spoke Nikias. Of the Athenians who came forward, most spoke for the expedition and not rescinding the vote, but a few spoke on the other side.

Thucydides 6.14–15.1

The debate about the Sicilian expedition is remarkable in many ways (see below **407–11**), but not least for this evidence that the Athenians essentially made up procedure as they went along.

Crowd pressure affects Assembly behaviour

204 Because of the fervent enthusiasm of the majority, anyone who did not care for the proposal was afraid that if he raised his hand in opposition, he would be judged unpatriotic, and so he kept quiet.

Thucydides 6.24.4

There was clearly a great deal of 'peer pressure' in the Athenian Assembly (see also **186, 409**) – but Thucydides' claim in both passages can only have been based on the subjective impression of some of his informants, perhaps wise after the event; Thucydides himself was in exile at this time (summer 415).

Elections in the Assembly

205   The election of generals, cavalry commanders and other military officers is held in the Assembly in whatever way the people see fit. This election is held by the first prytany after the sixth in whose term of office the omens are good.

[Aristotle] *Constitution of the Athenians* 44.4

Presumably the law specified that 10 generals should be elected, but did not prescribe how this was to happen.

Khoregoi appointed in the Assembly

206   For since no *khoregos* has stood for the Pandionid tribe for the third year running, and the Assembly had come round at which the law enjoins the arkhon to allot *aulos*-players to *khoregoi*, and since argument and abuse broke out, with the arkhon accusing the *epimeletai* of the tribe and the *epimeletai* accusing the arkhon, I came along and undertook voluntarily to be *khoregos*.

Demosthenes 21.13 (348–46)

Just as various activities had to happen in front of the Council, so other activities had to happen in front of the Assembly. That matters to do with the Dionysia were among these is consonant with the Assembly meeting in the theatre after the Dionysia (above **180**). For the *epimeletai* of the tribes see **100–102**.

Ambassadors elected in the Assembly

207   You elected as ambassador with full powers the man (Theramenes) whom the year before (405 BC), after his election as general, you had rejected at his vetting, because you thought he was ill-disposed to your democracy.

Lysias 13.10 (c.399)

Foreign affairs and the appointment of ambassadors were entirely in the hands of the Assembly.

Speakers might be given a rough reception in the Assembly

208   SOKRATES: If I had tried long ago to do politics, I should long ago have lost my life and have been no use either to you or to myself. Please do not be angry if I tell the truth. No man on earth who conscientiously opposes you or any other democratic assembly, and tries to prevent numerous unjust and illegal acts from occurring in the city, can survive. The genuine champion of justice, if he intends to survive even for a short time, must live a private life and abstain from politics.

Plato *Apology* 31d–32a

Sokrates' claim here is surprising, and reminds us of the extent to which passions might run high in the Assembly, and those who made themselves unpopular there might be subject to unofficial sanction in other aspects of their lives.

The Assembly as law-court

209 The Assembly had met to give audience to Nikias, Lamakhos and Alkibiades, the generals in command of the expedition to Sicily – Lamakhos' flagship was already lying offshore – when Pythonikos rose before the people and said: 'Fellow Athenians, you are launching this wonderfully-equipped expedition on hazardous enterprise. But I shall prove that general Alkibiades has been holding celebrations of the Mysteries in a private house with friends. If you will grant immunity to him whom I indicate, one who has not been initiated, a slave belonging to someone here present, will describe the Mysteries to you. Treat me as you will if I am not telling the truth.' Alkibiades denied the charge at great length; so the *prytaneis* decided to clear the meeting of those who had not been initiated and themselves to fetch the lad indicated by Pythonikos. Off they went and came back with a slave of Alkibiades called Andromakhos.

Andokides 1.11–12 (400)

The Assembly here spontaneously turns itself into a court, once more inventing procedure in response to events. For what followed see **247, 373–7**.

210 Speusippos, a member of the Council, proposed handing them (the men declared by Lydos to have profaned the Mysteries) over to the appropriate court. Whereupon my father furnished sureties and brought an action against Speusippos for making an unconstitutional proposal. The case was tried before 6,000 Athenians, and from all those jurors Speusippos obtained fewer than 200 votes.

Andokides 1.17)400)

This is both the first known use of the prosecution against an unconstitutional proposal and the only case where all 6,000 of the jurors – the whole panel – were employed in a single trial.

The trials of the generals at Arginousai

211 The Athenians lost twenty-five ships, crews and all, apart from a few men who were carried to land; the Peloponnesians lost nine Spartan ships, out of a total of ten, and more than sixty allied ships. The Athenian generals decided that Theramenes and Thrasyboulos who were trierarkhs and some of the taxiarkhs should sail with fifty-seven ships to the waterlogged ships and the men on board on them, while they themselves went with the rest of the fleet to attack the ships under Eteonikos which were blockading Mytilene. They wanted to carry out these moves, but wind and a storm which grew violent prevented them. After setting up a trophy, they bivouacked there.

Xenophon Hellenika 1.6.34–5

The most notorious of all occasions when the Assembly turned itself into a court was the trial of the generals who had been in charge at the sea battle at Arginousai. Xenophon and Diodoros have slightly different versions of the background, but the basic sequence of events is the same.

212 When the Athenians learnt of their success at the Arginousai Islands, they praised the generals for the victory, but they were furious that they had left unburied those who had died to preserve their supremacy. Since Theramenes and Thrasyboulos had returned to Athens first, the generals assumed that it was they who had denounced them to the people in the matter of the dead; so they sent the people a dispatch attacking them. In it they explained that it was Theramenes and Thrasyboulos whom they had ordered to pick up the dead. This dispatch was the main cause of their downfall; for although they could have had help in the trial from Theramenes and his supporters, who were eloquent speakers and had many friends and, most important of all, had taken part in the events of the sea battle, they had them, on the contrary, as adversaries and bitter accusers. When the dispatch was read out before the people, they were immediately angry with Theramenes and his supporters, but when they had spoken in their own defence, the result was that their anger was once more directed at the generals. Consequently, the people gave them notice that they would be tried and ordered them to hand over the command of the forces to Konon, whom they absolved of blame, and they voted that the other generals should return home forthwith.

Diodoros 13.101.1–5

213   The Athenians at home deposed all these generals apart from Konon. As colleagues for him they elected Adeimantos and Philokles. [2] Of the generals who had fought in the sea battle, Protomakhos and Aristogenes did not return to Athens. When the other six – Perikles, Diomedon, Lysias, Aristokrates, Thrasyllos and Erasinides – sailed home, Arkhedemos, who at the time led the Athenian people and managed the two-obol benefit, imposed a fine on Erasinides and then prosecuted him before a jury court, alleging that he held money from the Hellespont that belonged to the people; he also accused him of misconduct as a general. The court decided to imprison Erasinides. [3] After this the generals explained to the Council about the sea battle and the severity of the storm. When Timokrates proposed that the other generals too should be imprisoned and handed over to the Assembly, the Council imprisoned them.

[4] After this a meeting of the Assembly was held, at which a number of the people, and especially Theramenes, attacked the generals, saying that they ought to render an account of their failure to pick up the shipwrecked men. As proof that they implicated no one else, Theramenes produced a dispatch which the generals had sent to the Council and Assembly, in which they blamed nothing but the storm. [5] After this each general spoke in his own defence, but only briefly because, in accordance with the law, they were not allowed to make a full-length speech. They explained their actions, claiming that they themselves were to sail against the enemy, and that they had assigned the recovery of the shipwrecked men to certain capable trierarkhs and former generals, men like Thermenes and Thrasyboulos. [6] If they had to blame anyone in the matter of the recovery, there was no one else but those to whom the task had been assigned. 'We shall not,' they added, 'just because they accuse us, falsely allege that they were to blame. It was only the severity of the storm that prevented recovery.'

As witnesses the generals offered the helmsmen and many others who had sailed with them, and their arguments were beginning to persuade the people. [7] Many private persons stood up and offered to be sureties, but it was resolved to adjourn to another meeting; for it was by then late, and they could not have made out the hands. The Council was to draft and introduce a resolution on how the men should be tried.

[8] After this came the Apatouria, at which fathers and their kinsmen meet one another. So Theramenes and his supporters arranged for a large number of men who were wearing black cloaks and had their heads close-shaven to come to the meeting of the Assembly pretending that they were kinsmen of the dead. They also induced Kallixenos to attack the generals in the Council. [9] Then they held a meeting of the Assembly, at which the Council introduced its own resolution. It was moved by Kallixenos and ran as follows: 'Resolved that, since the Athenians have heard at the previous meeting both the accusers of the generals and their defence, they now all proceed to vote by tribes; and that two urns be set up for each tribe; and that in each tribe a herald proclaim that whoever finds the generals guilty of not picking up the victors in the sea battle shall cast his vote in the first urn, and whoever finds them not guilty shall cast his vote in the second; [10] and that, if found guilty, they shall be sentenced to death and handed over to the Eleven, and their property shall be confiscated, and a tenth of it given to the goddess (Athene).'

[11] A man came forward who claimed that he had been saved by clinging to a barrel of barley-groats. The men who were dying had charged him, if he survived, to report to the people that the generals had not picked up men who had proved most valiant in the service of their country. [12] Now Euryptolemos son of Peisianax and some others served a summons on Kallixenos, alleging that he had made an unconstitutional proposal. Some people applauded their action, but the majority shouted that it was a scandal if the people should be prevented from doing whatever they wanted. [13] Thereupon Lykiskos moved that these men should be judged by the very same vote as the generals, unless they withdrew their summonses. Once more the mob shouted its approval, and they were compelled to withdraw the summonses. [14] Furthermore, when some of the *prytaneis* refused to put the question to the vote illegally, Kallixenos again mounted the platform and urged the same accusations against them, and the people loudly demanded that those who refused should be prosecuted. [15] The *prytaneis* were cowed, and they all agreed to put the question, except for Sokrates son of Sophroniskos. He said that he would act only in accordance with the law. [16] After this, Euryptolemos mounted the platform and spoke as follows in defence of the generals.

'Men of Athens, I have mounted the platform partly to accuse Perikles, though he is my kinsman and intimate, and Diomedon, who is my friend, partly to speak in their defence, and partly to recommend the measures that I think best for the whole city. [17] I accuse Perikles and Diomedon because they persuaded their colleagues to change their mind when they wanted to send a dispatch to the Council and to you, explaining that they had ordered Theramenes and Thrasyboulos, with forty-seven ships, to pick up the shipwrecked men and that they failed to do so. [18] And so are the two generals now to share the blame with those who blundered on their own, and are they now, in return for the humanity they showed then, to run the risk of death, thanks to the machinations of those men and certain others?

[19] 'Certainly not, if you take my advice and follow the just and righteous course, whereby you will best learn the truth and not discover later to your regret

that you yourselves have offended most grievously against the gods and your own selves. The advice that I give you is such that, if you take it, you cannot be deceived either by me or by anyone else, and that with full knowledge you will punish the guilty in whatever way you wish, either all of them together or each one separately: give them one day, if not more, to defend themselves, and do not trust others more than yourselves.

[20] 'Men of Athens, you all know that the decree of Kannonos is very severe. It lays down that if anyone wrongs the people of Athens, he shall defend himself in chains before the Assembly, and if he is found guilty, he shall be executed and thrown into the chasm, and his property shall be confiscated, and a tenth given to the goddess. [21] Under this decree I bid you try the generals, and, by Zeus, if it so please you, my kinsman Perikles first of all: it would be shameful for me to value him higher than the city as a whole. [22] If you do not wish to do this, try them under the following law, which applies to temple-robbers and traitors: if anyone has betrayed the city or stolen sacred property, he shall be tried before a jury court, and if he be convicted, he shall not be buried in Attica and his property shall be confiscated. [23] By whichever of these laws you choose, men of Athens, let the men be tried, each one separately, and let the day be divided into three parts, in one of which you gather and vote on whether you judge them guilty or not, in another of which the prosecution presents its case, and in the third of which the defendant presents his case.

[24] 'If this is done, the guilty will incur the severest punishment, and the innocent will be set free by you, men of Athens, and not perish unjustly. [25] You yourselves will be granting a trial in accordance with the law and out of respect for the gods and your oaths, and you will not be fighting on the same side as the Spartans by putting to death – without a trial, in violation of the law – the men who captured seventy of their ships and defeated them. In fear of what, do you make such excessive haste? [26] In fear that you will be debarred from executing and acquitting whomever you please if you proceed in accordance with the law, but will still be able to do so if you proceed in violation of the law – by the method that Kallixenos persuaded the Council to propose to the people, that is, the single vote method? [27] But perhaps you might put to death an innocent man. Remember how painful and useless it always is to repent later – especially when one's error involved a man's death. [28] You would do a dreadful thing if, after granting Aristarkhos, who first overthrew the democracy and then betrayed Oinoe to our enemies the Thebans, a day in which to defend himself as he saw fit and all his other rights under the law, you now deprive the generals, who have done everything to your satisfaction and have defeated the enemy, of these same rights? [29] Do no such thing, you men of Athens, but guard the laws which are your own and which above all have made you mighty. Attempt nothing without their sanction.

'And now come back to the actual circumstances in which the generals are thought to have made their mistakes. When, after winning the battle, they sailed back to shore, Diomedon urged that they should all put out to sea in line and pick up the wreckage and the shipwrecked men, while Erasinides urged that they should all sail as fast as possible against the enemy at Mytilene. But Thrasyllos said that both objectives would be accomplished if they left some ships there and sailed with the rest against the enemy. [30] If that plan were approved, there would be left behind three ships from the squadrons of each of the eight generals, and the ten ships of the taxiarkhs, the ten Samian ships and the three of the nauarkhs. All these came to forty-seven, four for each of the lost vessels, which were twelve in number. [31] Among the trierarkhs left behind were Thrasyboulos and Theramenes, who at the previous meeting of the Assembly had accused the generals. With the rest of the ships they would sail against the enemy fleet. Now which of these actions did they not perform competently and well? It is therefore just that those detailed to attack the enemy should render an account of what they did not do well, and that those who were detailed to pick up the shipwrecked men but who failed to carry out the generals' orders should be tried for not picking them up. [32] This much, however, I can say in defence of both parties: the storm made it quite impossible to carry out any of the operations planned by the generals. As witnesses of this you have those who were saved by chance, among whom is one of our generals who survived on a waterlogged ship. They urge that he, who needed rescue himself at the time, should be judged by the same vote as those who did not carry out their orders.

[33] 'Do not, then, men of Athens, in the face of our victory and good fortune, act like men who are vanquished and unfortunate. Do not, in the face of divine compulsion, appear unreasonable by returning a verdict of treason rather than helplessness on men who could not carry out their orders because of the storm. It would be far more just to honour the victors with garlands than to yield to the persuasion of wicked men and sentence them to death.'

[34] So saying, Euryptolemos moved that the men be tried under the decree of Kannonos, each one separately; the proposal of the Council was that they all be judged by a single ballot. When these two proposals were put to the vote, they first of all chose the resolution of Euryptolemos; but when Menekles lodged an objection under oath, a second vote was held, and they chose the Council's resolution. They then convicted the generals who had fought in the battle, eight in number, and the six in Athens were executed.

[35] Soon after, the Athenians regretted their action, and voted that complaints should be brought against all those who had deceived the people, that they should give sureties until they could be tried, and that Kallixenos should be included among them. Complaints were brought against four others as well, and they were confined by their sureties. Later, however, in the civil disorder in which Kleophon was put to death (404), they escaped before trial. Kallixenos returned when the Peiraieus party returned (403), but he was hated by all and died of starvation.

Xenophon *Hellenika* 1.7

This long account provides rich information both about Assembly procedure and about the sorts of arguments that the Assembly was prepared to countenance. The central issue is whether the Assembly is so sovereign that it can do what it likes, or whether the Assembly too has restricted powers. The reaction to the Arginousai trial was such as to ensure that the Assembly never again acted in a comparable way.

11   LAW COURTS

For samples of Athenian laws see above **19–28**; for the Council as a court see **138, 155, 163, 167, 170–73**; for the Assembly as a court see **209–13**.

How the Athenians made their laws

214   Of all these, none is our discovery or new, but the ancient law, which he has broken, orders laws to be made in the following way: if anyone thinks that one of the current laws is not good he is to bring a case against it, and propose a replacement law which he would bring in if that law was repealed, and when you have heard the case you are to choose the better law. [90] For Solon, who laid down this way of making laws, did not think that it was right that the *thesmothetai*, who have been chosen by lot over the laws, should hold office only when they have been scrutinized twice, in the Council and among you in the court, but the laws themselves, which govern how they hold their magistracy and how you all live, should be made at a particular chance moment and be valid never having been scrutinised. [91] For I tell you that then, when they made laws in this way, they used the existing laws and did not make new ones. But when some men got a lot of political influence, as I gather, and made it possible for themselves to make laws, whenever anyone wanted and in any way they happened to, there were so many laws that contradicted each other that you voted laws arguing in opposite directions most of the time [92] and the matter could have no bound. The laws are no different from decrees; indeed the laws according to which it is necessary to frame decrees are more recent than the decrees themselves. In order that I might not just make a claim but show the law itself which I am talking about, take and read the law according to which the *nomothetai* were formerly appointed.
LAW
    [93] You understand, men of Athens, how Solon orders the laws to be well made: first amongst you, in those who have taken the oath, amongst whom other things too are validated, and then repealing the opposite laws, in order that there might be a single law on each issue and that this might not trouble ordinary individuals and made them inferior to those who know all the laws, but rather so that all could know the same things and learn simple and clear principles of justice. [94] And as a preliminary he ordered that they be displayed in front of the statues of the Eponymous Heroes and handed over to the Secretary and that he read them at the Assemblies in order that each of you, having heard them many times and considered at leisure that they were just and expedient, might then make them law. When there are so many just provisions, Leptines has not kept any of them – otherwise you would not have ever been persuaded, in my opinion, to make this law.

Demosthenes 20.89–94 (355)

This passage is not only one of the best sources we have for the actual procedure of law-making in Athens (the claimed law on law-making at Demosthenes 24.20–23 is not genuine, see Canevaro 2013b), but is also good evidence for what fourth-century Athenians understood the rationale to be for the procedure adopted. Demosthenes has obviously crafted his account to emphasise the extent to which Leptines, against whose law he is speaking, had breached the rules, but the fundamental principles outlined here are reliable. For the claims about Solon see **5**.

215 It is clearly laid down for the *thesmothetai* annually to correct the laws in the Assembly, after examining in detail and considering whether one law has been written up that is in opposition to another law, or an invalid law among the valid laws, or if more than one law has been written up about each matter. And if they discover any such thing, the law orders them once they have written it on boards to display it before the Eponymous Heroes, and the *prytaneis* are to hold an Assembly advertised as for the *nomothetai*, and the president of the *proedroi* is to hold a vote, to repeal some laws and keep others, in order that there may be one law about each thing and no more. Read me the laws.

LAWS.

So, men of Athens, if the story they tell was true and there were two laws about proclamations, I think there would be no avoiding the *thesmothetai* having discovered it, and the *prytaneis* having handed over to the *nomothetai* the question of which law should be repealed, either the one granting power to speak or the one forbidding it. Since neither of these has happened they are clearly proven not only to be saying something not true but something that could not possibly happen.

Aiskhines 3.38–40 (330)

For the rôle of the *thesmothetai* see 246–7.

Procedures preparatory to court appearance

216 They choose by lot the Forty, four from each tribe, to whom plaintiffs apply for hearings of other cases. They used to be Thirty and gave hearings travelling around the demes, but after the oligarchy of the Thirty they have become Forty. They are competent to judge cases up to 10 drakhmas, and hand over to the arbitrators cases involving over this value. When they have taken the case, if they are unable to bring about an agreement they make a decision, and if the decision pleases both parties and they abide by the decision, the case is at an end. But if one of the opposing parties refers the case to the court, they put the testimonies and the summonses and the laws into containers, keeping separate the prosecutor's and the defendant's, and once they have sealed these and have attached a record of the decision of the arbitrator written on a tablet, they hand all over to the four men who handle cases for the tribe to which the defendant belongs. These men take them and bring them to the court, those under 1000 dr. to a court of 201, those over 1000 to a court of 401. It is not possible to employ in court any laws or challenges or depositions other than those which come from the arbitrator and are deposited in the containers. The arbitrators are those in their sixtieth year.

[Aristotle] *Constitution of the Athenians* 53.1–4

The practice of admitting only witness testimonies which had been deposited at the point of arbitration seems to have been adopted in the 370s.

Examples of charges

217   I, Deinarkhos, son of Sostratos of Korinth, charge Proxenos, with whom I lodge, with damage to the tune of 2 talents. Proxenos has done me damage, having received me into his own house in the country, when, having left Athens I came back from Khalkis, by plotting to steal the 285 gold staters which I brought from Khalkis, to Proxenos' knowledge, and entered his house with, and silver vessels worth not less than 20 minas.

Dionysios of Halikarnassos *Deinarkhos* 3

This and **218** are offered as sample charges. The detail offered here contrasts with the generalized claims of **218**, and suggests that practice may have varied widely.

218   The prosecutor's oath from the trial goes like this – for it is still deposited, even now, according to Favorinus, in the Metroon: 'Meletos, son of Meletos, of the deme of Pitthos took the oath and laid this charge against Sokrates, son of Sophroniskos, of the deme of Alopeke: Sokrates commits an offence in not worshipping the gods whom the city worships, but introducing other and new gods; he commits an offence in corrupting the young. Penalty assessed at death.'

Diogenes Laertios *Lives of the Philosophers* 2.40

Diogenes reports substantially the same charge as is reported by Xenophon at *Memorabilia* 1.1.1. In both this and **217** the charge itself does not state the law under which it is brought (in this case impiety), but only the way in which it is held that the law had been broken. The presence of a suggested penalty is because in the case of impiety there was no statutory penalty (contrast **20** and **21** above), and so the prosecutor had to suggest a penalty, with the defendant able to suggest an alternative (see generally Todd (1993) 134–5).

The rôle of the arkhon

219   The following public and private lawsuits will fall to him [the arkhon], and he holds the preliminary investigation (*anakrisis*) and he introduces them to the jury court: maltreatment of parents – on this charge whoever wishes may prosecute without risk of penalty; maltreatment of orphans – the suit is against the guardians; maltreatment of heiresses – the suit is against the guardians or the husband; maltreatment of an orphan's estate – also against the guardians; mental incapacity – when a man is accused of squandering his property through mental incapacity...

[Aristotle] *Constitution of the Athenians* 56.6

220   When the preliminary investigations (*anakriseis*) happened before the arkhon and they submitted their case on behalf of these children as being legitimate sons of Euktemon, when they were asked by us who was the children's mother and whose daughter she was they were unable to answer, and when we drew attention to this and the arkhon ordered them to reply according to the law [*gap in text*] Gentlemen, imagine going to court about the legitimay of children and claiming there was no case to answer, but not being able to show who the mother was or any relation of the children. But then they claimed that she was a Lemnian and had an adjournment made. Later when they came to the preliminary investigation, before anyone could ask, they immediately said that the mother was Kallippe and she was the daughter of Pistoxenos – as if they had done enough if they simply provided the name Pistoxenos. And when I asked who he was, and whether he was still alive or not, they said that he died on campaign in Sicily...

Isaios 6.12–13 (364)

This description gives some impression of the drama of the pre-trial proceedings.

The frequency of court action

221 They (the Athenians) have to judge more public and private lawsuits and examine more officials than all the rest put together.

Old Oligarch 3.2

222 STUDENT: This, you see, is a map of the whole world. Here's Athens.
STREPSIADES: What do you mean? I don't believe you: I can't see the jurors in session.

Aristophanes *Clouds* 206–208 (419/8, in this version)

223 Furthermore we must remember that the Athenians have to celebrate festivals, during which they cannot hold trials, and that they celebrate twice as many as other cities.

Old Oligarch 3.8

224 It is impossible for the Assembly and the courts to meet on the same day.

Demosthenes 24.80 (summer 353)

The breadth of Athenian involvement in the courts

225 CHORUS (of Wasps): Some of us mete out justice where the arkhon sits, some of us before the Eleven, and some in the Odeion ...

Aristophanes *Wasps* 1108–9 (422)

226 Demosthenes held the office of commissioner for the repair of walls... and so he was handling public funds and imposing fines, like the other officials, and presiding in court...

Aiskhines 3.27 (330)

The choice of jury

227 Jury service is open to men over thirty years old, as long as they are not in debt to the public treasury or (otherwise) deprived of their civic rights. If anyone acts as juror who may not do so, an injunction is brought against him and he is taken to court; if he is convicted, the jurors penalise him additionally whatever they think he should suffer or pay. If a fine is imposed upon him he has to be bound until he pays both his former debt, which was the occasion for the injunction, and the additional punishment which the court has imposed upon him. Each juror has a boxwood ticket bearing his name, patronymic and demotic

and one letter from the letters up to K. For the jurors from each tribe have been distributed into ten sections, roughly equal numbers under each letter.

[Aristotle] *Constitution of the Athenians* 63.3–4

228 [Most] courts consist of 500...but when it is necessary...[two courts] come together in the Heliaia...before 1500 jurors: that is, three [courts combined].

[Aristotle] *Constitution of the Athenians* 68.1

We do have one claim that a case was heard by the whole panel of 6000 jurors (see above **210**). The complicated arrangements described in the *Constitution of the Athenians* seem to have come into force only during the middle and later part of the fourth century.

229 Men over the age of 50 who have the reputation for having lived best. These judge cases of homicide.

Souda s.v. *Ephetai*

230 Public lawsuits for impiety fall to him (the Basileus), and when one man is disputing with another about a priesthood. He holds inquiries for *genē* and priests in all disputes about religious matters. All cases of homicide fall to him, and he is the one who makes the proclamation that the killer is excluded from the things specified by law. Cases of homicide and wounding, if anyone kills or wounds intentionally, are held on the Areopagos, and for poisoning, if anyone kills by this means, and for arson. These are the only cases tried by council of the Areopagos.

[Aristotle] *Constitution of the Athenians* 57.2–3

For the court of the Areopagos see **1, 14, 41–3, 446**. For the Basileus see **352**.

Court fees

231 The *prytaneia* were the specified fees which the prosecutor and defendant had to deposit before a case. If they did not pay them the magistrates who brought cases to court struck off the case. Whoever lost the case paid the fees of both, and the jurors received the fee.

Pollux 8.38

This rule was designed to deter abuse of the law allowing anyone to bring a prosecution. The modern deterrent of legal costs did not apply as prosecutor and defendant were required to plead for themselves. For problems with *sykophantai* (vexatious prosecutors) see **190, 259**.

Fines for bringing prosecutions that get no support

232 He obtained a case against me for 10,000 dr. but when I put forward a witness that the case was not admissible because arbitration had already taken place, he did not attack my witness, knowing that if he did not take a fifth share of the votes he would incur a fine of one sixth of the sum; but he persuaded the magistrate and filed the suit again, on the grounds that all he risked was the *prytaneia*.

Isokrates 18.11–12 (perhaps 400–399)

233   SOKRATES: Anyone can see that if Anytos and Lykon had not come forward
to accuse me, he (Meletos) would have lost a thousand drakhmas for not having
obtained a fifth of the votes.

Plato Apology 36ab

234   LAW: If someone commits hubris against someone, a child or woman or man,
free or slave, or does anything illegal against any of these, let any Athenian who
wishes and is competent to do so indict him before the *thesmothetai*, and let the
thesmothetai introduce the case to the Heliaia within 30 days of the indictment
being placed, unless some public business prevents it, or else as soon as it is
possible. Whomsoever the Heliaia condemns shall have his penalty assessed
immediately, whatever he seems to deserve to suffer or to pay. All who bring
indictments according to the law, if any of them fails to proceed with the charge,
or proceeds but fails to take a fifth of the votes, he is to pay 1,000 dr. to the
public treasury. If someone is condemned to pay a fine for hubris, let him be
bound, if he committed the hubris against a free man, until he pays up.

Demosthenes 21.47 (348–46)

This law on hubris is both a good example of a law which does not specify what the offence is – so that
hubris becomes what the prosecutor can convince the court is hubris – and a good example of the contrast
between the vague definition of the substantive offence and the detailed prescription of the procedure to be
followed. For the formulation of Solon's laws see above **14–28**. On hubris see **270**.

235   If someone...sees a murderer going around in the sanctuaries or through the
agora he can lead him away to the prison... And having been so led away he
will not suffer anything before he is judged, but if he is convicted he will be
punished by execution; but if the man who led him away does not get one fifth
of the votes he will incur a fine of 1,000 dr.

Demosthenes 23.80 (352)

Compare the discussion of the different effects of different legal procedures in **18**.

The jurors, their pay and their attitudes

236   The common people of Athens seem ill-advised in compelling the allies to sail
to Athens for court cases. But they respond by enumerating all the benefits
accruing to the common people of Athens from this practice. First of all, they
take enough money in the form of the allies' legal deposits to pay the jurymen
each year.

Old Oligarch 1.16

237   For some time the jurors were given two obols; subsequently, after serving as
general, Kleon raised the rate to three obols at the height of the Peloponnesian
War.

Scholiast on Aristophanes Wasps 88

For the introduction of jury pay see above **14**.

238   The jurors receive 3 obols.

[Aristotle] Constitution of the Athenians 62.2

239   LEADER OF CHORUS (of Wasps): Out of this mini-pay I have to buy barley-groats, firewood and fish for three.

Aristophanes *Wasps* 300–301 (422)

240   AISKHYLOS: When they (the Athenians) count the enemy's territory as their own and their own as the enemy's, and count the fleet as their resource and any other resource as bankruptcy.
DIONYSOS: Right, except that the juror gulps the money down, unaided.

Aristophanes *Frogs* 1463–66 (405)

241   PAPHLAGON: Aged jurors, brethren of the three-obol rate, whom I feed by shouting accusations, right or wrong, come to my aid ...

Aristophanes *Knights* 255–257 (424)

The (comic) implication here is that those who prosecuted a lot were popular with jurors because they kept the courts active and therefore ensured that paid work was available.

242   BDELYKLEON: From this total set aside a year's pay for the six thousand jurors – 'no more yet dwelt within the land'. We get, do we not, one hundred and fifty talents?

Aristophanes *Wasps* 661–63 (422)

The sum here assumes that all 6,000 jurors worked 300 days a year at half a drakhma (= one 12,000th of a talent) a day: ((6,000 x 300) ÷ 2) x 6,000 = 150; but that gives a quite unreal wages bill of 150 talents. The maximum number of working days was not 300 but something like 239: 354 – (40 + 60 + 15) = 239, where 354 is the number of days in the lunar year, 40 is the number of Assembly meetings, 60 is the number of major national festival days and 15 is the number of days of ill omen. Not all jurors worked on all 239 days.

The oath taken by jurors

243   OATH OF THE JURORS IN THE HELIAIA COURT:
I will vote according to the laws and decrees of the Athenian people and of the Council of 500. And I will not vote that there should be a tyrant or an oligarchy: even if someone puts an end to Athenian democracy or speaks or puts something to the vote contrary to this, I will not obey. And I will not vote for the abolition of private debts or the redivision of the land of the Athenians or the houses. And I will not bring back those in exile, nor those condemned to death in court, and I will not pardon those who have remained contrary to the existing laws and decrees of the Athenian people and of the Council nor will I allow any other to do so. And I will not confirm a man in a magistracy when he is subject to scrutiny for another magistracy – the nine arkhons and the recorder and all who are allotted on this day with the nine arkhons and the herald and embassies and delegates. And I will not allow the same man to hold the same magistracy twice nor the same man to hold two magistracies in the same year. I will not receive gifts for the sake of judgement in court, neither I myself nor any other man or woman for me with my knowledge, not by any manner or means. And I was born not less than 30 years ago. I will listen to the prosecutor and the defendant both alike and I will vote on the matter which is the subject of the prosecution. I swear by Zeus, Poseidon, Demeter, and I curse destruction on myself and my

own house if I transgress any of these, and if I keep my oath may many good things happen to me.

Demosthenes 24.149–151 (summer 353)

The genuineness of the text giving the jurors' oath is disputed, though some of the clauses are certainly well attested elsewhere. If genuine it makes very clear the very political rôle that the Athenian courts played.

The voting procedure

244 When the pleadings are concluded, the men who have been chosen by lot to take charge of the voting pebbles hand over to each of the jurors two ballots, one perforated and one solid, openly so that the litigants can see, in order that no one will receive either two perforated or two solid ballots. Then the person who has been chosen by lot for this takes away the staves of the jurors. In return for them each of the jurors receives, when he votes, a bronze token with the number 3 on it. For when he returns it he receives 3 obols. This is done to make sure that all will vote. For nobody gets a token unless he votes.

[Aristotle] Constitution of the Athenians 68.2

245 DIKAIOPOLIS. I also know the minds of the old (jurors): they have their eye on nothing but biting with their ballots.

Aristophanes Akharnians 375–6 (425)

Fourth-century bronze ballots have been found, some of which are inscribed 'public vote', see Osborne (2008) 6.10.

The rôle of the *thesmothetai*

246 The *thesmothetai* have the power, first, to prescribe the days on which the jury courts are to sit... They introduce all...public suits for unconstitutionality... and generals' scrutinies. There fall to them also public suits in which a prosecutor's deposit is levied: for being a foreigner...for bribery... They introduce the vettings of all officials, claims to citizenship rejected by demesmen...

[Aristotle] Constitution of the Athenians 59.1–3

247 After the various informations had been laid, the question of rewards arose; for Kleonymos' decree had offered 1,000 drakhmas and Peisandros' had offered 10,000. Conflicting claims were made by the informers mentioned – by Pythonikos, on the grounds that he had first made a denunciation to the Assembly, and by Androkles on behalf of the Council. So the people decided that those members of the court of the *thesmothetai* who had been initiated should hear the several informations and adjudicate. They voted the major award to Andromakhos and the minor to Teukros. At the festival of the Panathenaia Andromakhos received 10,000 drakhmas and Teukros 1,000.

Andokides 1.27–8 (400)

For the earlier stage of proceedings in the Assembly see above **209**. For the whole story of the mutilation of the Herms and the Profanation of the Mysteries see **373–7**.

Allocation of cases and allotment of time

248 ...they call up the cases. If they handle private matters they call up private parties, in number four from each of the types of suit determined by the law. The parties swear that they will speak to the matter at issue. When they handle public matters, they call up the public litigants, and they only judge one case. There are water-clocks with small outlet tubes; into these they pour the water by which the pleadings must be measured. 10 measures are allowed for cases involving an amount of more than 5,000 dr. and 3 measures for the second speech; 7 measures for those under 5,000 dr. and 2 for the second speech; 5 measures for those under 1,000 dr. and 2 for the second speech; and 6 measures in the case of adjudications in which there is no second speech.

[Aristotle] *Constitution of the Athenians* 67.1

249 When a prosecution for unconstitutionality comes before the jury court [of the *thesmothetai*], the day is divided into three parts. The first water is poured in for the accuser, the laws and democracy; the second water for the defendant and those who speak on the questions at issue; but when the question of unconstitutionality has been decided by the first ballot, then the third water is poured in for the assessment of the penalty and the intensity of your anger.

Aiskhines 3.197 (330)

250 SOKRATES: I am convinced that, voluntarily at least, I have wronged no man, but I have failed to persuade you of this, because we have had so little time for discussion. If it were your practice, as it is with other nations, to allow not one day but several to capital trials, I believe that you would have been persuaded.

Plato *Apology* 37a

The Spartans were well known for continuing capital trials over several days, Plutarch *Moralia* 217a, cf. Thuc. 1.132.5.

What swayed a jury?

251 The prosecutor, gentlemen of the jury, can say whatever he wants and can lie, but your verdict on me should, I think, be based not on the slanders of the prosecution but on an examination of my whole life.

Hypereides *Defence of Lykophron* 14 (probably 333)

252 THE LAWS OF ATHENS: Much might be said ... on behalf of the law, now to be broken, which enjoins that judicial findings are binding.

Plato *Kriton* 50b

253 In the lawcourts they (the common people) put their self-interest before justice.

Old Oligarch 1.13

254 Gentlemen of the jury, you readily allow your generals and speakers to make substantial gains. It is not the laws that allow them to do this but your gentleness and generosity. You lay down but one condition: the money they get must further your interests, not oppose them.

Hypereides *Against Demosthenes* 25 (323)

The comic view of the courts

255 SLAVE: He (the slave's master) loves it, this juror business; and he groans if he can't sit on the front bench. He doesn't get even a wink of sleep at night, but if in fact he does doze off just for a moment, his mind still flies through the night to the waterclock... And by god, if he saw any graffito by the doorway saying 'Demos, son of Pyrilampes, is beautiful', he would go and write beside it, '*kemos* (the ballot-box) is beautiful' ...

Straight after supper he shouts for his shoes, and then off he goes to the court in the early hours and sleeps there, clinging to the court-pillar like a limpet. And through bad temper he awards heavy sentences to all the defendants and then comes home like a bumble bee with wax plastered under his fingernails. And because he's afraid that some day he may run short of voting-pebbles, he keeps a whole beach in his house. That's how mad he is ...'

Aristophanes *Wasps* 87–111 (422)

Aristophanes' *Wasps* is a satire on the obsession of elderly Athenians with jury service and their prejudice and gullibility. The harshness of the jurors (cf. **245**) is marked by having them form a chorus of wasps, their gullibility by having the chief character called Philokleon (= lover of Kleon); his son Bdelyleon (= Kleon-hater) tries to re-educate his father.

256 PHILOKLEON: And our conduct is subject to no examination. This is true of no other office.
BDELYKLEON: Yes, that is impressive.

Aristophanes *Wasps* 587–8 (422)

257 BDELYKLEON: If there is any juror at the door, let him come in. No admittance once proceedings have begun.
PHILOKLEON: Which is the defendant? He won't escape conviction.
BDELYKLEON: Now listen to the indictment. Prosecution initiated by Dog (*kyon* cf. Kleon) of Kydathenaion against Labes (cf. Lakhes, the general) of Aixone for wrongdoing, in that he ate one Sicilian cheese all by himself. Penalty proposed: a fig-wood collar.
PHILOKLEON: No, a dog's death, if he's convicted.
BDELYKLEON: The defendant Labes now appears before the court.
PHILOKLEON: The villain! What a thievish look he has! He thinks he can deceive me by grinning like that. But where's the prosecutor, Dog of Kydathenaion.
DOG: Bow-wow!

Aristophanes *Wasps* 891–903 (422)

258   BDELYKLEON: Good sir, have pity on those in distress. Labes here eats up
his giblets and bones, and never stays in one place. But the other one – what a
creature he is! He just guards the house. He stays at home but demands his share
of whatever is brought him; if he doesn't get it, he bites.

PHILOKLEON: Oh dear! Whatever is it that is softening me? Some malady is
encircling me. I am beginning to be won over.

BDELYKLEON: Come, I beg you, pity him, father. Don't destroy him. Where
are his children? Come up, you poor things. Beg and beseech him, with
whimpers and tears.

PHILOKLEON: Down, down, down, down you go.

BDELYKLEON: I will stand down, although that 'down' has deceived so very
many in the past. All the same, I will stand down.

PHILOKLEON: Devil take you. What a mistake to gulp down soup. I wept
away my resolve only because I'm full of soup.

BDELYKLEON: So he's not getting off?

PHILOKLEON: It's hard to tell.

BDELYKLEON: Come, dear father, adopt the better course. Take this pebble,
shut your eyes, dash past to the second urn and acquit him, father.

                                                Aristophanes *Wasps* 967–88 (422)

259   INFORMER: You there, where are you from?

MEGARIAN: I'm Megarian, a dealer in pigmeat.

INFORMER: Then I expose these pigs as enemy goods, and you too.

MEGARIAN: There we go! Back comes the source from which our troubles
sprang.

INFORMER: You'll suffer for talking Megarian. Let go of that sack.

MEGARIAN: Dikiaopolis! Dikiaopolis! I am being exposed.

DIKAIOPOLIS: Who by? Who is exposing you? Market regulators, aren't you
going to keep out informers? What gives you the idea that you can expose
without a wick?

INFORMER: Am I not to expose the enemy?

DIKAIOPOLIS: You'll be sorry if you don't run off and do your informing
somewhere else.

MEGARIAN: What a blight this is on Athens.

                                             Aristophanes *Akharnians* 818–29 (425)

The figure named 'Informer' here and in the following passage is the *sykophantes*. There has been a good
deal of modern debate about how the *sykophantes* should be regarded and whether there were individuals
in Athens who made money out of prosecution. The term becomes a widely used term of abuse that labels
a litigant as vexatious, but the Aristophanic picture is of individuals who target legal actions, such as *phasis*
(the exposing of illegal trade and similar actions), where the successful prosecutor received a monetary
reward. For the debate see Osborne 1991/2010 and Harvey 1991. For the 'market regulators' see **275**. The
choice of a Megarian as the one denounced here is significant. Not only was Megara the city neighbouring
to Athens, but a dispute with Megara was an important factor in bringing about the Peloponnesian War (see
below **388–9**). Athenian action against Megara was held to have reduced Megarians to desperate poverty.

260 INFORMER: Dear me! How distressing it is that, good and patriotic fellow that I am, I am so badly treated.

JUST MAN: You – patriotic and good?

INFORMER: More than anyone.

JUST MAN: Then answer me this.

INFORMER: What?

JUST MAN: Are you a farmer?

INFORMER: Do you think I'm off my rocker?

JUST MAN: A merchant, then?

INFORMER: I claim to be, when necessary.

JUST MAN: Well, have you learnt a trade?

INFORMER: Certainly not.

JUST MAN: Then how on earth have you managed to keep alive, if you don't do anything?

INFORMER: I supervise the affairs of the city and of all private persons.

JUST MAN: You do? What are your qualifications?

INFORMER: I am the man who wishes.

JUST MAN: Then how could you be a good fellow, you villain, when nothing is your concern and you incur hatred?

INFORMER: Isn't it my concern, you nitwit, to benefit my own city to the best of my ability?

JUST MAN: Does meddling benefit the city?

INFORMER: No, but coming to the help of the established laws does, and not conniving if anyone breaks them.

JUST MAN: Doesn't the city appoint jurors to office for this very purpose?

INFORMER: But who prosecutes?

JUST MAN: The man who wishes.

INFORMER: That's me! So the city's affairs are my concern.

JUST MAN: Good heavens, what a worthless protector the city has! Why don't you become anyone who wishes – to keep quiet and live a life a leisure?

INFORMER: You're describing the life of a sheep.

Aristophanes *Wealth* 899–922 (c. 388)

A range of offences which caused harm to a person or group that was not able to bring a prosecution (the gods, the state) could be prosecuted by anyone who wished to.

261 CHORUS (of Knights): Glorious is your empire, Demos, seeing that all men fear you like a tyrant, but you are easily led astray, you enjoy being flattered and deceived, and you gape at the speaker of the moment. Your mind is both at home and out to lunch.

DEMOS: No mind at all lurks inside your long hair, if you think that I'm half-witted. I choose to play the fool like this. I positively enjoy my daily dose, and it is my pleasure to keep one thieving leader, and when he is full up, to snatch him up and strike him down.

Aristophanes *Knights* 1111–30 (424)

Self-presentation by defendants in court

262   SOKRATES: There is one thing, gentlemen of Athens, that I entreat and beg
of you: if you hear me defending myself in the same language that it has been
my habit to use at the tables of the bankers in the Agora, where many of you
have heard me, and elsewhere, do not be surprised and do not make a
disturbance. The facts are these. This is my first appearance in a court of law,
at the age of seventy; so I am a complete stranger to the language of this place.

Plato *Apology* 17cd

263   SOKRATES: It may be that one of you, remembering his own case, will be
annoyed that whereas he, standing trial on a less serious charge than this, begged
and besought the jury in floods of tears and paraded his infant children to excite
maximum sympathy, and many of his relatives and friends as well, I for my part
intend to do no such thing, even though I face, as it might appear, the gravest
of dangers.

Plato *Apology* 34bc

264   SOKRATES: I have often noticed that some people of this kind, despite their
reputation, go to extraordinary lengths when they come up for trial, thereby
showing that they think it will be a fearful thing if they lose their lives – as
though they would live for ever if you did not put them to death! In my view
they bring shame on the city. Any visiting Greek might suppose that the flower
of Athenian manhood, whom their fellow-citizens select for public office and
other high honours, are no better than women. Men of any reputation at all must
not do such things to you, Athenians; and if we do, you must not allow it. You
must instead make plain that you will be much quicker to convict anyone who
stages these pathetic scenes and makes a laughing-stock of the city than anyone
keeps quiet. Apart, gentlemen, from the question of the city's good name, I do
not think it right for anyone to entreat the juror or to get off by so doing; he
should instead expound the facts and persuade. The juror does not sit to dispense
justice as a favour, but to determine where justice lies. He has sworn not to
gratify those he pleases, but to judge according to the law.

Plato *Apology* 35a–c

The absence of a judge directing the jury, and the fact that individuals defended themselves, rather than
being defended by professional lawyers, made it inevitable that notions of relevance were relatively loosely
policed, and that there was less clarity than in a modern court about what should affect the decision about
guilt and what affect the severity of any sentence.

265   Now he (Eratosthenes) cannot even have recourse to the expedient, so habitual
in this city, of offering no defence against the charges, but making other
statements about themselves which sometimes deceive you: they represent to
you that they are good soldiers, or that as trierarkhs they have captured many
enemy ships or won over cities that were previously hostile. Just tell him to
explain when they (the Thirty) killed as many of the enemy as they have of
Athenian citizens.

Lysias 12.38–9 (403/2)

266   SOKRATES: He who would be a competent speaker has no need of the truth about the just or the good, or about men who have been made such by nature or upbringing. In the courts no one pays any attention whatever to the truth about these matters – only to plausibility. Plausibility is nothing but probability, and it is to probability that he who would be a scientific speaker must attend. Sometimes both prosecution and defence should pass over the facts if they are improbable and concentrate on probability. Say goodbye to the truth, and in your speeches pursue probability at all costs.

Plato *Phaidros* 272de

Class bias in the Athenian courts?

267   Perhaps Aphobetos and his brother Philokhares will speak up for him. There are many justifiable complaints to make against both of them. It is necessary, men of Athens, to speak frankly, not holding anything back. We, let me tell you Aphobetos and Philokhares, have considered you worthy, you who paint alabaster boxes and drums, and these brothers who are scribes and common or garden men, (that is no evil, but it doesn't deserve the generalship) of embassies, and military commands and the greatest honours...

Demosthenes 19.237 (343)

This and other passages, including those below, suggest that there was plenty of subtle allusion to social class in the courts, and that speakers took advantage of jurors' prejudices, and their dislike of prejudice, in various ways, depending on the result that they hoped to achieve. See Todd (1990).

268   So summon Straton himself who suffered such things; for he may, of course, stand here (although deprived of his civic rights). This man, men of Athens, for all that he may be poor, is not depraved. However, he, a citizen who had campaigned with his age class in all the campaigns, and had done nothing terrible, stands here now in silence, deprived not only of all other goods common to all, but even of the possibility of speaking or wailing. He cannot even tell you whether what he has suffered is just or not. He has suffered this at the hands of Meidias and Meidias' wealth and arrogance against his poverty, helplessness and being one of the many. If he broke the law and took the 50 drakhmas from him and manifestly pronounced in Meidias' favour the case which he arbitrated against Meidias, he would still enjoy his civic rights, and with no trouble would share equally with all the rest of us. But since he looked beyond Meidias to what was just, and feared the laws rather than Meidias' threats, he has been thrown by this man into such and so great a disaster.

Demosthenes 21.95–6 (348–6)

269   If someone poor who does something wrong because of his need is liable to the final penalty, are we going to pardon someone rich who does the same things through base desire for gain? Where is our vaunted all having equal shares and democracy, if you sort these things out like that?

Demosthenes 51.11 (after 361)

270   Bear in mind that the poor have no share in the dangers that go with property, but that we all alike share violence directed at the body. So, whenever you punish those who deprive others of property you benefit only the rich, but when you punish those guilty of hubris you help yourselves... [19] None of you, noticing that I am poor and one of the masses, should decide to deny me the just penalty imposed. For it is not right to make the punishments on behalf of those who have no repute less than those on behalf of those with famous names, nor to think the poor worse than those who have much. After all you would be dishonouring yourselves if you were to make such a decision about citizens.

Isokrates 20.15, 19 (soon after 402)

'Hubris' was a term used to cover a wide range of actions that brought shame to the victim, ranging from slighting the gods to beating up a fellow-citizen or even a slave. See also above **234**.

271   Enough accusations have been made against Epikrates. You must bear in mind that you have often heard these men saying, when they want to destroy someone contrary to justice, that unless you condemn those whom they order you to, your pay will give out.

Lysias 27.1 (c.390)

Decisions in the courts directly affected state revenues from which payments were made to jurors; cf. **163**.

12   MAGISTRATES AND OFFICIALS

The arkhonship

272   The appointment of the arkhons was based on good birth and wealth, and it was they who became members of the Areopagos. That is why membership of the Areopagos has remained to this day the only public office held for life.

[Aristotle] *Constitution of the Athenians* 3.6

For more on the arkhonship see above **39,44**. For their rôle in the legal system see **219–20**. For the Areopagos see **1,14** and **44**. The criterion of wealth remained formally in place even after the arkhons were chosen by lot.

The number and range of magistrates and officials

273   More than twenty thousand men were supported from the tribute, the taxes and the allies. There were 6,000 jurors, 1,600 archers, and also 1,200 cavalry, the Council of 500, 500 guards of the dockyards, and also 50 guards on the Akropolis; about 700 internal officials...

[Aristotle] *Constitution of the Athenians* 24.3

Scholars have been unable to verify all of these figures, but they appear to be of the right order of magnitude: see Hansen (1987).

274   First, there are ten treasurers of Athene, one appointed by lot from each tribe, from the *pentakosiomedimnoi* in accordance with Solon's law – the law is still in force; the men appointed hold office even though they may be quite poor.

They take over the statue of Athene, the Victories, the other equipment and the money in the presence of the Council.

Next there are ten *poletai* (Sellers), one appointed by lot from each tribe. They are responsible for all leases and let out contracts for the mines and taxes... They sell confiscated property...

There are ten *apodektai* (Receivers), appointed tribally by lot: they take over the tablets and delete the sums paid in the presence of the Council in the Council-house, and give back the tablets to the public slave again. If anyone misses his payment, he is recorded there and is obliged to pay double the missing sum or go to prison...

Ten *agoranomoi* (market regulators) are appointed by lot, five for the city and five for Peiraieus. They are required by the laws to oversee all goods on sale, to ensure that what is sold is in good condition and unadulterated...

The Eleven are appointed by lot. They are responsible for the men in the prison... When thieves, kidnappers and cloak-snatchers are hauled before them, the Eleven put them to death, if they admit their guilt; if they dispute it, they bring them before the jury court. If they are then acquitted, they let them go; if not, they put them to death.

[Aristotle] Constitution of the Athenians 47.1–2; 48.1; 51.1; 52.1

Many passages cited above to illustrate the rôle of the Council have mentioned boards of magistrates. These extracts fill out the picture.

275   DIKAIOPOLIS: As regulators of the market I appoint the three picked by lot, these leather straps...

DIKAIOPOLIS: If he (Lamakhos) squawks, I'll summon my market regulators.

Aristophanes Akharnians 723–4; 968 (425)

Behind this joke lies the reality that many Athenian magistracies demanded – and since they were open to all needed to demand – only a minimum of knowledge.

For more on magistrates and officials see index s.v. *apodektai*, arkhons, basileus, *epimeletai, kolakretai, poletai,*

13   THE ARMY AND NAVY

The politics of military power

276   So, first of all, I will say this, that it is fair enough that in Athens the poor and the common people should seem to have more power than the noble and rich, because it is the common people who row the ships and so render the city powerful; it is the steersmen, boatswains, under-boatswains, look-out men, and shipwrights who render the city powerful, far more than the hoplites, the noble and the respectable. Since this is so, it seems fair that they should all share in the offices of state by the processes of lot and election, and that anyone of the citizens who wishes should have the right to speak.

Second, all those offices that bring safety to the state as a whole when they are in respectable hands, danger when they are not, in these offices the common people do not require any share. They do not think that it is proper for them to share in the generalship by having it allotted, nor in the cavalry command. For they recognise that they derive greater benefit by not holding these offices themselves but allowing the most capable men to hold office. But all those offices which involve the receipt of money and benefit for one's household, these the common people seeks to hold.

Old Oligarch 1.2–3

The Old Oligarch places at the very beginning of his discussion of Athenian democracy this analysis of the logic of Athenian practice with regard to the military forces and their officers, and the effect which their place in Athens military efforts had on the political power of different sectors of Athenian society.

Becoming a soldier

277   When I was released from the ranks of children, I was a border-guard (*peripolos*) of the countryside of Attica for two years, and I will provide my fellow-ephebes and the officers as witnesses of this to you.

Aiskhines 2.167 (343)

Since Aiskhines was born in 390 we are dealing here with the events of c.372. It is not clear how universal service as an ephebe was in these years. Formal obligation to do ephebic service may have been introduced only in the 330s with the law of Epikrates (**280**).

278   Two years ago I went out to Panakton, after garrison duty had been assigned to me.

Demosthenes 54.3 (uncertain date)

The date of this speech is quite uncertain, and it is not clear whether the garrison duty here is as an ephebe or as part of the regular hoplite force (which we know to have manned the border forts in 357 and 341).

279   When you have done what I say, I submit, not only would the city be better off for money, but it would be more willing to obey, better ordered, and better at fighting wars. For those assigned to be trained would do this much more carefully if they received greater subsistence allowance in the gymnasium than they do when under the command of gymnasiarkhs in the torch races; and those assigned to guard duty in the guardposts and serve as light-armed troops and border-guards (*peripoloi*) in the countryside, would do these much more if subsistence was supplied for all these tasks.

Xenophon, *Ways and Means* 4.51–2

Xenophon has maintained that the state should take over the silver mines and so generate income to fund other desirable enterprises, amongst which garrison service figures largely.

280   Another character mentioned by Lykourgos in the speech 'About Administration' is Epikrates, saying that a bronze statue was set up because of the law about the ephebes. They say he obtained a property worth sixty talents.

Harpokration *s.v. Epikrates*

Although the precise date of Epikrates' law is uncertain it falls somewhere in the middle of the 330s, following the Athenian defeat at Khaironeia.

281   There are ten eponyms of the tribes and 42 of the age grades. The ephebes who are enrolled were formerly written up onto whitened boards and the arkhon under whom they were written up and the eponym of the year that had served as arbitrators in the preceding year were listed against them; but now they are written up on a bronze stele and the stele stands in front of the Council chamber by the eponymous heroes.

[Aristotle] *Constitution of the Athenians* 53.4

For the registration of young men as ephebes see above **59**. For the arbitrators see above **216**. The reform in question will be consequent on the law of Epikrates. Use of bronze for inscriptions is uncommon at Athens, and none of these bronzes survive. It may be that bronze was used because the lists were relatively ephemeral in their use and the bronze could be melted down and re-used.

282   You have an oath which all citizens swear when they are inscribed into the deme records (*lexiarkhikon grammateion*) and become ephebes, not to bring shame upon the sacred arms, not to leave the ranks but to defend their fatherland and to hand it on better.

Lykourgos *Against Leokrates* 76 (330)

For the full text of the oath see RO 88.

283   Kallikrates of Aixone proposed: since the ephebes of Kekropis in the arkhonship of Ktesikles (334/3) have been well-disciplined and done all that the laws ordain that they should and have obeyed the *sophronistes* elected by the people, to praise them and crown them with a gold crown from 500 drakhmas for their good order and discipline. And to praise the *sophronistes* Adeistos son of Antimakhos of Athmonon and crown him with a gold crown from 500 drakhmas because he has looked after the ephebes of the Kekropid tribe well. And to inscribe this decree on a stone stele and stand it in the sanctuary of Kekrops.

Hegemakhos son of Khairemon of Perithoidai proposed: since the ephebes of Kekropis established at Eleusis looked after all that the Council and people commanded them well and enthusiastically and show themselves well disciplined, to praise their good order and good discipline and crown each of them with a wreath of olive, and to praise their *sophronistes* Adeistos son of Antimakhos of Athmonon and crown him with a crown of olive when he gives his scrutiny, and inscribe this decree on the dedication which the ephebes of Kekropis dedicate.

Protias proposed: the demesmen have decided, since the ephebes of Kekropis looked after the guarding of Eleusis well and enthusiastically and their *sophronistes* Adeistos son of Antimakhos of Athmonon, to praise them and crown each of them with a crown of olive, and inscribe this inscription on the dedication which the ephebes of Kekropis in the arkhonship of Ktesikles dedicate.

Euphronios proposed: the demesmen have decided, since the ephebes inscribed in the arkhonship of Ktesikles have been well disciplined and done all that the laws ordain that they should, and the *sophronistes* elected by the people shows that they have been obedient and have done everything else enthusiastically, to praise them and crown them with a gold crown from 500 drakhmas for their good order and discipline; and to praise their *sophronistes*, Adeistos son of Antimakhos of Athmonon, and to crown him with a gold crown from 500 drakhmas because he has looked after the demesmen and all the others of the Kekropid tribe well and enthusiastically; and to inscribe this decree on the dedication which the ephebes of Kekropis and the *sophronistes* dedicate. The tribe. The Council. The Eleusinioi. The Athmoneis.

RO 89 (*IG* ii² 1156) 26–66 (332)

This is one of a number of surviving inscriptions honouring groups of ephebes belonging to different tribes (collected in Reinmuth 1971). It nicely indicates the range of central and local groups that were involved with the ephebes.

Generals and other infantry officers

284 All the military officers are elected. They used to elect one general from each tribe, but now they elect all ten from the whole people... [3] Ten taxiarkhs are elected, one from each tribe; each of them commands his tribal regiment and appoints the company commanders. Two cavalry commanders are elected from the whole citizen body...

[Aristotle] *Constitution of the Athenians* 61.1; 3–4

For the political rôle of the general see above **191–4**.

285 A man may hold the military offices repeatedly, but none of the other offices except that one can serve on the Council of 500 twice.

[Aristotle] *Constitution of the Athenians* 62.3

286 CHOROS: Lamakhos, you who throw glances that are like lightning, help! You with the gorgon plume, manifest yourself! Lamakhos, my friend, my fellow-tribesman! Is there a taxiarkh about, or a general, or a wall-stormer? Let him come to my aid!

Aristophanes *Akharnians* 566–71 (425)

This nicely illustrates the way in which a soldier might turn to his friends, his fellow-tribesmen, who would be stationed around him, and then to the officials posted over him – the taxiarkh and the general.

287 'But,' Sokrates said, '...the general must be able to prepare everything for the war, and able to provide supplies necessary for the soldiers, and be inventive and effective, careful and persevering and shrewd, both friendly and harsh, both straightforward and subtle, a good protector and a good thief, lavish and rapacious, generous and grasping, steady and aggressive; and a man must have a great many other qualities, natural and acquired, if he is to be a good general. Still, it is a fine thing to be a tactician, and a well-ordered army is a very different thing from a badly ordered one.'

Xenophon Memorabilia 3.1.6

288 Sokrates once saw Nikomakhides coming away from the elections and asked, 'Nikomakhides, who have been elected as generals?' And he said, 'The Athenians are not such as to choose me, Sokrates, worn out serving in the ranks and being a *lokhagos* and taxiarkh and with all these wounds from the enemy (and he stripped and showed the scars of his wounds as he said this), but they have elected Antisthenes, who has never fought as a hoplite and hasn't done anything to notice in the cavalry and who knows only about piling up money...'

[11] 'I accept that, but you pass over the question of what advantage is it to be able to be a good household manager if it is necessary to fight? Surely,' said Sokrates, 'this is where it will be most valuable of all. The good household manager, knowing that nothing is so advantageous and profitable as that the fighting force beats the enemy and nothing so disadvantageous and punitive as being defeated, will enthusiastically look out and prepare what helps achieve victory, and will consider carefully and guard against what brings defeat. He will fight energetically, if he sees that his preparations can bring victory, and no less, if he is unprepared, he will guard against engaging in battle. Don't despise men who are household managers, Nikomakhides. Looking after private matters differs only in scale from looking after communal matters; in other respects they are just alike, and the most important thing is that neither can happen without men, and individual affairs aren't done through one set of men and community affairs done through another set. Those who look after community affairs do not use any other men than those who look after individual household management. Those who know how to use those men do both individual and communal business well, and those who do not know make a mess of both.'

Xenophon Memorabilia 3.4.1, 11–12

As with much in the *Memorabilia*, Sokrates is being a devil's advocate here, stressing precisely the skills likely to be little valued among generals. But the passage suggests that there was popular discussion about the merits both of particular candidates for general and of the type of person who made the best general.

289 Generals differ from one another in the following way: some produce men who are willing neither to labour nor to run risks, who do not even think that it is worth obeying, except in as far as they are forced to, but even make a big thing of opposing their officer. These same generals do not produce men who know to be ashamed if something disgraceful happens. But officers who are godlike, good and knowledgeable, have the same men, and often others whom they have recruited, ashamed to do anything disgraceful and thinking that it is better to obey and priding themselves that, one and all, they do what they are told, and, when it is necessary to labour, labour without being despondent. Just as some individuals love working, so, under good officers, love of work and wanting to be seen doing something fine by their officer can be instilled into the whole army. The officers towards whom the followers are thus disposed are the strong commanders, certainly not the ones who have the best body among the soldiers or are best with the bow or the spear and have the best horse and face the dangers first in the manner of cavalry or peltasts, but those who can instil it in the soldiers to follow even through fire and every danger.

Xenophon *Oikonomikos* 21.4–7

290   CHORUS: Believe me, though there is much to talk about, I don't know what to say. So intense is the pain I feel, when I look at the present state of the city. While we old men ran it, we did not run it like this. To start with, we citizens had generals from the greatest families, pre-eminent in wealth and blood, to whom we prayed as if they were gods, which they were. As a result, we enjoyed security; but now, whenever we happen to be campaigning, we elect scum as generals.

Eupolis *Demes* fr.117 K-A (produced in 412)

The contrast between the present and the more heroic past is a regular feature of Old Comedy; see Strauss (1993). Modern scholars, however, have generally agreed that over the course of the fifth and fourth centuries generals came to be more professional, and the rôles of political and of military leadership came to be separated, so that whereas in the fifth century Kimon or Perikles or Alkibiades were prominent both in politics and as generals, in the fourth century generals such as Iphikrates or Phokion played little part in politics, while politicians like Demosthenes and Lykourgos were not military leaders.

291   Since some offices require experience, in relation to these it is a good idea to harness some of the younger men always in order that they might be trained by those who know and administer the city none the worse. So Hagnon once advised the Athenians over the generals, using the example of hunting, for there, he said, those who love hunting always try out puppies. ... [172] It is necessary that the man who will hold greater offices should serve other offices first, something recommended in the case of the generalship. It is strange if a man who has not been taxiarkh or phylarkh should straightaway be general.

Theophrastos, *On the Choice of Magistrates*, Ms. Vat. Gr. 2366B 105–129, 172–183 from *Transactions of the American Philological Association* 106 (1976) 230–233.

The issue of continuity:

292

Tribe	441/0	440/39	439/8
Erekhtheis	Sokrates of Anagyrous		?[Sokrates]
Aigeis	Sophokles of Kolonos		Demokleides
Pandionis	Andokides of Kydathenaion	Hagnon and Phormio	Phormio
Leontis	Kreon of Skambonidai		?Ch..........
Akamantis	Perikles and Glaukon	Perikles	Perikles and Glaukon
Oineis	Kallistratos of Akharnai		Kallistratos of Akharnai
Kekropis	Xenophon of Melite	Antikles	Xenophon of Melite
Hippothontis	Lampides of Peiraieus	Thoukydides	
Aiantis		Tlepolemos	Tlempolemos (sic)
Antiokhis	Kleitophon of Thorai		

From a mixture of literary and epigraphic sources we are able to reconstruct with some confidence the lists of generals for three successive years in the middle of the fifth century (for details see Develin 1989). This enables us to see the high degree of turnover among the Athenian generals. Note that in 441/0 and 439/8 Akamantis has two generals, at the expense of Aiantis in the earlier year and of Hippothontis or Antiokhis in the later. For the election procedure see Mitchell 2000.

293   The laws prescribe for the orator and the general, men who consider that they deserve the trust of the people, to beget children according to the laws, to own land within the boundaries of the territory, and only when he has deposited all the worthy pledges to reckon himself worthy to be a champion of the people.

Deinarkhos 1.71 (323)

This is the only source that claims that children and land ownership were legal requirements of a general, let alone of an orator. The claim is not likely to be factually true, but it shows well how Athenians thought that Deinarkhos could claim this.

294   LAMAKHOS: Is that how you talk to a general, beggar that you are?
DIKAIOPOLIS: I, a beggar?
LAMAKHOS: Then what are you?
DIKAIOPOLIS: What am I? A good citizen, not an office-hunter, but ever since war broke out, an active soldier; whereas you, ever since war broke out, have been a paid officer.
LAMAKHOS: I was elected –
DIKAIOPOLIS: By three cuckoos.

Aristophanes *Akharnians* 593–598 (425)

295   After the defeat of Thoukydides and his ostracism, Perikles acquired supremacy by holding the annual office of general for no fewer than fifteen years on end.

Plutarch *Perikles* 16.3

For the conflict between Perikles and Thoukydides see **186–8**.

The responsibility of the general

296   In fact, the citizen body did not stop being angry with Perikles until they had
punished him with a fine; but soon afterwards, as is the way of the mob, they
once more elected him general and entrusted all their affairs to him: they were
now less sensitive to the grief that each felt for his personal losses, and they
thought that he was the best man to meet the needs of the city as a whole.

Thucydides 2.65.3–4

297   When the news of the sea battle reached the Athenians at home, they were
furious with Alkibiades, because they thought that he had lost the ships through
his own negligence and indiscipline, and they elected ten new generals: Konon,
Diomedon, Leon, Perikles, Erasinides, Aristokrates, Arkhestratos,
Protomakhos, Thrasyllos, Aristogenes. Alkibiades was out of favour with the
fleet too; so he took one warship and sailed off to his forts in the Khersonese.

Xenophon Hellenika 1.5.16–17

See also above **212–13** on the trial of the generals after the battle of Arginousai.

298   If the fact that they are often condemned to death does not make the generals
bad, so neither are sophists bad.

Aristotle Rhetoric 1397b24–5

Hansen (1974) reckons that during period 432–355 160 generals are known, of whom 33 were impeached,
27 convicted, and 19 sentenced to death. Knox (1985) calculates that of the 41 best known fifth- and fourth-
century politicians, eight were executed and additionally 17 served terms of exile.

299   Apparently I, the orator and adviser, am to be given no share of the responsibility
for what happened according to the proposal and plan, but am to be held alone
responsible for what went wrong with the generals' command.

Demosthenes 18.212 (330)

As this passage makes clear, there were two sides to the story of the lack of responsibility of speakers in the
Assembly and the responsibility of military officers.

300   PERIKLES: I have many other reasons for hoping that you will win through if
you can agree not to enlarge your empire in wartime and to run needless risks.
I am more afraid of our own mistakes than of the enemy's plans.

Thucydides 1.144.1

Hoplite conscription

301   DEMOS: First, all who row long ships, I will give full pay when they launch
the ships... Second, when someone has been put on the list as a hoplite, no
busybody will change it, but it will be inscribed just as it first was.

Aristophanes Knights 1366–71 (424)

302   They use the eponyms for army service too, and when they send out an age-class they prescribe from what arkhon and eponym until what men are required to campaign.

[Aristotle] *Constitution of the Athenians* 53.7

See above **281** for the eponyms of age-classes. On hoplite conscription see **318** and Christ (2001).

303   The politicians, giving reality to public enthusiasm, wrote a decree that the people should look to the common freedom of Greece and free the cities that were under garrisons and prepare 40 quadriremes and 200 triremes, and that all Athenians up to the age of 40 should campaign and 3 tribes be left to guard Attica and 7 tribes be prepared for expeditions abroad.

Diodoros 18.10.2

This was the call-up for the so-called Lamian War that broke out after Alexander's death in 323 BC. On this call-up see Hansen (1985) 83–8.

304   After that, the Corinthian war took place in which both I and my father were compelled to serve so that neither of us could take up the case.

Isaios 10.20 (378–71)

Given normal age of marriage for men of 30, this passage implies that call-up during the Corinthian War, which broke out in 395 BC, included men well over the age of 40.

305   They had sworn that they would list those who had not served, and then they broke their oaths.

Lysias 9.15 (c.395–87)

The date of the events in Lysias 9 is uncertain, as is Lysias' authorship, but this is likely to be a genuine fourth-century speech.

306   When I got back to the city the year before last, I had not yet lived here for two months when I was listed as a hoplite. When I realised what had been done, I straightaway suspected that there was something improper about my being listed. So I went to the general and made it clear that I had done a period of service. But I did not get at all a decent treatment. I was annoyed at being abused, but I kept quiet.

Lysias 9.4 (c.395–87)

Troop numbers in 431

307   Perikles thus encouraged them on the finances, and that there were 13,000 hoplites, not counting those in the forts and on the battlements who numbered 16,000. That was the number on guard initially when the enemy invaded, drawn from the oldest and youngest and as many of the metics as were hoplites... [8] He revealed 1200 cavalry with the *hippotoxotai*, 1600 archers and 300 triremes in sailing condition.

Thucydides 2.13.6–7, 8

These figures given by Thucydides in 2.13 are our best indication of the total population of Athens in 431; see Akrigg (2007) 29–31.

The Athenian cavalry

308   It is clear that those who are most capable, financially and physically, must provide the cavalry according to the law that either brings them into court or persuades them. I think that one should bring to court those whom, if one does not, one will seem to have been bribed not to. For if you do not compel those most able first, then one would straightway have to turn to those less able. But one can, I think, establish an enthusiasm for cavalry service in the young by relating all the glories in cavalry service, and reduce the opposition of those who have charge of them by teaching that they will in any case be compelled to maintain horses, if not by you then by someone else, because of their wealth.

Xenophon *Hipparkhikos* 1.9–11

For the examination of the cavalry by the Council see above **169**. On the Athenian cavalry see Spence (1993).

309   The following are the things that the hipparkh himself must concern himself with. First, how to sacrifice successfully to the gods on behalf of the cavalry. Second how to make spectacular processions at the festivals. And also all the other occasions when there has to be a display for the city, how to make the finest possible display, both in the Akademy and in the Lykeion and at Phaleron and in the Hippodrome.

Xenophon *Hipparkhikos* 3.1

The Akademy and Lykeion were both gymnasia (as well as being the places in which Plato and Aristotle, resectively, taught).

310   For when you returned you voted that the phylarkhs should list those who had been members of the cavalry in order to get the equipment allowance back from them. Well, no one could show that I was listed by the phylarkhs, or handed over to those handling the court cases nor that I repaid the allowance. Yet everyone can easily discover this, that the phylarkhs had to pay a fine if they did not publish a list of those who had the allowances. It is much more just for you to trust that document than this one: anyone who wanted to could easily get his name erased from this list, but those who had served in the cavalry had to be included in that list by the phylarkhs. What is more, Council, if I had been in the cavalry I would not have tried to deny it as if it were something terrible I had done, but I would have thought it right to prove that no citizen had suffered badly at my hands and to submit to examination. I see that you are of the same opinion, and that many of those who served in the cavalry then are members of the Council, and many of them have been elected as generals and hipparkhs.

Lysias 16.6–8 (c.392–89)

This passage describes what happened after the restoration of democracy in 403. Despite the protestations at the end of this passage it is clear that the Athenians continued to feel equivocal about the cavalry.

311 Thibron asked for 300 cavalry from the Athenians, saying that he would pay them. They sent some who had been in the cavalry under the Thirty, considering it an advantage for the people if they went away and perished.

Xenophon Hellenika 3.1.4

The cavalry, perhaps including Xenophon himself, had supported the Thirty, and as a result were subsequently suspected. This request for cavalry support from the Spartan Thibron may have been made in 400/399 precisely because the Spartans expected more support from the cavalry than from others in Athens.

312 Dexileos son of Lysanias of Thorikos. He was born in the arkhonship of Teisandros; he died in that of Euboulides, in Corinth, one of the five cavalrymen.

RO 7B (IG ii^2 6217) (394)

This is the only Athenian gravestone that gives dates of birth (this equates to 414/13) and death (394/3). One reason for that might be that Dexileos' youth will provoke especial pity, but it is likely that this is also intended to flag up that Dexileos himself had nothing to do with the cavalry under the Thirty (cf. **149, 310**), and that he lost his young life as a patriotic democrat. Dexileos' name also appeaers on a monument listing all the cavalry dead of that year; see further RO 7.

313 Well, I, gentlemen of the jury, stayed with you in the city the whole time and never received any base blame, nor was there any legal case between me and any of the citizens: I neither had to defend myself in any case nor did I prosecute another, but I continued to rear horses keenly the whole time according to my ability and beyond my property. I have been crowned by all the cavalry for my manly goodness and by my fellow officers. For you, gentlemen of the jury, first elected me as phylarkh, then as hipparkh to Lemnos. And I held office there for two years, the only one of the hipparkhs ever to have done so, and I additionally remained there for a third year, not wanting to rush head-first into exacting the pay for the cavalry from men who were citizens and badly off. And in this time no one there made a complaint against me, either privately or publicly, and I was crowned with three crowns by the people in Hephaistia and with others by the people in Myrine.

Hypereides Defence of Lykophron 16–18 (probably 333)

314 You have dared to speak against my relatives. You are so shameless and ungrateful that you express neither love nor respect for Philodemos the father of Philon and Epikrates, through whom you were enrolled among the demesmen, as the elders among the Paianians are aware. And I am shocked, Demosthenes, that you dare to abuse Philon, and that in the presence of the most reputable citizens of Athens, who have assembled here to pass judgement on the city's best interests and who are now paying attention to our lives rather than our words. Do you expect that they would rather pray that there should be ten thousand hoplites like Philon, with bodies like his and souls so decent, or thirty thousand perverts (*kinaidoi*) like you?

Aiskhines 2.150–151 (343)

The exchange of abuse here is notable both for the evidence it gives for homosexuality being a potential matter for negative comment, even when no exchange of money for sex is in question, and because of the polar opposition between the *kinaidos* and the hoplite. This remains an isolated passage, however, and arguably Winkler (1990b) makes too much of it.

Going to war

315 The demesmen mustered before setting out. I knew that some of them who were good and patriotic citizens were short of provisions, and I said that the haves should provide what was necessary for those in need. Not only did I so advise the others, but I myself gave thirty drakhmas to each of two men, not because I saw myself as being rich but to set a good example to the others.

Lysias 16.14 (c.392–89)

The deme was not a formal military unit, but clearly fellow-demesmen went to war together. For mustering by *trittys* see above **104**.

316 When the officers whom you had elected to command me assigned me to my position at Poteidaia and Amphipolis and Delion, I remained at my post like anyone else and faced death...

Plato *Apology* 28e

The campaigns to which Sokrates here refers occurred during the Arkhidamian War when Sokrates himself was in his 40s.

Military offences and their prosecution

317 Everyone who is convicted of theft or bribery – and in this case their dependents, everyone who leaves the ranks or is found guilty of refusing military service or cowardice or refusing to fight in a sea battle, or who throws away his shield, or who three times bears false witness, or falsely witnesses a summons, or harms his parents – all these are deprived of their civic rights (*atimoi*) but they retain their property

Andokides 1.74 (400)

318 Some dare to say that no one is liable to the charge of leaving the ranks or cowardice. For no battle took place and that the law ordains that if someone backs out of the ranks because of cowardice, while the others are fighting, then the soldiers are to judge the case against him. But the law does not give orders just about this, but also about all those absent from the infantry ranks. Read me the law.

LAW.

You hear, gentlemen of the jury, that the law concerns both things, both those who when there is a battle retreat backwards and those who are absent from the infantry army. And consider who it is that ought to be present. Is it not those who belong to this age-class? Is it not those whom the generals list? I think, gentlemen of the jury, that the defendant alone of the citizens is liable to the whole of the law. For he would justly be convicted of failure to serve in the army, since after he had been listed he did not march out with you; of abandoning the ranks, since alone he did not present himself in the camp to be marshalled with the others; and of cowardice, since when he ought share risks with the infantry he chose to serve in the cavalry.

Lysias 14.5–7 (395)

For hoplite conscription see above **301–2**. For prejudice against the cavalry see **311**.

319   What I think that you ought to hear, and what will be proof of this man's boldness and daring, I will now mention. For in Corinth, when he arrived after the battle against the enemy and the campaign to Koroneia, he got into a fight with the taxiarkh Lakhes and struck him, and when the citizens had marched out in full force he seemed to be the most ill-disciplined and depraved and so, alone of Athenians, was proclaimed as excluded from the army by the generals.

Lysias 3.45 (after 394)

Death on campaign and its commemoration

320   Consider also the argument from the date which they claim for the will. For they say that Astyphilos made this will when he sailed out to campaign at Mytilene. He appears on their account to have been prescient about everything that was about to happen. For he first campaigned against Corinth and then against Thessaly and then throughout the Theban war, and indeed he went off everywhere as platoon commander (*lokhagos*) wherever he perceived an army was being gathered. And not even on one of those trips did he leave a will. But the Mytilene campaign was his last, on which he died. Would any of you find it credible that, when Astyphilos had served other campaigns before and knew well that he would face dangers on all of them, fortune dealt so nicely that when on earlier occasions he had made no will even about a single item of his property, yet when he was about to go on his last campaign, and was sailing as a volunteer and particularly expecting to return safely – how is it plausible that he then left a will, sailed out and died?

Isaios 9.14–15 (between 371 and 355)

We do not have any very good idea of how likely death in campaigns was. Although it has been calculated that on average some 14% of combatants on the losing side and 5% on the winning died in a hoplite battle, casualties varied greatly from battle to battle. This history of a single individual gives an impression of the frequency of military action for a man who had was evidently keen to serve his city as a soldier.

For the commemoration of the war-dead see above **312** and LACTOR 1[4] **42**.

321   From now on the city will maintain their children at the public expense until they are grown up.

Thucydides 2.46.1

We do not know when maintenance for orphans was introduced in Athens, but this extract from the funeral speech ascribed to Perikles indicates that it was introduced before the Peloponnesian War.

322   What Greek person who had received a liberal education would not feel pain remembering that moment, if no other, in the theatre when once, at the time when the city was particularly well-governed and employed better advisers, on this very day when, just as now, the tragedies were about to happen, the herald came forward and presented the orphans whose fathers had died in war, young men decked out in full armour. He announced the finest of all pronouncements and the one best designed to encourage excellence: that the people had maintained until puberty these young men whose fathers, dying in war, had become good men, and now had armed them with this full set of armour and was sending them forward to their own affairs with good fortune and was summoning them to sit at the front. That was what he announced then, but not now...

Aiskhines 3.154–5 (330)

For Aiskhines' capacity to invent past Athenian practices in this speech see above **196**. But the substance of this claim is broadly confirmed by other sources.

The Athenian navy: Athenian investment in the 480s

323   In the arkhonship of Nikodemos (483/82), when the mines were discovered at Maroneia and the city had a surplus of 100 talents from the minings, some advised distributing the money to the people, but Themistokles prevented this. He did not say what he would use the money for, but told the Athenian to lend a talent to each of the hundred richest Athenians, and then if what they spent the money on pleased them to consider the expense public, and if it did not, to fetch in the loans from the individuals. He got the money on these conditions and had a hundred triremes built, with each man getting one trireme built. It was these triremes with which they fought the battle of Salamis against the barbarians.

[Aristotle] *Constitution of the Athenians* 22.7

There seems a link between this version of the story and the claim that the battle at Salamis improved the political position of the Areopagos Council, which was largely made up of wealthy men.

324   Before this, another proposal of Themistokles had fortunately prevailed. The Athenians had a large sum of money in their treasury, the yield of the mines at Laureion. They were about to share it out among the citizens at the rate of ten drakhmas a man, when Themistokles persuaded them to drop the distribution and use the money to build 200 ships to help in the war with Aigina. The outbreak of this war at that time saved Greece by forcing Athens to become a naval power.

Herodotos 7.144.1

Herodotos' story and that in the Aristotelian *Constitution* differ in detail (and in the number of ships) but agree about the source of the funds and the rôle of Themistokles. For the true history of the Athenian navy see van Wees (2013)

325   Themistokles also persuaded them to complete the walls of Peiraieus – they had been begun earlier, in his year of office as arkhon (493/92). He realised that it was a fine site, with its three natural harbours, and that if they became a naval people, it would assist them greatly in the acquisition of power – he had been the first to dare to say that they should take possession of the sea – and he forthwith began to join in laying the foundations of their empire.

Thucydides 1.93.3–4

The creation of the Peiraieus anticipates by a decade, on these versions, the enlargement of the Athenian navy, but both become part of a Themistoklean master-plan.

326 The Council and people decided, Akamantis held the prytany, Phelleus was secretary, Antigenes was arkhon, Siburtios was president, on the proposal of Alkibiades, that the generals with Perikles should lend money from the current *apodektai* to the ship-makers. Whatever they lend the *trieropoioi* are to pay back. The generals are to send those ordered to sail to man the ships as quickly as possible, and if they do not they are to be brought to the law-court and charged with treachery. The generals are to bring to court anyone not willing to go. The Council is to see to the bringing of the ships which the ship-makers send from Macedon in order that they may send them to Athens as quickly as possible and they may be manned and the army brought to Ionia to look after security there as well as possible. If anyone fails to do any of this he is to owe ...00 dr. sacred to Athena. A crown to be given as the people decides to the first man to come and bring a ship. And since Arkhelaos both now and in former time is good to the people of Athens and assists the shipmakers sent from Athens to [*gap in text*] camp and they decided wood and oars and all the rest that they needed, to praise Arkhelaos as a good man and keen to do all the good he can to the Athenian people and in return for all his benefits to the city and the Athenian people to inscribe him and his children as *proxenoi* and benefactors on a stone stele on the Akropolis...

ML 91 (407/6)

This inscription confirms the combination of public and private enterprise that the Athenians employed to establish and maintain their fleet (cf. **324** above).

Athenian trierarkhs

327 Four hundred trierarkhs are chosen for each year: there are disputes to settle from any of them who want to argue the case.

Old Oligarch 3.4

We do not know exactly how the trierarkhic system worked in the fifth century. Clearly some expense was involved for the individual, but we do not meet the same complaints about this expense as in the fourth century, perhaps simply because of the greater prosperity of fifth-century Athens. The claim that there were 400 trierarkhs is problematic, since this is a larger number than the number of ships in the Athenian navy in the fifth century (300 ships according to Perikles in Thucydides 2.13.8).

328 PAPHLAGON. I'll make you a trierarkh who has to spend his own money. You'll have an old vessel, which you'll never stop spending on and repairing; and I'll arrange for you to get a sail that's rotten.

Aristophanes *Knights* 912–918 (424)

329   For when the city lost the ships at the Hellespont and was deprived of its power, I was so far different from most trierarkhs that with few others I saved my ship, and different from even these in that I alone sailed into the Peiraieus and did not give up my trierarkhy. Others were happy to be released from liturgies but despondent at the present situation, regretted what they had spent and hid what was left, considered that the community as a whole was done for and looked to their own interests, I did not share their opinion but persuaded my brother to be co-trierarkh with me, paid the sailors from our own resources, and got on with harming the enemy.

Isokrates 18.59–60 (400–399)

This passage nicely illustrates the potential independence of the trierarkhs – admittedly here in extreme circumstances at the end of the Peloponnesian War.

330   How will the generals enlist one of us if they are enrolling men into a symmory or if they are appointing trierarkhs? Of if there is some military campaign, how will it be clear which of the two of us is listed?

Demosthenes 39.8 (c.348)

In the fourth century responsibility for a trierarkhy was shared among a group of men known as a symmory. The statement here arises in a case about the problems of two people sharing the same name.

331   I served as trierarkh five times and I fought in four naval battles. I paid the capital levy many times during the war, and I performed my other public services as well as any citizen. My purpose in spending more than the city required was that you should think better of me, and that if some reverse should befall me, I should give a better account of myself in court.

Lysias 25.12–3 (c.399)

It is relatively common for Athenians to boast in court of the money that they have spent as trierarkhs as a way of demonstrating what good citizens they are (**370–71**).

332   Phanostratos has been trierarkh seven times already, he has borne all the liturgies and he has won most of the victories there are to win. And Khairestratos here has been trierarkh, he has been a *khoregos* for tragedies, he has been gymnasiarkh for the torch race. And they both have paid all the capital levies among the 300...

Isaios 6.60 (364)

333   Of the three sons (of Euthymakhos of Otryne), Arkhippos lost his life while serving as a trierarkh at Methymna...

Demosthenes 44.9 (date uncertain)

Paying sailors

334   If we take a loan (from Olympia and Delphi) we will be able to steal away their foreign sailors with greater pay. For Athenian power is bought by money rather than home-grown.

Thucydides 1.121.3

This is a claim made by the Corinthians as they attempt to persuade the Spartans and the other allies in the Peloponnesian League to make war on Athens.

335 The fleet had been lavishly equipped at great expense to the trierarkhs and to the city. The treasury was giving a drakhma a day to each sailor and providing unmanned vessels – sixty warships and forty troop transports – and the best petty officers to go with them. The trierarkhs were giving bonuses, additional to their pay from the treasury, to the *thranitai* and the petty officers and had also spent heavily on standards and fittings. Each one of them took great pains to ensure that his own vessel should excel in appearance and speed.

Thucydides 6.31.3

Thucydides here describes the naval force prepared for the expedition to Sicily in 415.

Who rowed Athenian triremes?

336 Those who heard (about the plan for an oligarchic coup on Samos) went after each of the soldiers individually to persuade them not to hand over power, and particularly approached the crew of the Paralos, who were Athenians and freeborn to a man sailing in the ship and were always of course laying into oligarchy even when it was not present.

Thucydides 8.73.5

Thucydides talks of the crew of the Paralos – one of the 'state' triremes – being all freeborn Athenians as if that was unusual.

337 Diodoros from Aphy[tis], Satyros from Samos, Arkhedemos from Pep[arathos], Philton from Pepar[ethos]...

Gerys of Apollo–, Ktitas of Epikrat[es], Euphron of Arkhede[mos], Apollonios of Aristomenes, Herakleides of Philonikhides, Strombikhides of Kharidemos, Phoinix of Eukheros, Nauson of Theophilos; trierarkhs: Protomakhos from Kephi[sia], Pausistratos from Ste[iria]; marines: Khairemon from Agryl[e], Mnesias from Agryle, Phourarkhos from Agry[le], Amphikles from Agry[le], Hippodamos from Agry[le], Iason from Agryle.

IG i³ 1032 83–6, 266–85 (last decade of fifth century)

These are two extracts from a long list of sailors on Athenian triremes, probably dating to the last decade of the fifth century, that must originally have contained 500 or more names. Slave rowers are listed separately from citizens and identifiable because given their owner's name (e.g. Nauson of Theophilos), while citizens are given demotics (only, and not fathers' name, cf. **36** above, (e.g. Iason from Agryle)), metics are called 'metic', and foreigners are given an ethnic (e.g. Sabyras from Samos). With the group of marines all from the same deme compare **315** above.

338 Remember, men of Athens, when Philip was reported in Thrace besieging Heraion Teikhos for the third or fourth year. Well, it was the month Maimakterion then. After there had been a lot of argument and a lot of debate amongst you, you voted to launch 40 ships and to man them with those up to the age of 45 and to raise 60 talents by a capital levy.

Demosthenes 3.4 (349/8)

339   You voted (362/1) that the trierarkhs should launch the ships and bring them
to the jetty, and that the Councillors and demarkhs should make lists of the
demesmen and deliver sailors and in haste to make an expedition and bring help
in every direction. This proposal of Aristophon's won the day.
DECREE.
Well, you have heard the decree, gentlemen of the jury. When the sailors
drafted by the demesmen for me did not come but were few in number and those
not fit to row, I let them go, mortgaged my own property, borrowed money, and
was the first to crew my ship having hired the best sailors I could, giving each
of them big gifts and advances. What is more, I equipped the ship with all private
equipment, and I took no public equipment, and of the trierarkhs I adorned the
ship as beautifully and elegantly as I could.
[15] In as far as I had, in my love of honour, manned my ship with good
rowers, in the same way I suffered the greatest desertion of all the trierarkhs.
For in the case of the others, quite apart from anything else, the crews were
drafted and stayed on their ships waiting to get safe home whenever the general
released them, but my sailors, confident of their ability to row, went off to
wherever they could get the most pay, thinking that their present prosperity was
better for them than their future fear if they were ever caught by me.
[Demosthenes] 50.6-7; 15–16 (probably 359)

Apollodoros was the son of a man who had been granted Athenian citizenship, and seems to have been
always over-anxious to prove his worth as a citizen. His recruitment of sailors here suggests that there was
a pool of mercenary sailors available for hire, his loss of those same sailors that there was plenty of demand
for such men.

Keeping the navy up to the mark

340   Let them record the names of the trierarkhs. No one is to be allowed to launch
a ship with fewer than 140 men or to beach it with fewer than 120 men, nor to
brace a ship with fewer than 50(?) men, nor to bring a ship round to anchor with
fewer than 100 men, nor [*lacuna*] not even one. Nor [*lacuna*] The trierarkh and
the steersman of each ship are to see that everything is looked after as well as
possible. And if any trierarkh or steersman or anyone else breaks the rules, he
is to be fined 1000 drakhmas which are to be consecrated to Athena, and the
epimeletai of the shipyards are to punish him. The secretary of the Council is
to write up this decree on a stone stele and the *kolakretai* are to give the money,
and the *poletai* are to put it out to tender.
IG i³ 153.5–23 (440–25)

This decree dates from between 440 and 425 and appears to be a general regulation about the conduct of
trierarkhs and others responsible for triremes. These rules were presumably required because the trireme
itself was public property and it is was important that those responsible for it in any given year handled it
safely.

341   If it was the person for whom most supporters would speak, Council, to whom
the decree ordered you to give the crown, I would have been mad if I thought
I was worthy of taking it, when my only supporting speaker is Kephisodotos
here while they have very many. But, as it is, the people ordered the treasurer

to give the crown to the man who got his trireme ready first, and I have done that. So I say that I should be crowned... [4] For when you made a decree to shackle and try in court whoever did not get his ship moored at the jetty before the new moon, and when you had ratified this, I moored and received a crown from you for this. These men did not even get launched and so were liable to be shackled. So how would you not be doing something completely bizarre if you should be seen crowning those who have allowed such a prize to be carried off? Well, I spent my own money on the equipment which the city has to provide to the trierarkhs, and did not take anything from the city, while they used your equipment and did not contribute any of their own resources to this.

Demosthenes 51.1, 4–5 (after 361)

342 Polyeuktos son of Kallikrates of Hestiaia proposed: the Council has decided that since the jurors condemned Sopolis son of Smikythos of Kydathenaion when those in charge of the shipyards under the arkhon Antikles (325/4) indicted him, because he did not give back the wooden equipment for ten triremes on behalf of Kephisodoros the brother of Smikythos who had been made treasurer and they fined him more than double, and since Sopolis' oars have been brought into the shipyards and Sopolis' property has been registered to be confiscated as public property along with the oars of Sopolis brought into the shipyards, and since Polyeuktos who registered the property for confiscation has released the amount required by the laws and the proceeds of the confiscation for the fine, those in charge of the shipyards under the arkhon Hegesias (324/3) are to record Sopolis as having given back 3 dr. for each of the oars that have been brought into the shipyard for him, whichsoever the treasurer takes when he has counted the number of the oars and the total of the money, and the secretary of the Eleven and Dikaiogenes the general and Opsigonos, the public slave in the shipyards, are to erase from the money owed by Sopolis whatever the treasurer reveals that he has taken, in the presence of the relatives of Sopolis and of the man who registered the property of Sopolis for confiscation. And if those in charge of the shipyards under the arkhon Hegesias do not record the fact on a stone stele when the city receives back the oars, or if the secretary of the Eleven does not erase the proceeds of the oars from Sopolis' debt according to the decree of the Council, let each of them owe 3,000 dr. to the public treasury and let Sopolis and Sopolis' family have a case for wrongful retention of the value of those oars whichsoever the city has received from Sopolis and Sopolis' family. And an impeachment may be brought against them before the Council just as if someone commits an offence concerning some matter to do with the shipyards. This whole decree is for the security of the country since it concerns the exaction of money.

IG ii^2 1631 350–403 (323/2)

This fascinating decree gives some indication of the complexity of running the Athenian navy when so much private enterprise was involved and encouraged from trierarkhs so that there was a constant mixing of private and public property. For the procedure of registering property for confiscation see Osborne 1985/2010.

343 These were exacted by the officers in the shipyards in the arkhonships of Euboulos and Lykiskos and Pythodotos and Sosigenes (345–41 BC). Of the tribe

Erekhtheis. Euthunos of Lamptrai, who was Treasurer of the Trieropoiic fund in the arkhonship of Arkhias (346/5) 3,600 dr., having received oars from us from the shipyard, of those which were handed in which he himself brought in 1,800 were unsatisfactory. Amutheon of Euonymon, in charge of the shipyards in the arkhonship of Phrasikleides (371/0), 252 dr.; Ktesibios of Lamptrai, in charge of the shipyards in the arkhonship of Elpinos (356/5), 55 dr.; Lykon of Kephisia, in charge of the shipyards in the arkhonship of Nausinikos (378/7), whose heir was Agatharkhos of Hamaxanteia, this man gave back 300dr..

IG ii^2 1622.379–411 (342/1)

14 DEMOCRACY AND RELIGION:
REGULATING CULT ACTIVITIES AND PIETY.

The number of Athenian festivals

344   The common people recognise that every poor person individually is unable to sacrifice and feast, to erect temples, or to live in a great and beautiful city, but they have found a means of achieving this end. The city frequently makes many sacrifices publicly, and the common people enjoy the feasts and obtain a share in the sacrifices.

Old Oligarch 2.9

345   To start with, they (the Athenians) have to celebrate more festivals than any other Greek city – and during festivals it is less possible for anyone to transact state business.

Old Oligarch 3.2

Although the number of Athenian festivals seems to be something of an obsession of the Old Oligarch (see also **223**) there is little doubt that the Athenians did celebrate a great many festivals, and that those festivals were unusually elaborate. There seems to have been a tendency to enhance festivals with competitive elements, particularly in the years just after the Kleisthenic reforms (see Osborne 1991/2010). The festivals celebrated by demes, phratries, etc. further enhanced the active religious life of the Athenians. See generally Parker (1996), (2005).

346   We have indeed provided for ourselves the most relaxations for the mind from labours, celebrating with games and sacrifices throughout the year and with handsome private provision, the daily pleasure of which frightens away any anxiety.

Thucydides 2.38.1

The organization of and expenditure on festivals

347   The common people have subverted those who spend their time in gymnasia or who practise music, poetry and drama; they consider that it is not a good thing because they know that they cannot practise these pursuits themselves. In the case of providing financial support for festivals, for activities in the gymnasia and for manning triremes, they know that it is the rich who put up the money for these activities, while the common people enjoy their festivals and contests, and are provided with their triremes. The common people think that they deserve to take money for singing and running and dancing and sailing in the ships, so that they get more and the rich become poorer. And in the lawcourts they put their own self-interests before justice.

Old Oligarch 1.13

At the City Dionysia three tragic poets competed, each offering three tragedies and a satyr play and each being provided with a chorus of 15 men. Five comic poets competed, each offering one comedy and each being provided with a chorus of 24 men. There were also inter-tribal competitions in dithyramb (in origin a hymn to Dionysos), for men and for boys, each tribunal chorus being 50-strong. All these choruses rehearsed for months and were maintained the while by *khoregoi*. So, for this one festival, 1165 men and boys underwent months of subsidised training. The tribal teams that competed in some events at the Panathenaia and other festivals were maintained by gymnasiarkhs. Trierarkhs appointed annually recruited oarsmen for, commanded and maintained, one of the three hundred Athenian warships. The trierarkhy was the only military liturgy. See further **327–35**..

348   I gather that he is saying that I am being impious by putting an end to sacrifices. If I were responsible for the laws about the inscription I would have allowed that Nikomakhos could say such things about me. But as it is, I think that he should obey the established laws which we all share. I am amazed if he does not recall, when he asserts that I am being impious in insisting that we sacrifice the sacrifices ordained on the boards and the stelai according to the written instructions, that he is also accusing the city. It was you who made these decisions. In addition, if you think this is terrible, that is all the more reason for thinking that those who only sacrificed according to the boards are doing wrong. Yet, gentlemen of the jury, you should not learn about piety from Nikomakhos but consider past events. Our ancestors, who sacrificed according to the boards, handed on to us the greatest and most blessed of Greek cities, so that we ought to make the same sacrifices as they did, if for no other reason than the good fortune which has stemmed from those rites. How could anyone be more pious than me, when I hold firstly that we must sacrifice in the ancestral way, and secondly that we make those sacrifices which are particularly expedient for the city and those that the people voted and we can afford from our present income? But you, Nikomakhos, have done the opposite of this. By inscribing more sacrifices than had been ordered you have become responsible for the money available for these things being spent and there being deficiencies in the ancestral sacrifices. Immediately, last year, there were 3 talents worth of sacrifices that could not be made of those which were written on the boards. Yet it is not possible to claim that the city's income was insufficient: if Nikomakhos had not added 6 talents and more worth of sacrifices there would have been sufficient for the ancestral sacrifices and the city would have had 3 talents to spare.

Lysias 30.17–20

The sacrifices made by the Athenians at public expense were laid down in the Athenian law code. This is not so much because they had to be carried out as because the law code listed everything that the Athenians had decided should be the case 'as a rule'. The law-code was revised repeatedly in the political turmoil of the last decade of the fifth century (above **51**) and in the process the very question of what the Athenians did or did not sacrifice became a political issue, leading to the trial of Nikomakhos (on which see further Todd 1996).

349   To the kitharodes: to the first, a crown of olive, 1,000 dr. gold, 500 dr. silver; to the second 1,200 dr.; to the third 600 dr.; to the fourth 400 dr.; to the fifth 300 dr.; to the men players of the *aulos*: to the first 300 dr. in form of a crown, to the second 100 dr. [*gap in the text*]

To the boy who wins the *stadion*: 50 amphoras of oil; to the second, 10; to the boy winning the pentathlon, 30 amphoras of oil, 6 to the second; to the boy winning the wrestling, 30 amphoras of oil, to the second 6; to the boy winning the boxing, 30 amphoras of oil, to the second 6; to the boy winning the *pankration*, 40 amphoras of oil, to the second 8; to the beardless youth winning the *stadion*, 60 amphoras of oil, to the second 12; to the beardless youth winning the pentathlon, 40 amphoras of oil, to the second 8; to the beardless youth winning the wrestling, 40 amphoras of oil, to the second 8; to the beardless youth winning the boxing 40 amphoras of oil, to the second 8; to the beardless youth winning the *pankration* [*gap in the text*] to the second 8; to the pair of costly horses 140 amphoras of oil, to the second 40; in the combats of war: to the horse winning the single horse race, 16 amphoras of oil, to the second 4; to the pair of horses winning, 30 amphoras of oil, to the second 6; to the pair winning in the procession, 4 amphoras of oil, to the second 1; to the man hurling javelin from horseback, 5 amphoras of oil, to the second 1. Prizes: to the boy *pyrrhikhistai*, an ox, 100 dr.; to the beardless youth *pyrrhikhistai*, an ox 100 dr.; to the men *pyrrhikhistai*, an ox 100 dr.; to the tribe victorious in *euandria*, an ox, 100 dr.; to the victorious tribe, an ox, 100 dr.; to the victorious torchbearer, a hydria, 30dr.

IG ii² 2311.5–14, 23–77 (380s)

This extract from the list of prizes at the Panathenaia shows that amphoras of oil were not the only prizes, that prizes were not restricted to winners, and that in team events the prize was an animal intended surely for immediate sacrifice and consumption. Shear (2003) suggests that just over 2,000 amphoras were given as prizes annually.

350   The people chooses by lot ten *hieropoioi*, called the *hieropoioi* in charge of the sacrifices, who see to the sacrifices ordered by oracles, and if there is need of obtaining good omens they obtain good omens with the seers. It also appoints by lot another ten, called the annual *hieropoioi*, who sacrifice certain sacrifices and administer all the penteteric festivals except the Panathenaia. The penteteric festivals consist of: first, to Delos – there is also a heptateric festival here –, second, the Brauronia, third, the Herakleia, fourth, the Eleusinia, fifth, the Panathenaia. None of these happen in the same year. But now another festival of this kind has been added, the Hephaisteia, which was first introduced in the arkhonship of Kephisophon (329/8).

[Aristotle] *Constitution of the Athenians* 54.6–7

It is not possible for 5 festivals, each occurring at four-yearly intervals, all to occur in different years, but [Aristotle] seems to mean that the four administered by the annual *hieropoioi* fall in different years – which sensibly gives them one festival to organize each year. It looks as if the fifth festival was added to this list when the original text of the *Constitution of the Athenians* was revised in the 320s.

351 The arkhon appoints the three wealthiest men from all the Athenians as *khoregoi* for the tragedies. He used to appoint five for the comedies, but now the tribes provide for these. Then he takes the *khoregoi* provided by the tribes for the Dionysia, for the men and the boys and for the comedies, and for the Thargelia for the men and the boys – there is one *khoregos* for each tribe at the Dionysia, one for every two tribes at the Thargelia, with the tribes providing in turn – and he manages the exchanges for these and brings to court the cases if anyone claims to have served the liturgy before or not to be eligible because he has served another liturgy and the period of his exemption has not yet passed, or not to be of the required age. For it is required that the *khoregos* for the boys be over 40 years old. He also appoints *khoregoi* for Delos and leaders of the pilgrimage for the *triakonter* taking the youths. He looks after processions, both the procession for Asklepios when the initiates stay indoors, and the procession of the Great Dionysia with the officials – whom formerly the people elected, ten in number, and they supported the expenses for the procession by themselves, but now it allots one from each tribe and gives them 100 minas for the equipment. He also looks after the procession at the Thargelia and the one for Zeus Soter. He administers the contest at the Dionysia and that at the Thargelia. So he looks after these festivals.

[Aristotle] *Constitution of the Athenians* 56.3–5

Like the organization of the navy, the organization of festivals in Athens was not only extremely expensive (something over 100,000 dr. a year; see Davies [1967]) but involved a very large number of officials.

352 The Basileus first looks after the Mysteries with the officials whom the people elects, two from all the Athenians, one from the Eumolpidai and one from the Kerykes. Then he looks after the festival of Dionysos at the Lenaion: this is both a procession and a contest. The procession the Basileus and the officials look after together, but the Basileus arranges the contest. He also sets up all the contests involving torches, and he administers all what one might call the ancestral sacrifices. Cases of impiety are allotted a court before him and if anyone disputes against someone else about a priesthood. He gives judgement for *genē* and priests in all disputes over rituals. All homicide cases are allotted a court before him and he is the man that announces prohibition from the things specified in the laws.

[Aristotle] *Constitution of the Athenians* 57.1–2

On the Eleusinian Mysteries see further **355, 358–66**. For other duties of the Basileus see **230**.

The intimate relationship of politics and religion

353 The polemarch sacrifices the sacrifices both to Artemis Agrotera and to Enyalios, and he administers the Funeral Games for the dead in war and makes offerings to Harmodios and Aristogeiton.

[Aristotle] *Constitution of the Athenians* 58.1

The sacrifice to Artemis Agrotera was introduced in celebration of the victory at Marathon and involved the sacrifice of 500 goats. Whether the funeral games were 'ancestral' as Thucydides 2.34.1 states or began in 464, as Pausanias 1.29.4 states is disputed. It seems unlikely that they could go back before the time of Kleisthenes.

354   Well, this man is so impious and polluted and capable of doing or saying anything, whether it is true or false, against an enemy or friend, or whatever, that he did not even draw the line, although he has accused me of murder and had me summarily arrested on such a charge, but allowed me to act as *hieropoios* for the entry sacrifices for the Council, and sacrifice and carry out the preliminary ritual on behalf of you and the whole city, and he allowed me as leader of the sacred embassy to lead the communal pilgrimage to Nemean Zeus on behalf of the city, and overlooked my having been chosen along with two others from all the Athenians to be *hieropoios* for the Semnai Theai [Furies] and my carrying out those preliminary rituals.

Demosthenes 21.114–5 (348–46)

This list of religious rôles well illustrates the extent to which those active in public life were constantly involved in sacrificial activities. For the entry sacrifices of the Council see above **130**.

355   So I want to tell you, men of Athens, how much you punished a man who had already been condemned by the people for offences at a festival, and to show what some people did that brought your anger upon them, in order that you can compare these with what this man has done. Well, first, in order that I might mention first the last offence to have occurred, the people condemned Euandros of Thespiai for offences at the Mysteries, on the accusation of Menippos, a man from Karia. The same law applies to the Mysteries as to the Dionysia, and that law was made later than this. So, what did Euandros do, Athenians, that you condemned him? Listen to this. He had secured the conviction of Menippos in a commercial case, but had not been able previously to apprehend him, as he claimed, and arrested him when he was visiting at the Mysteries. You condemned him for that, and in addition to everything else, when he entered into the court you wanted to punish him with death, but when the prosecutor had been persuaded, you both compelled Euandros to give up the case he had formerly won – it was a matter of two talents – and you then added the damages which the man reckoned he had suffered in staying for the court case. This one man, from a private affair which involved no hubris gave such a penalty simply for having broken the law.

Demosthenes 21.175–7 (348–46)

356   The law makes priests and priestesses subject to scrutiny, both all as a group and each one separately, both those who only receive perquisites and those who offer prayers to the gods on your behalf, and not only individually but for the *genos* as a group, the Eumolpidai and the Kerykes and all the others.

Aiskhines 3.18 (330)

357   Resolved to pay back to the Gods the money that is owed them, since the 3,000 talents from Athene, of our own currency, which were voted on, have been brought up to the Akropolis... Resolved to elect Treasurers for this money, by lot, when the other magistracies are filled, just as the Treasurers of Athene. And let these fulfil their office as Treasurers of the monies of the Gods on the Akropolis in the Opisthodomos as divine law sanctions, and let them join in opening, closing, and sealing the doors of the Opisthodomos with the Treasurers of Athene.

ML 58.2–18 (probably late 430s)

The wealth of sanctuaries was considered available for use, particularly as a source of loans (cf. **334**), but it was not thought right to alienate it. When, from time to time, Greek states at war seized the resources of sanctuaries, this was strongly condemned. Here the Athenians are punctilious in repaying what they have borrowed from the gods. For the rôle of the Council and the continuation of this passage see above **161**.

City and sanctuary: the case of Eleusis

358   The Council and people decided, when Paraibates was secretary: the *hieropoioi* of the Eleusinia are to sacrifice the first sacrifices and the rest for the festival at Eleusis: to Ge, to Hermes Enagonios, to the Graces, a goat; before the Eleusinia to Poseidon a ram; to Artemis a goat, to Triptolemos Telesidromos, a ram; to Plouton [...] and the two goddesses, a bull and two other victims at the festival.

IG i^3 5 (early fifth century)

The sanctuary of Demeter and Persephone (also known as 'Kore') at Eleusis was from an early date an exceptional sanctuary. This was partly because its unusual rituals involved initiation (*myesis* – hence the name 'mystery cult') and the revelation of secret information to those initiated, and in consequence a special sort of building for this to happen in (the 'Telesterion'), but partly because it was open to and attracted Greeks from all over the Greek world, and not simply from Athens. The sanctuary remained an Athenian sanctuary, however, and the Athenian Assembly assumed responsibility for its overall running, though the rituals themselves remained in the hands of two families, the Eumolpidai and the Kerykes and of officials drawn from those families. For all these inscriptions see Clinton (2005).

359   In the case of involuntary acts just the simple amount; in the case of voluntary acts: double. The ordinary initiates and the highest grade of initiates and their servants to be covered by a truce with all their possession whether they be foreign or Athenian. The time of the truce is to begin during the month Metageitnion from the full moon and for Boedromion and until the 10th of Pyanopsion. The truce to be in all the cities which use the sanctuary and for Athenians there in the cities themselves. And for the Lesser Mysteries the truce is to be during the month Gamelion, from the full moon, and for Anthesterion and until the tenth of Elaphebolion.

IG i^3 6 B.4–47 (before 460)

The almost two-month truces allowed pilgrims to travel to and from Eleusis safely.

360   The *hieropoioi* are to receive half an obol a day from each initiate. The priestess of Demeter is to receive at the Lesser Mysteries an obol from each initiate, and at the Greater Mysteries an obol from each initiate. All the obols are to belong to the Goddesses apart from 1,600 dr. From the 1,600 dr. the priestess is to pay the expenses until it is used up. The Eumolpids and the Kerykes are to receive from each initiate 5 obols from males and 3 obols from females. No initiate can be initiated with paying the fee except for initiate from the hearth. The Kerykes are to initiate [*number missing*] initiates each and the Eumolpids are to do the same. [*Gap in the text*] more to be scrutinised for 1000 drakhmas. All Kerykes and Eumolpids who have come of age may initiate. Of the sacred money [*gap in the text*] to the Athenians [*gap in the text*] while they want, just as the money of Athene on the Akropolis. The *hieropoioi* are to hand over the money and it is to be kept by the Treasurers on the Akropolis. [*Gap in the text*] orphans [*gap in the text*] orphan children and initiates [*gap in the text*] initiates at Eleusis [*gap in the text*] in the hall within the sanctuary, and those in the city [*gap in the text*] in the Eleusinion. The priest at the altar and the Phaidountes of the two Goddesses and the priest [*gap in the text*] each are to receive [*gap in the text*] from each initiate.

IG i³ 6C.6–50 (before 460)

361 Let the *prytaneis* bring to the Council the *theosesinoi* whenever they ask. Thespieus proposed: in other respects I agree with the Council, but choose five men from the Athenians, these to have 4 obols each from the *kolakretai*, and one of these to be elected secretary. These are to look after the moneys of the two Goddesses just like those who looked after the works on the Akropolis and the cult statue. No possibility of refusing office on oath. Those selected are to approach the Council and describe and ask for it if they want anything for the goddesses. They are to serve for a year having sworn themselves in between the altars at Eleusis, and for the future men are to be chosen in the same way every year. They are to look after the annual income received by the two Goddesses, and if they learn that anything has perished they are to restore it. The *logistai* are to audit at Eleusis what is spent at Eleusis and in the town of Athens what is spent in the town, summoning the architect Koroibos and Lysanias in the Eleusinion, and at Phaleron in the sanctuary what is spent at Phaleron. He is to spend what is especially necessary after consultation with the priests and the Council for the future. He is to recall the money beginning from the magistracy which he handed over to Ktesias. The decree to be written on a stele at Eleusis and in the town of Athens and in the Eleusinion at Phaleron. Lysanias said: in other respect I agree with Thespieus, but the counting of the money which the treasurers handed over---

IG i³ 32.4–38 (449–447)

It is notable that these complicated arrangements were introduced at the Assembly as an amendment (to a measure that has largely been lost). The primary concern here is that proper track is kept of the moneys expended on the Eleusinian cult both at Eleusis and at the related cult centres in Athens and Phaleron.

362 Timoteles of Akharnai was secretary. The Council and people decided, Kekropis held the prytany, Timoteles was secretary, Kykneas was president. The draftsmen brought these proposals: Athenians to give first fruits to the two goddesses according to ancestral custom and to the oracle from Delphi, at a rate of not less than one *hekteus* of barley per hundred *medimnoi* and half a *hekteus* of wheat per hundred *medimnoi*. If anyone has more or less grain than that the first-fruits to be calculated at that rate. The demarkhs are to collect the grain in the demes and to hand it over to the *hieropoioi* from Eleusis at Eleusis. To build three stores at Eleusis according to ancestral custom where it seems best to the *hieropoioi* and the architect to be suitable, from the money of the two goddesses. The corn received from the demarkhs to be deposited here. The allies are to contribute first-fruits in the same way. The cities are to choose collectors of the grain and the cities are to collect the grain as seems best to them. When it is collected it is to be sent to Athens. Those bringing it are to hand it over to the *hieropoioi* from Eleusis at Eleusis. If they do not take it within five days of its arrival being announced, although it was handed over by those from the city from which the grain is, let them be subject to 1,000 dr. fine each at scrutiny. They are to accept the grain from the demarkhs in the same way. The Council is to select heralds to announce to the cities the decision of the People, in the current instance as soon as possible, in the future at whatever time it decides. The hierophant and the dadoukh at the Mysteries are to command that the Greeks give first-fruits of their grain according to ancestral custom and the oracle from Delphi. Having recorded on a board the amount of grain from the demarkhs deme by deme and from the cities city by city, they are to deposit it in the Eleusinion at Eleusis and in the Council chamber. The Council is to announce to all other Greek cities, where it seems to it to be possible, describing how the Athenians and the allies give first fruits and instructing them, but not ordering them, to give first-fruits if they want, in the ancestral fashion and according to the Delphic oracle. The *hieropoioi* are to receive from any city that sends in the same way. There should be sacrifice from the sacred cake according to the instruction of the Eumolpidai, and an offering of three animals, of which the first is to be an ox with gilded horns, to each of the two goddesses from the wheat and the barley, and to Triptolemos and to the god and to the goddess and to Euboulos, a perfect victim for each, and for Athene an ox with gilded horns. The rest of the barley and wheat is to be sold by the *hieropoioi* with the Council and offerings dedicated to the two goddesses, in whatever form the People of Athens decides, and it is to be inscribed on the dedications that the dedication is made from the first fruits of the grain, and which of the Greeks has given first-fruits. May many blessings be on those who do this, and good and plentiful crops, who do no wrong to the Athenians or the city of the Athenians or the divine.

Lampon said: in other respects I support the drafters of the first fruits of the harvest for the two goddesses. The secretary of the Council is to write their regulations and this decree on two stone stelai and set up the one at Eleusis in the sanctuary and the other on the Akropolis. The *poletai* are to put the inscribing out to tender. The *kolakretai* are to give the money. These clauses about the first fruits of the harvest for the two goddesses are to be inscribed on the two stelai, and the new arkhon is to intercalate a second month of Hekatombaion. The Basileus is to bound the sanctuaries in the Pelargikon, and for the future it shall not be allowed to set up altars in the Pelargikon without the permission of Council and people, nor to quarry stone there or remove earth or stone. If anyone breaks any of these rules let him be fined 500 dr. and let the Basileus bring an impeachment to the Council. And on the matter of the first-fruits of oil, let Lampon bring a written proposal to the Council in the ninth prytany; and the Council must bring it to the people.

ML 73 (430s)

This decree, dating to the middle of the 430s shows the Athenians thinking how to make political and economic capital out of the reputation of the sanctuary at Eleusis across the whole of Greece, and in particular from Demeter's fame as the giver of cereal crops. The Athenians have evidently consulted the oracle (at Delphi) about this, and received qualified support.

The amendment to the decree is moved by a well-known religious figure, Lampon, a seer. He seems to have tried to use his reputation for religious knowledge not simply to tidy up the proposal but to bring in on the back of it further ideas of his own, some of them only vaguely related to the matter in hand. In the end there seems to have been impatience in the Assembly and Lampon is told to sort out some matters with the Council and return to a later Assembly.

363   In the arkhonship of Alkaios, the Overseers from Eleusis, for whom Philostratos of Kydathenaion was secretary, received from the *hieropoioi* at Eleusis [*gap in the text*] and his fellow magistrates the money from the first fruits of grain of the goddesses [*gap in the text*] Under the Council for which Prepis was first secretary, in the arkhonship of Aristion, the Overseers from Eleusis for whom Philostratos of Kydathenaion was secretary, received from the *hieropoioi* at Eleusis, Theoxenos of Kephale and his fellow magistrates, silver from the first fruits of grain of the goddesses 6dr. In the Council for which Kharinos was first secretary, in the arkhonship of Astyphilos, the Overseers from Eleusis for whom Philostratos of Kydathenaion was secretary, received from the *hieropoioi* at Eleusis, Demokritos of Alopeke and his fellow magistrates, silver from the first fruits of grain of the goddesses, 31 dr. Under the Council for which [*gap in the text*] was first secretary, in the arkhonship of Arkhias, the Overseers from Eleusis to whom Philostratos of Kydathenaion was secretary [*text breaks off*]

IG i³ 391 (422/1)

This appears to record some of the income resulting from the decree recorded in the previous item.

364   Gods. In the [*number lost*] prytany of Pandionis, on the twenty-first day of the prytany, in [*location lost*]. [*Name lost*] of Ikaria of the *proedroi* put the matter to the vote. Meid- [*part of name and patronymic lost*] of Eleusis said: the *nomothetai* decided: otherwise according to the law of Khairemonides concerning the first-fruits, but the people to have the power to decide on the best way to collect the first-fruits of grain for the goddesses. The Council currently in power after the arkhonship of Thoudemos (353/2) is to see that the first-fruits for the goddesses happen and all the rituals are sacrificed on behalf of the Athenian people, from the sacred cake as the Eumolpidai specify and the sacrifice for Zeus and Demeter and Kore and Triptolemos and the god and the goddess and for Euboulos and Athene [as the people decided]. The Council [will choose ten *hieropoioi* and will send the first-fruits and] will make all the sacrifices according to the law, [with no freedom not to contribute voted for], just as if it was done according to a decision of the Athenian people. The secretary of the Council is to inscribe this law in addition to the earlier law of Khairemonides on the stele in front of the Metroon, and the treasurer of the people is to give 20 drakhmas for the inscription from the expenses in connection with decrees.

IG ii² 140 (353/2)

Detailed changes to the regulations for the Eleusinian sanctuary continued to be made at various points in the fourth century. Note that this incription was erected in the Athenian agora, rather than at Eleusis.

365   Total amount of barley: 1,153 *medimnoi*, 4 *hemihekteis* (=1/3 *medimnos*) and
2 *khoinikes* (=1/24 *medimnos*). Out of this one *medimnos* for barley groats for
the two goddesses; sixteen *medimnoi* minus three *khoinikes* (=3/48 *medimnos*)
to the *hieropoioi* from the Council for the holy cakes. We sold 1,027 *medimnoi*,
one *hekteus* and 21/2 *khoinikes*, good measures added to these 64 *medimnoi*,
one *hekteus* and 21/2 *khoinikes*. Total value of the barley: 3,082 dr. 3 obols, the
barley having been sold at 3 dr. a *medimnos* as the People ordered. Total amount
of wheat: 80 *medimnoi*, 10 *hemihekteis*, and a *khoinix*. From these, for a sacred
cake for the two goddesses, one medimnos, and for the *hieropoioi* from the
Council 10 *medimnoi* and an additional quantity of 5 *hemihekteis*. We sold 72
medimnoi, a *hekteus* and a *khoinix*, with three *medimnoi* and three *khoinikes* as
good measure. Total value of the sixty-two *medimnoi* of wheat 173 dr., 1 1/2
obols, the wheat having been sold at six drakhmas a *medimnos* as the people
ordered apart from ten *medimnoi* whose price was 50 dr. Total cash value of
the first-fruits for the goddesses 3510 dr. 51/2 obols. From these the following
expenses were made: to the *hieropoioi* from the Council the sum which the
People ordered for each sheep and goat, 30 dr. for 43 animals, total 1290 dr.
For each ox, 400 dr.; three oxen, 1200 dr.

IG ii² 1672.279–90 (329/8)

These detailed accounts of the Eleusinian sanctuary reveal the amount of grain offered to the goddesses by
the demes of Attica as 'first-fruits', and also the expenditure of the sanctuary on both directly religious and
other matters. On Attic grain production see Garnsey (1985); on 'good measure' see Johnstone (2011) 49–53.

366   In Metageitnion, at the Eleusinia: an ox, 90 dr.; a ram for Kore, 12 dr.; three
pigs, 9 dr.; priestly services 6 dr. 4 1/2 obols; a *hekteus* of barley groats: 4 obols;
a *khous* of wine.

IG ii² 1358.43–5 (first half of the fourth century)

Religious figures and their influence

367   The people decided, on the proposal of Athenodoros. The people voted on what
Euthydemos the priest of Asklepios says: in order that the preparatory offerings
which Euthydemos priest of Asklepios ordains might be made and also the other
sacrifice on behalf of the Athenian people, the people voted that the Overseers
of Asklepios should make the preparatory sacrifice which Euthydemos ordains
from the money from the quarry and when this has been taken away the rest of
the money is to be devoted to the building of the temple. In order that the
Athenians may distribute as much meat as possible, the *hieropoioi* in office are
to look after the feast in its public aspect. They are to distribute the meat of the
leading ox to the *prytaneis* and the nine arkhons and to the *hieropoioi* and those
in charge of the procession, and the rest of the flesh they are to divide up for
the Athenians [*some further instruction lost*].

IG ii² 47.23–39 (date uncertain)

This is a rare case when we see a man with a particular priestly office using the special knowledge and
prestige that that gave him to persuade the Athenian Assembly to do something advantageous to the cult for

which he was responsible – in this case use the income from a quarry to fund sacrifices. The cult of Asklepios was introduced to Athens only in the late fifth century.

368   EUTHYPHRON: Why, even in my own case, when I say something about religion in the Assembly and foretell the future, they laugh at me as though I were mad. And yet all my predictions have come true.

Plato *Euthyphron* 3bc

Not every attempt to use claims to religious knowledge in the Assembly met with popular enthusiasm.

Public responsibility for the things of the gods

369   The herald of the Council is to summon these magistrates to be present on whichsoever day the *prytaneis* give notice. The *prytaneis* are to call Eukles the public slave to come to the Akropolis to record the things in the Khalkotheke. When the building is opened they are to examine by kind everything and record the total numbers and the prytany secretary and the other public record secretaries are to write a copy. And when everything has been examined and written down, the secretary of the Council is to write it on a stone stele in front of the Khalkotheke. The Treasurer of the Council is to give 30 dr. from the expense account of the Council ordained by decree, for the writing of the stele. The secretary of the Council is to make a copy of what is written about the things in the Khalkotheke from the stele. When this is ready the *prytaneis* are to give notice about this in the Council chamber, whenever it is possible, and when the Council has heard the record read out, if there is need of anything, it is to make a preliminary proposal and bring it to the people in order that the people might hear and consider how to remedy deficiencies in order that things might be as finely and piously organised as possible for the goddess.

IG ii^2 120.9–32 (362/1)

This decree illustrates not only Athenian public concern for proper administration of matters concerning the gods but also the rôle of public slaves. The Khalkotheke was a building immediately west of the Parthenon in which objects made of bronze were stored.

Festivals as opportunities to gain popular and political support

370   Nikias...was very rich, and he used his riches as a means to political leadership. He distrusted his ability to compete in the glib buffoonery by which Kleon catered to the pleasure of the Athenians, and he tried to win over the people with expenditure on choruses and athletic events and other such displays of munificence. In their cost and elegance he surpassed all his predecessors and contemporaries. Two of his dedicatory offerings still stand *in situ* in my day: the statue of Pallas (Athene) on the Akropolis – the one that has lost its gilding – and the temple in the precinct of Dionysos with the tripods commemorative of his choral victories. He won many such victories and was never defeated... Also recorded is the splendour of his munificence at Delos – well worthy of the god (Apollo).

Plutarch *Nikias* 3.1–4

Religious festivals and their need for sponsors created possibilities for individuals to buy themselves popularity and political credit (cf. above **331–2**). This passage is also good evidence for Nikias' style, on which see further **405–6**.

371   Aristophanes possessed land and a house worth more than 5 talents, but he spent 5,000 dr. as *khoregos* on behalf of himself and his father, and spent 80 minas as trierarkh. He has paid not less than 40 minas in capital levies on behalf of both. He spent 100 minas on the voyage to Sicily. He provided 30,000 dr. for the sending out of triremes when the Cypriots came and you gave them 10 ships and pay for peltasts and money to purchase arms. And the total of all these comes to only a little less than 15 talents.

Lysias 19.42–3 (388–7)

The resources of sanctuaries in Attica

372   In the demarkhy of Autokleides. Of the moneys of Nemesis the total in the hands of the 200-drakhma-borrowers: 37,000 (drakhmas).

ML 53.1–9 (450–440)

This inscription, which dates to the middle of the fifth century, records the resources of the sanctuary of Nemesis in the deme of Rhamnous in the north-east of Attica. It shows both the large sums of money possessed by such sanctuaries and the way in which they served as banks.

The affair of the Mutilation of the Herms and the profanation of the Mysteries

373   During these preparations, nearly all the stone Herms in the city of Athens – square figures, of which, by local custom, there are many both in the porches of private houses and in temples – had their faces mutilated in a single night. No one knew who the perpetrators were, but large public rewards were offered for their detection, and in addition it was decreed that if anyone – citizen, foreigner or slave – knew of any other impious deed that had been committed and was willing to give information, he could do so with immunity. They took the matter seriously: they regarded it as an ill omen for the expedition and also as a manifestation of a revolutionary conspiracy aimed at the overthrow of the democracy.
    [28] Information was accordingly given by some metics and domestic slaves, not about the Herms, but about previous mutilations of other statues by young men in drunken revelry, and also of mock celebrations of the Mysteries held in private houses. In this latter charge Alkibiades was implicated. His bitterest enemies seized on this charge because he stood in the way of their undisputed leadership of the people. Thinking that if they could secure his exile, they would occupy first place, they magnified the matter and loudly proclaimed that both the affair of the Mysteries and the mutilation of the Herms were aimed at the overthrow of the democracy, and that none of it would have happened without him. As evidence they cited his generally undemocratic and unconventional lifestyle.
    [29] Alkibiades rebutted the charges there and then, and he offered to stand trial before sailing – the preparations for the expedition were now complete – to establish whether he was guilty of any of these offences; if found guilty of any offence, he would be punished; if acquitted, he would hold his command.

He protested against their receiving allegations against him in his absence. If he were guilty, he begged them to put him to death at once. It would be imprudent to send him out in command of so large a force with so serious a case still undecided. But his enemies feared that he would have the expeditionary force on his side if he went on trial at once, and that the people might relent and protect him because it was thanks to him that the Argives and some Mantineians were joining in the expedition; and so they did all they could to defeat the proposal. They incited other speakers to urge that he sailed forthwith and did not delay the launch; on his return he should be tried within a fixed number of days. They wanted him to come back when summoned and face trial on a graver charge, which they would find it easier to produce in his absence. It was decreed that Alkibiades should sail.

Thucydides 6.27–29

Immediately before the great naval expedition against Syracuse was due to sail to Sicily in 415, the statues of Hermes throughout the city were found to have been vandalized. The unprecedented public investigation that followed turned up evidence for a further irreligious act, a parody celebration of the Eleusinian Mysteries. The attempt to discover those responsible led to a group of wealthy men, including Alkibiades (see **134, 209, 247**). These men were put on trial, condemned, and their property confiscated. How successful the Athenians were at discovering the truth was unclear at the time and remains unclear. Whether or not the culprits were correctly identified, the affair reveals very clearly the link between politics and religion.

374   They (the Athenians) found the Salaminia (in Katane). It had come from Athens for Alkibiades, who was to sail home to answer charges brought against him by the city, and for other members of the expedition who had been informed against for impiety – some of them with Alkibiades in connection with the Mysteries and others in connection with the Herms. Once the expedition had sailed, the Athenians pursued as vigorously as ever their enquiries into the facts about the Mysteries and Herms. They did not vet the informers, but in their suspicious mood accepted every accusation. On the evidence of worthless people they arrested and imprisoned excellent citizens. They thought it more important to get to the bottom of the matter and discover the truth than to let any accused person of good character escape unexamined in view of the worthlessness of the informer. The people had heard that the last phase of the tyranny of Peisistratos and his sons had been harsh and also that it had not been overthrown by Harmodios and themselves but by the Spartans, and so they were constantly afraid and looked at everything with suspicion.

Thucydides 6.53

375   With this (the last years of the tyranny of Hippias) in mind and recalling all that they knew about it from hearsay, the Athenian people turned awkward and suspicious of those accused in the matter of the Mysteries. They thought that it had all been done to further an oligarchic or tyrannical conspiracy. This made them angry: many persons of consequence were already in prison, and there was no sign of a let-up. They turned daily more savage and arrested still more people. And then one of those in prison, thought to be the most guilty, was persuaded by a fellow-prisoner to lay information, whether true or not. Both possibilities are entertained, and no one from that day to this has been able to say for certain who the perpetrators were. His fellow-prisoner managed to persuade him that, even if he had not done it, he should save himself by gaining immunity and free the city of its current suspicions. He would be surer of safety if he confessed after being granted immunity than if he denied it and were brought to trial. Accordingly, laid information involving himself and others in the affair of the Herms.

The people of Athens were delighted to get at what they thought was the truth, having previously thought it intolerable not to be able to identify those who were plotting against them. They immediately released the informer and all the others whom he had not accused. Those he had accused they brought to trial. All whom they had arrested they executed; those who had fled they condemned to death, and they set a price on their heads. In this it was not clear if those who suffered had been punished unjustly, but the rest of the city received immediate and manifest relief.

As for Alkibiades, the Athenians, urged on by the same enemies as had attacked him before he sailed, took a harsh view of him. Since they thought that they had got at the truth of the affair of the Herms, they believed more strongly than ever that the affair of the Mysteries, in which he was implicated, had been his doing, with the same idea in mind, namely, the conspiracy against the democracy.

Thucydides 6.60-61.1

376   Thessalos son of Kimon, of the deme Lakiadai, denounces Alkibiades son of Kleinias, of the deme Skambonidai, for offences committed against the two goddesses, Demeter and Kore (Persephone): mimicking the Mysteries and showing them to his companions in his own house, wearing such a robe as the hierophant wears when he displays the holy objects, and calling himself the hierophant, Poulytion the dadoukh, and Theodoros of Phegaia the herald, and hailing the rest of his companions as initiates and *epoptai*, contrary to the rules and regulations of the Eumolpidai, Kerykes and priests of Eleusis.

Plutarch *Alkibiades* 22.3

Plutarch claims here to be quoting the words of two charges brought against Alkibiades for profaning the Mysteries.

377   Of Euphiletos son of T[imotheos of Kydathenaion]
On both counts. House [*text missing*].
15 drakhmas   1,500 drakhmas

ML 79.88–90 (414)

This is part of the so-called Attic Stelai, a set of inscribed slabs recording the sale by the ten *poletai* of goods confiscated from those convicted of involvement in the profanation of the Mysteries or the mutilation of the Herms or, as in the case of Euphiletos, both. His house fetched 1,500 drakhmas, on which a further 1% tax was payable. See further Lewis (1966).

Part III: Democracy in Action

Note D: The elite and the mass in democratic Athens

Part I of this book gave the evidence for the most important changes to the Athenian constitution across time. Part II of this book gave the evidence for the working of the most important institutions within Athenian democracy. But changes in who is entitled to do what, and rules about what those who are, individually or corporately, given a particular rôle to play may and may not do tell us rather little about how the political system as a whole worked. In Part III an attempt is made to get closer to understanding democracy in action, through contemporary descriptions of what actually happened in the Assembly, through understanding how democracy was theorized, that is what the underlying assumptions were behind how people acted and where the arguments lay, and through seeing how the system was subverted or how Athenians feared that it would be subverted.

The central problem of democracy is how to discover what is in the best interest of the community as a whole, and how to ensure that it is the best interest of the community as a whole, rather than a sectional interest, that prevails. In Athens itself, as the passages in section 16 show, the debate on this issue turned particularly on whether or not people could become experts in politics. Was politics a craft that could be learned, so that some citizens ended up better at seeing what was in the public interest than others? Or was politics different, and was this an area where all individuals were equally capable of making the assessment, though any of them might get the assessment wrong in particular cases, so that the more people involved in making a decision the more likely it was that the decision would be the correct one?

In classical Athens there was no agreement about the question of political expertise. Athenian practice was built upon assumptions that all could contribute equally, but the privileged position of the generals in politics relies upon the view that they are peculiarly likely to know what ought to be done. Plato records Protagoras' justification for all alike having a rôle in political decisions, but he himself, above all in his *Republic*, gave eloquent arguments for restricting political power to the experts (the 'philosopher kings'). So too, in the contemporary world, practices such as jury selection assume that all are equally well-placed to take decisions in legal cases – albeit under the advice of a judge – but candidates for election to Parliament or local councils try to show that they are better prospects for good political decisions than others.

Although modern law-courts retain the ideal of the unbiased verdict, modern politics has long since given that up. The system of political parties accepts that different groups within society will make decisions in their own interest, and simply give the electorate the opportunity to exercise its prejudices in favour of one group of another. Although there are points in Athenian politics where it is clear that voting became factional, the factions were often split over foreign policy rather than over domestic questions (cf. **414** below). Not that domestic and foreign policy issues could be divided: the great fourth-century debate over how to divide funds between the stratiotic fund (essentially a war-fund) and the theoric fund (essentially a benefit fund) illustrates this nicely (see **415**). It is a notable feature of the analysis by the Old Oligarch that he takes it for granted that the rich always act in their own interests, the poor in theirs. But in general the Athenians seem to have remained idealists, believing that it is possible in a mass meeting to agree to what was in the common interest, not in a particular sectional interest.

Was that belief well-founded? How successful was the mass of the people assembled on the Pnyx at securing the best advice from those who tried to persuade it? Did the people in the Assembly or in the law-courts tyrannise the rich minority? The rhetoric of the law-courts features both rich men pleading their virtue by parading the extent to which they have used private means to the benefit of the city as a whole (particularly through the liturgy system and through contributing to capital levies) and claims that at other times law-courts have been swayed to condemn individuals because doing so will enrich the public treasury. We cannot know the truth of allegations of biased judgement from jurors, and it would be naïve to deny that courts were capable of such action. But arguably what is most important is that such behaviour was alleged and extravagant liturgical expenditure was claimed. For the parading of exemplary practice, good and bad, ensured that jurors kept in mind the issue of the common good, that they asked themselves whether the behaviour to which they were being alerted was the behaviour appropriate to someone working for the common good, and that they asked themselves whether it was the common good that they themselves were working for.

In the case of the Athenian Assembly the mechanisms of control were different in detail but similar in principle. In the fifth century politicians who were perceived to be using tactics that were more divisive than productive were liable to be ostracized – removed from the city for 10 years, though without suffering loss of property or any other stigma. After 415 ostracism was no longer employed, but individual proposals were subject to review in a law court under the procedure known as *graphe paranomon*, indictment of an illegal proposal (see **210**, and there was a similar procedure to deal with the proposal of unsuitable laws). This procedure was used a great deal in the fourth century – indeed might at times itself be abused in order to cause political delay. But the presence of the possibility of review imposed a control which meant that although the people as such could not be held to account, their decisions could be reviewed.

Alongside these institutional mechanisms, the telling of exemplary tales played an important part. Most obviously cautionary were the stories of notorious moments at which the Athenians all agreed that they had got it wrong. One of these was the Mytilene debate (**202, 393–5**), where the Athenians themselves came to agree (though not immediately – they took a similar decision a few years later about the revolt of Skione) that the original decision to execute all the men of Mytilene as a punishment for the revolt of the city had been too harsh, another their decision to execute the generals who had failed to pick up the shipwrecked sailors after the successful naval battle at Arginousai (**212–3**). On the other side, the annual speech over the war dead, of which the speech by Perikles at the end of the first year of the Peloponnesian War recorded by Thucydides is the most famous surviving example, gave an occasion for running through the virtues of the Athenians and of the way in which Athenian democracy worked. The various examples of this that survive show how in this speech a model Athens was invented and repeated from year to year by different speakers, and there is little doubt that the idealism of these speeches rubbed off on Athenians in general, as it has also rubbed off on modern readers.

The attempts to dress up past behaviour as good or bad, the construction of an allegation that an individual, a decree or a law was working or would work in a way harmful to the city, the telling of stories about past virtue or past error – all of these are matters of rhetoric. The Athenians liked to think that rhetoric was a recent invention, and critics of democracy saw rhetoric as something that had been encouraged by democracy but was potentially also its downfall (cf. Plato *Gorgias*). Such claims are implausible – the techniques of persuasion by careful construction of arguments to ensure that the listeners hear what they want to hear and don't hear uncomfortable truths are as much on show in the speeches in the *Iliad* and *Odyssey* as in any fifth-century work. But there is no doubt that the importance of rhetoric became more obvious in the democratic city because addressing mass audiences was so fundamental to democratic decision-making. It was the possibility that rhetoric might be teachable, and hence the citizen who had been able to buy a rhetorical education able to exercise greater political influence than the citizen who had not, that lay behind much of the discussion about political expertise. We are fairly certain that when Aristophanes in *Clouds* presents Sokrates as a teacher of rhetoric he is not giving a faithful picture of the historical Sokrates and his activities, but he was clearly touching on a raw Athenian nerve in his exploration of those who make the worse argument seem the stronger (cf. **382, 403**).

The Athenians had two responses to the threat of professional rhetoric. One was to attempt to exclude the professional. There was no place in the Athenian law-court for the lawyer. All prosecutors and defendants had to put their own case; the most they could do by way of getting assistance in the court was to call on others to speak alongside them, using up part of their speaking time. Outside the court, of course, they could employ a speech-writer to frame their case for them, and most of the law-court speeches that survive are precisely speeches written for others to deliver. In the Assembly the problem was different – it was the thought that a citizen who could speak well might sell himself to another and deliver views that were not his own in return for money or favours. One consequence of this was repeated allegations of bribery. Another was the banning of those who had sold their bodies for sex from speaking in the Assembly – if they had sold their bodies, how could one know whether they had not sold out completely? The idealist Athenian answer to the problem of rhetorical education this was to admit that rhetoric could be learned, but to insist that education in rhetoric happened through participation in the city itself (cf. Perikles' Funeral Oration in Thucydides 2.39.1, 2.41.1 and Hippias' remark in Plato *Protagoras* 337d on Athens being the 'very *prytaneion* of wisdom'). But if democracy educated, it could only educate those who participated.

Arguably the most important factor in enabling Athenian democracy to work was the high level of participation that was achieved. We have good reason to believe (see **65** above) that the Assembly in the fourth century was regularly attended by at least 6,000 people (20% of the citizen population). We can also calculate that over half the Athenian citizen body will have served on the Council of 500, a body whose central responsibility and heavy duties have been well illustrated above. In addition to this, Athenians found themselves caught up in various other groups (demes above all, but also phratries, *genē*, etc.) which ran themselves as miniature versions of the city's democracy. The expectation of political involvement ran so deep that Sokrates' denial that he has taken part in politics is made in the same breath as his admitting to having served as a member of the Council (**145**). This political habit will have been one of the main factors that prevent Athens from suffering from meetings being dominated by those whose sectional interest was most served (or threatened) by the proposals being voted on.[7]

7. For further discussion of the issues here see Ober (1989), Liddel (2007).

Note E: Framing a decision

In this section the passages chosen offer descriptions by observers, and in some cases by those themselves involved in politics, of how politics worked. They emphasise in particular what happened in the Assembly. But what happened in the Assembly had in important ways been predetermined, and it is important to understand how much politics took place outside the Assembly, and in particular in the Council.

The institutional rôle of the Council has been set out in section 9 above. It is important to preface what I will go on to say here by emphasizing that the Council of 500 was a determinedly amateur body. That is, since no one could serve for more than one year at a time, or more than two years in total, there could be no experts in the Council. The most experienced could only call on one year of previous Council service. Although there were enough routine matters that the Council dealt with that even one previous year would help, that limited experience will have meant that there were many situations that arose which no one on Council in a particular year had ever met before.

The most important way in which the Council shaped the politics of the Assembly was by framing Assembly decisions. The Assembly could not discuss anything that was not put on its agenda by the Council – although it could ask for the Council to put something on its next agenda (cf. **362**). The Council could put a matter on the agenda for discussion without a recommendation as to what the Assembly decision should be (as in **147**), but this seems to have been unusual. Normally the Council produced not simply a list of items for discussion but a series of recommendations as to what to do.

Our best evidence for the recommendations made by the Council comes from Athenian decrees. Athenian decrees purport to contain the recommendations made by the Council that were subsequently approved by the Assembly, either as they stood or with amendments. In fact it is clear that the record of decisions has been somewhat edited before being written up, and the Council must normally have said rather more to the Assembly about why it was recommending a particular course of action than is recorded on the stone. The stone record is economical with the truth – almost certainly for political reasons, to avoid re-opening the political debate that lay behind the decision.[8]

Regardless of editing, we can learn a great deal from the texts of Athenian decrees – and particularly if we compare the contents of decrees with the contents of surviving political speeches, whether in the historians or among the works of the orators. Political speeches stress what is in the Athenian best interest – whether it is a matter of going to war, making a treaty, suppressing the revolt by an ally, or engaging in the practice of honouring citizens who benefit the city. Speakers concentrate on persuading the Athenians either to adopt or not to adopt a particular course of action. Only relatively rarely do they try to change the course of action.

The debate over the Sicilian expedition, though in other respects not at all typical, offers a good example. As Thucydides tells the story, an initial meeting of the Assembly has decided to make a 60-ship expedition against Syracuse. A second meeting is supposed to discuss how to implement that, but Nikias tries to persuade the Athenians to overturn the original decision. Alkibiades reiterates the reasons for launching it. The people are persuaded to stick to their original resolution and so Nikias then tries to persuade them that in that case the expedition should be much larger (Thucydides 6.8–26; see below **407–11**). Even though the matter in hand at this second

8. I discuss this further in Osborne 1999/2010.

Assembly is one of detail, Nikias tries to return to the matter of principle, and only when compelled to does he deal with matters of detail.

Matters of detail were, by contrast, exactly what the Council was required to focus upon. As surviving inscribed decrees reveal, the proposals that came from the Council were often worked out in very specific detail (**326, 357, 362, 364, 367, 369**). This is hardly surprising. It must have been difficult enough debating details in a body of 500 men (one wonders if the *prytaneis* were expected to take a lead in this), but settling details in a gathering of 6,000 men would have been impossible – no wonder that when Lampon tried to engage in detailed discussion of first-fruits he was sent off to talk to the Council and get them to come back on the issue (**362**). Nevertheless, as the modern saying goes, 'the devil is in the detail'. Exactly how the details were worked out will have affected what the overall reaction to the measure was. What is more, the requirement to read out the whole proposed action to the Assembly must have encouraged brevity – and on occasions that brevity seems to have brought with it failure adequately to think through the consequences (cf. **157**).

What the Council did gave political leaders difficult choices. Their options were essentially to support or to oppose – we have quite a number of amendments to decrees preserved, but few of these were moved by well-known political figures (though Hyperbolos' name appears among them). Amendment was a high-risk strategy, both because proposing an amendment was liable to suggest that you were someone who fussed about details, and because even if the amendment was passed a 'Yes, but' speech could never be as powerful as a 'Yes, certainly' or 'Not at all' speech.

In this light it is worth revisiting the Sicilian debate. We might wonder what would have happened had the decision to invade not started with the report to the Assembly of the Egestan embassy. It was the need to hear this embassy that put the item on the agenda – most plausibly without a specific Council recommendation beyond 'to consider what the Egestans say'. The enthusiastic reaction to the Egestans and decision to send 60 ships under Alkibiades, Nikias and Lamakhos then obliged the Council to come up with a proposal for the next Assembly on how to get this despatched. By that time saying 'Not at all' was hardly an option. But had the Council initially proposed not just the details of how to get the expedition away, but the very idea of an expedition, Nikias would surely have stood a much greater chance of persuading the Athenians that this was not the right way to go. Instead he comes out of this as a man whose objection is to the detail.

Historians give us, as is apparent from section 9 above, rather little description of what went on in the Athenian Council. But we should not for that reason neglect it. The Athenian insistence on getting the ordinary man, who had no special experience, to frame political decisions was an important way of keeping political control out of the hands of any particular group of politicians. However skillful their rhetoric was, they could exercise it only on the material that the Council gave them. Twice in their lifetime political leaders could themselves serve on the Council, but this could never be enough to enable them to give any long-term steer to Athenian policy by that means. Every policy initiative in Athens had to pass the 'ordinary man' test – it had to get itself past 500 men, chosen by lot according to quotas for each deme in a way that precluded any political grouping dominating proceedings. Such a way of working is unlikely to have been efficient – there must have been a great deal of 'reinventing the wheel' from year to year – but it did offer one important way in which the ordinary Athenian remained firmly in control of Athenian political life.

15 POLITICS IN ACTION

378 If anything bad results from the people's plans, they allege that a few men working against them ruined their plans; if something good results, they take the credit for themselves.

Old Oligarch 2.17

The development of political rhetoric

379 The leader of the embassy was Gorgias the rhetorician, who in eloquence far surpassed all his contemporaries. He was the first man to devise manuals of rhetoric and so far excelled his rivals in sophistry that he received from his pupils a fee of 100 minas. Now when he went to Athens and was introduced to the people, he addressed them on the subject of the alliance, and the novelty of his style dumbfounded the Athenians, clever and fond of argument though they are.

Diodoros 12.53.2–3

380 PROTARKHOS: Well, Sokrates, I have often heard Gorgias insist again and again that the art of persuasion far surpasses all other arts; for it would bring everything into voluntary subjection without using force.

Plato *Philebos* 58ab

381 PROTAGORAS: The rest (of the sophists) maltreat the young: though the young have fled from specialised studies, they take and thrust them back against their will into such studies, teaching them arithmetic and astronomy and geometry and music, but if Hippokrates comes to me, he will learn only what he has come to learn, namely, good sense in private affairs – how best to manage one's estate; and good sense in public affairs – how to speak and act most effectively in politics.

Plato *Protagoras* 318d–319a

382 STREPSIADES: Ladies, I beg from you just this tiny favour, that I should be the best speaker in Greece by miles.
CLOUDS: We shall grant you that, and so henceforth no one will carry more resolutions in the Assembly than you.

Aristophanes *Clouds* 429–31 (419/8, in this version)

383 SOKRATES: What about the rhetoric addressed to the Athenian people and the free men comprising the peoples of the other cities? Just what do we find it is? Do you think that politicians always speak with their eye on what is best and aim to make the citizens as good as possible by their speeches? Or do they strive to gratify the citizens, despising the common interest for the sake of their own private interest?

Plato *Gorgias* 502de

Perikles and the Athenians

384   Perikles was also the first to introduce payment for service in the law courts,
seeking win popular support in the face of Kimon's wealth. For Kimon, who
had as much property as a tyrant, performed the public liturgies in a magnificent
manner, but also maintained a good many of his fellow demesmen. For anyone
who wanted of the deme of Lakiadai could go to him every day and receive a
reasonable maintenance; and his whole estate was unfenced so that anyone who
liked could enjoy the fruit. Perikles did not have enough property to match such
lavish liberality, so he followed the advice of [Damon son of] Damonides of
Oa, who appeared to be the instigator of most of Perikles' measures, and was
later ostracized for that reason. This man had advised Perikles, since he had less
property of his own, to 'offer the people what was their own', and so he
instituted pay for the judges. Some people blame him saying that the law courts
deteriorated as a result, since after that anyone rather than the better men were
eager to draw lots for law-court duties.

[Aristotle] *Constitution of the Athenians* 27.3–4

385   Perikles' enemies shouted out at meetings of the Assembly: 'The people of
Athens are in disrepute and ill spoken of because they have removed the
common funds of the Greeks from Delos to their own keeping, and their most
presentable excuse to give to their detractors, that they took the common funds
from there out of fear of the Persians and were guarding them in safety, Perikles
has removed. Surely Greece is grossly insulted and plainly subjected to tyranny
when she sees that with her enforced contributions to the war we are gilding
and embellishing our city, which, like an immodest woman, adorns herself with
precious stones and statues and thousand-talent temples.'

Plutarch *Perikles* 12.1–2

For Perikles' building programme see LACTOR 1[4] **66** and note. For opposition to Perikles see **186**.

386   A meeting of the Assembly was called (in spring 431) and the Athenians held
a debate, resolving to make up their minds and give a complete and final answer.
Many came forward to speak, supporting one side or the other and urging the
need to fight or the need to revoke the decree, which could not be allowed to
stand in the way of peace. Perikles son of Xanthippos also came forward to give
his advice. He was the leading citizen of his time and very able in both speech
and action. He advised them like this: 'Men of Athens, I hold always to the same
policy – no concessions to the Peloponnesians...'

Such was the speech of Perikles. The Athenians believed that his advice was
the best and voted as he wished.

Thucydides 1.139.3–140.1; 1.145

387   After the second invasion of the Peloponnesians [in 430], Athenian attitudes
had changed. Their land had been ravaged twice, and the plague and war both
lay heavily upon them. They blamed Perikles for inciting them to war and
causing their misfortunes, and they had become eager to treat with Sparta.
Accordingly they sent an embassy there, but it failed. Reduced to utter

desperation, they were vehement against Perikles. Perikles saw that they were annoyed at the situation in which they found themselves, and acting in just the way he had expected. He was still general, so he summoned an assembly wanting to encourage into them and distract their angry thoughts so as to render them calmer and more confident. Coming to the speaker's platform, he said the following:

'I expected this outbreak of your anger towards me, since I understand the reasons for it; and I have called an assembly with the aim of reminding you of the plan and blaming you if your anger against me is misdirected or if you mistakenly give way to misfortune. It is my opinion that if the city is generally sound, it benefits its private citizens more than if it prospers so far as individuals are concerned but fails as a whole. A man may prosper personally, but if his country is ruined, he is ruined along with it no less; whereas if he meets with misfortune in a prosperous country, he is much better protected.

Since therefore a city can support the misfortunes of the individual, but the individual citizen cannot support the misfortunes of his city, it must be right for all to defend her and not to do what you are now doing: shattered by your personal afflictions, you are letting go the security of the city and blaming not only me who advised fighting but yourselves who agreed. And yet in being angry with me you are angry with one who is, I believe, second to none in determining what has to be done and in expounding the same, and with one who loves his city and who cannot be bribed.'

Thucydides 2.59–60.5

388   DIKAIOPOLIS: Why do we blame all this on the Spartans? It was men of ours, I do not say the city – remember that, I do not say the city – but debased bits of humanity, mis-struck, worthless, counterfeit, unathenian, who began exposing the Megarians' little woollen cloaks, and if they saw anywhere a cucumber or a leveret or a piglet or a clove of garlic or some lumps of salt, it was declared Megarian and sold off on the same day. Now those were little local difficulties; but then some lads intoxicated from playing drinking games went to Megara and stole a whore called Simaitha. And after that the Megarians, garlic-inflamed by their sufferings, stole two of Aspasia's whores in revenge. And from that – from three prostitutes – broke forth the origin of the war over the whole of Greece. Then in his wrath Olympian Perikles lightened and thundered and threw all Greece into confusion, carrying laws drafted like drinking songs, that no Megarian should remain on land or in Agora or at sea or in the sky. Then when the Megarians were starving by degrees, they begged the Spartans to secure the reversal of the decree occasioned by the prostitutes. But we refused their many requests. And then it was shield-clashing time.

Aristophanes *Akharnians* 514–539 (425)

389   HERMES: Pheidias started it (the run-up to the Peloponnesian War) when he got into difficulties. Then terrified of suffering the same fate, Perikles, who feared your tempers and hard-biting style, in order not to fall into danger himself, set the city on fire throwing in the small spark of the Megarian Decree.

Aristophanes *Peace* 605–609 (421)

For further discussion of the Megarian decree see LACTOR 1⁴ **97–99** and **259**.

The nostalgic view of Perikles

390   A: He was the best speaker in the world! Whenever he came forward, like the
great sprinters, he out-spoke the politicians, even giving them a ten-foot start.
B: You're talking speed!
A: But besides his speed a certain credibility haunted his lips, such a spell did
he cast on us; and he was the only speaker to leave a mark on in his audience.

Eupolis *Demes* (produced in 412) fr. 102 K-A

Perikles' successors

391   But they reversed Perikles' entire strategy and adopted other policies,
seemingly irrelevant to the war, in the light of personal ambitions and personal
gain, with ill effects for Athens and her relations with her allies. If these policies
succeeded, they were rather a source of honour and gain to individuals, but if
they failed, they impaired the city's war effort. Perikles owed his power to his
prestige and his ability, and he also proved manifestly incorruptible. He handled
the masses as free men: he led them rather than was led by them, since he did
not say anything to please them in an effort to acquire power by improper means,
but contradicted them somewhat angrily because, thanks to his prestige, he
already enjoyed power. When he saw that they were unjustifiably elated or
arrogant, his words would reduce them to fear, and when again they were
irrationally downhearted, he would restore them once more to confidence. What
was still nominally a democracy became in fact the rule of the leading citizen.
His successors were more on a level with one another, and because each was
grasping at pre-eminence, they began to hand over the conduct of affairs to the
whims of the people. Consequently, many mistakes were made, as you would
expect in a large and imperial city, and in particular the Sicilian expedition,
which was not so much a miscalculation about the enemy to be attacked as a
failure of those who sent out the expedition to take the best additional measures
to assist those on it; instead, through personal slanders to do with the leadership
of the people, they blunted the edge of the expedition and for the first time
produced political turmoil at home.

Thucydides 2.65.7–11

392   While Perikles led the people, public life was in better shape, but when he died,
it became much worse. Then for the first time the people chose a leader who
was not well regarded by the upper classes, whereas in the past the upper classes
had always supplied the leader...

After the death of Perikles, the men of distinction were led by Nikias who
died in Sicily and the common people by Kleon son of Kleainetos. Kleon seems
most of all to have corrupted the common people by his impulsive behaviour,
and he was the first to shout on the platform and hurl abuse and harangue the
people with his clothes hitched up, while the others spoke in an orderly fashion.
Next after them Theramenes son of Hagnon led the others and Kleophon the
lyre-maker led the common people. Kleophon was the first to provide the two-
obol benefit. It continued to be paid for a while, but then it was abolished by
Kallikrates of Paiania, after he had first promised to add another obol to the

other two. Both of them were later condemned to death. The masses commonly come to hate those who induce them to do something wrong, especially if they have been deceived... The best Athenian politicians after the older ones seem to have been Nikias, Thoukydides and Theramenes. As to Nikias and Thoukydides almost everyone agrees that they were fine, upstanding, public-spirited gentlemen with a fatherly attitude to the city as a whole; as to Theramenes there is disagreement because in his time there was a constitutional upheaval.

[Aristotle] *Constitution of the Athenians* 28.1, 3, 5

Kleon as political leader:
1. The suppression revolt of Mytilene (Summer 427)

393 A meeting of the Assembly was summoned forthwith. Different opinions were expressed by different speakers, and Kleon son of Kleainetos, who had carried the previous motion to put the Mytileneans to death, the most forceful man in Athens and much the most influential with the people at that time, came forward again and spoke as follows:

'I have often thought that democracy was incapable of ruling others, and not least on the occasion of your current change of mind about Mytilene. Because you have no fear or suspicion of one another in daily life, your attitude to our allies is the same, and you do not regard the mistakes you make through yielding to their arguments, or the concession you make to pity, as weakness that is dangerous to yourselves and wins no gratitude from the allies. You do not see that your empire is a tyranny, exercised over disaffected conspirators, who obey you, not because of the damaging concessions you make, but because of your superior strength rather than their goodwill. It will be most alarming of all if we do not stand firm by any of our resolutions, and do not recognise that a city is stronger if it observes imperfect laws that bind than good ones that are ineffectual; that ignorance combined with self-control is more valuable than cleverness combined with indiscipline; and that inferior men usually order their cities better than the more gifted ...'

Thucydides 3.36.5–37.3

394 KLEON: You are easily deceived by any new argument and unwilling to comply with a proven one, slaves of every topical paradox, despisers of tradition; each one wishing that he could speak himself, but, failing that, competing with those who can speak by evidently following the argument immediately and by applauding a sharp remark before it is made; eager to anticipate what is said but slow to foresee its consequences; seeking, as it were, a different world from the one we live in, and insufficiently attentive to existing circumstances; quite overcome by the pleasures of the ear and more like the audience of a sophist than the government of a city.

Thucydides 3.38.5–7

395 So spoke Diodotos. These were the arguments that they had advanced on each side, and they were almost equally strong. The Athenians nevertheless proceeded to decide the debate. The show of hands was very close, but Diodotos's motion prevailed.

Thucydides 3.49.1

Kleon as political leader:
2. The Pylos affair (Summer 425)

396 Realising the disfavour with which he was regarded for having prevented the treaty (with Sparta), Kleon said that those who had brought the news were not telling the truth. When the messengers advised the Athenians to send inspectors if they did not trust them, the Athenians elected Kleon and Theogenes. Realising that he would now be compelled to say what had already been said by the men whom he was slandering or be proved a liar if he said the contrary, he advised the Athenians, who he saw were resolved to continue the campaign, that, instead of sending inspectors and wasting time and opportunities, they should, if they thought the news was true, sail against the enemy. Pointing at Nikias son of Nikeratos, one of the generals, whom he hated, he declared sarcastically that if the generals were real men, it would be easy to sail with a force and take those on the island, and that that was what he would have done, had he been in office.

[28] The Athenians were murmuring at Kleon and asking why he did not now sail if he thought is so easy, and, mindful of his criticism, Nikias told him that, so far as the generals were concerned, he might take whatever force he liked and try. Thinking at first that Nikias' offer was only a pretence, Kleon was willing to go, but when he had realised that in fact Nikias was ready to make over the command, he withdrew, saying that Nikias was general, not himself. He was now alarmed, for he had not thought that Nikias would have the nerve to make way for him. Again Nikias bade him take the command against Pylos, and he called the Athenians to witness. The more Kleon backed off from the expedition and tried to retract what he had said, the more the Athenians, as is the way of the mob, urged Nikias to hand over the command and shouted at Kleon to sail.

Since he could not escape from his own words, he took on the expedition, and, coming forward, said that he was not afraid of Spartans and would sail without taking a single Athenian, but only the Lemnian and Imbrian forces in Athens, light-armed troops who had come from Ainos to help, and four hundred archers from elsewhere. With them and the troops already at Pylos, he said that within twenty days he would either bring back the Spartans alive or kill them on the spot. There was some laughter among the Athenians at his boasting , but men of sense were pleased to reflect that of two good things they would obtain one: either they would be rid of Kleon, which they thought more likely, or, if they were mistaken, he would reduce the Spartans for them. [29] After he had settled everything in the Assembly and the Athenians had voted him the command of the expedition, he chose Demosthenes, one of the generals at Pylos, as his colleague and made haste to sail.

Thucydides 4.27.3–29.1

The Aristophanic parody of politics as played by Kleon

In *Akharnians* (425) Aristophanes indicates that he had been prosecuted by Kleon after his *Babylonians* of 426 had 'attacked the magistrates'. In 424 Aristophanes made his whole play, *Knights*, an attack on Kleon, who is thinly disguised as the character Paphlagon, who in the course of the play is supplanted as the favourite slave of Demos (= the people) by the even more vulgar Sausage-Seller.

397   DEMOSTHENES: As this oracle says, you are to become a very great man.
SAUSAGE-SELLER: Tell me how I, a mere sausage-seller, am to became a real man.
DEMOSTHENES: Look, it's for precisely that reason that you are to become great – because you are base and brash and a product of the Agora.
SAUSAGE-SELLER: I can't think I am worthy to exercise such power.
DEMOSTHENES: Oh dear. Why on earth do you think you're unworthy? There must be something good on your conscience. You aren't one of the fine and upstanding?
SAUSAGE-SELLER: Good heavens, no. I'm base-born all right.
DEMOSTHENES: I congratulate you on your good fortune! What an asset for you in public life.
SAUSAGE-SELLER: But, my good man, I've had no education, except for reading and writing, and I'm really bad at them.
DEMOSTHENES: That's your one handicap – knowing them, even really badly. Leading the people no longer calls for a man of education or good character. It's a job for a disgusting ignoramus.

Aristophanes Knights 177–193 (424)

398   SAUSAGE-SELLER: I can't imagine how I'm to manage the people.
DEMOSTHENES: Child's play. Do what you always do. Stir up all their affairs together and make mincemeat of them, and always try to win the people over by sweetening them with some artfully prepared phrases. The other leadership qualities you have: a hideous voice, low birth and market origins. You have everything you need for public life.

Aristophanes Knights 211–19 (424)

399   SAUSAGE-SELLER: It is worth hearing what happened. For I was hurrying from here, right behind him, and he was in there breaking thundering words as he went on the attack against the cavalrymen, telling marvellous tales and piling in steep claims and saying 'conspirators' very persuasively. The whole Council as it listened became full of false-orach, it looked mustard and knit its brows. I, when I realized that it was accepting the words and being deceived by the lies, said: 'Come, Gods of Worthlessness, Gods of Wool-pulling and Folly and Monkey-business, Protector of the Drunk and disorderly, and you, Agora, in which I was educated as a child, grant me boldness, a fluent tongue and a shameless voice.' As I was thinking this, a bugger farted from the right. I bowed in worship. Then striking the barrier with my arse, I knocked it out of its slots, and opening my mouth wide I cried out: 'Council, I have come with good news, and want to be the first to announce this to you. From the time when the war broke out, I have never seen cheaper sardines'. Immediately serenity came across their faces; then they were garlanding me for my good news. And I said to them, making it a secret, that they should quickly impound all the craftsmen's bowls in order to buy the most sardines for an obol. They clapped and opened their mouths wide in wonder at me. But Paphlagon had an idea, since he knew what words most pleased the Council. He moved the following resolution:

'Gentlemen, it seems to me that in response to the good fortune that has been announced we should sacrifice a hundred cows to the goddess for the good news.' The Council blew back in his direction again. I, when I realized that I was being worsted by his bullshit shot over his head with two hundred cows and advised to make a vow of a thousand goats for Artemis Agrotera for tomorrow if anchovies should fall to one hundred for an obol. The Council turned eagerly to me again. But he, when he heard this, was shocked and began babbling. Then the *prytaneis* and the Archers dragged him off, and the Councillors stood around making a din about the sardines. He besought them to wait for a short moment 'in order to learn what the herald from Sparta is saying, for he has come about peace'. But they all cried out as from one mouth: 'About peace? now? that, my good fellow, is because they noticed that sardines were so cheap with us. We don't need peace. Let the war proceed.' They called out for the *prytaneis* to let them go, and then they leapt over the barriers in all directions. I ran off and bought up all the coriander and onions in the market, and then I gave them to them when they were at a loss as to seasoning for the sardines and I was flavour of the month. They all praised me and cheered me so that I've come here with the whole Council bought for an obol's worth of coriander.

                                                              Aristophanes *Knights* 624–82 (424)

This passage is interesting for its parody of forms of argument – both the conjuring up of conspiracies and the straight appeal to the material desires of the audience – and also for situating this debate not in the Assembly but in the Council. See further **136–138**.

400   DEMOS: O dearest of friends, come here, Agorakritos. You've done me a power of good, boiling me.
SAUSAGE-SELLER: Did I? But, my good fellow, you do not know what you were like before, nor what you got up to. Otherwise, you would consider me a god!
DEMOS: What did I do before? Tell me what sort of person I was.
SAUSAGE-SELLER: To start with, whenever someone spoke in the Assembly saying, 'O Demos (people), I am your lover, I'm fond of you, I care for you, I am the only one to advise you', whenever someone used opening words like these well, you flapped your wings and bellowed.
DEMOS: I did?
SAUSAGE-SELLER: And then in return he deceived you and walked away.
DEMOS: What are you saying? They did this, and I never noticed it?
SAUSAGE-SELLER: Yes, by Zeus, your ears opened up like an umbrella and then shut again.
DEMOS: Had I become so mad and senile?
SAUSAGE-SELLER: Yes, by Zeus, and if two speakers were holding forth, one saying to build warships and the other spend money on state pay, the man advocating pay went and outran the trireme man. So why are you hanging your

head. Aren't you going to stay?

DEMOS: I'm ashamed of my old misdeeds.

SAUSAGE-SELLER: But you weren't to blame for this, don't worry, it was those who deceived you over this. Now tell me, suppose some abusive prosecutor says: 'There will be no barley-groats for you jury unless you convict in this case', what would you do to this speaker?

DEMOS: Raise him up and throw him into the pit, with Hyperbolos hung around his neck.

Aristophanes Knights 1335–1363 (424)

Once more here claims are made for the people being moved by material self-interest, but here the material self-interest takes, at least in part, the form of greed on behalf of the city as a whole. This passage also draws attention to the people's susceptibility to flattery.

Kleon's successors

401   SOSIAS: I'd no sooner fallen asleep than I saw an assembly of sheep in session on Pnyx; they were holding staves and wearing a little cloaks; and then I dreamt that these sheep were being harangued by a voracious whale with the voice of a blazing sow.

XANTHIAS: Yuck!

SOSIAS: What's the matter?

XANTHIAS: Stop, stop! Don't go on. Your dream reeks of rotten leather.

SOSIAS: Then this loathsome whale took a balance and began weighing out some beef-fat (*dēmon*).

XANTHIAS: The wretch! Wanting to divide our people (*dēmon*).

Aristophanes Wasps 31–41 (422)

402   CHORUS LEADER: In a ring round his (Kleon's) head licked a hundred heads of damned flatterers.

Aristophanes Wasps 1033–4 (422)

403   SOKRATES: How could this fellow (Strepsiades) ever learn getting off or summonsing or persuasive vacuity? And yet Hyperbolos managed to learn it for a talent.

Aristophanes Clouds 874–76 (419/8, in this version)

404   HERMES: Now listen to what Peace has just asked me: 'Who is the current master of the stone (platform) on the Pnyx?'

TRYGAIOS: Hyperbolos currently occupies that spot. You, what are you doing? Why are you turning your head away?

HERMES: She's abandoning the people because she's angry that they have chosen such a worthless protector.

TRYGAIOS: We shan't go on using him, but just at the moment the people, bereft a guardian and feeling naked, have put him on for temporary protection.

HERMES: She wants to know how that will help the city.

TRYGAIOS: We shall take better decisions.

HERMES: How so?

TRYGAIOS: Because he's a lamp-maker. Hitherto we were going in the dark; but now we shall decide everything in lamplight.

Aristophanes *Peace* 679–92 (421)

For Hyperbolos see **406**.

A different political style: the case of Nikias

405 But when the Athenians had also suffered the defeat at Amphipolis and Kleon had died and Brasidas too, who were those on both sides most opposed to peace – the one because of his good fortune and the honour he got from war, the other because he thought that in a time of quiet his wrongdoing would be more manifest and his slanders would be less believed – then those most eager for leadership on both side, Pleistoanax son of Pausanias king of the Spartans and Nikias son of Nikeratos, who at that time had the greatest reputation for generalship, grew much more keen on peace. Nikias wanted to preserve his good fortune while he was without defeat and esteemed, for the present to be free of labours himself and responsible for ending them for the citizens, and for the future to leave a name for managing the city without failure. He thought that the way to achieve this was to avoid risks and put himself least into the hands of fortune, and that it was peace that provided the least risk.

Thucydides 5.16.1

406 The dissension between Alkibiades and Nikias became so acute that recourse was had to the procedure of ostracism... People loathed the lifestyle of Alkibiades and dreaded his audacity... His wealth made Nikias an object of envy, but above all his lifestyle struck them as unfriendly and unpopular and indeed antisocial, oligarchic and alien. Since he often resisted their desires and tried to force them against their wishes to adopt the expedient course, they found him objectionable. But, to put it simply, it was a contest between youthful warmongers and elderly peacemakers, the former voting against Nikias and latter against Alkibiades.

'But in time of strife, the villain too has his share of honour', and so in this case also the people, by splitting in two, made room for the most ruthless and depraved men. One of these was Hyperbolos of Perithoidai, whose boldness did not derive from any influence of his, but he acquired influence through his boldness. His credit in the city was a discredit to the city. At this time he thought himself beyond the reach of ostracism – he was indeed a fitter candidate for the pillory – and he expected that when one of the two rivals had been banished, he would become a match for the survivor. He was obviously delighted at their dissension, and incited the people against both.

When Nikias and Alkibiades and their followers became aware of his skulduggery, they conferred secretly. By combining and uniting their two factions into one, they gained the upper hand, and so it was neither Nikias nor Alkibiades who was ostracised but Hyperbolos instead.

For the time being the people were delighted and amused, but later they were annoyed to think that this procedure had been degraded by its application to such an unworthy man. They thought that even punishment conferred some dignity, or rather they regarded ostracism as a punishment for men like Thoukydides and Aristeides but as an honour for Hyperbolos and an excuse for him to boast that his skulduggery had earned him the same fate as the best men. And so Platon the comic poet says of him somewhere:

> Indeed he met a fate appropriate for the men of old,
> But inappropriate for his own branded person:
> The *ostrakon* was not devised for such as he.

In the event, no one was ever ostracised after Hyperbolos – he was the last, as Hipparkos of Kholargos, a kinsmen of the tyrant (Peisistratos), had been the first.

Plutarch Nikias 11.1–6

For the ostracism of Thoukydides see above **188**, **295**.

The decision to invade Sicily

407 The Athenians called a meeting of the Assembly, and after hearing from the Egestans and their own ambassadors a report that was encouraging, but untrue, on matters generally and on the money in particular, to the effect that there was plenty available in the temples and the treasury, they voted to send sixty ships to Sicily, under the command of Alkibiades son of Kleinias, Nikias son of Nikeratos, and Lamakhos son of Xenophanes, those generals to have full powers.

Thucydides 6.8.2

408 Nikias had been chosen to command against his will, and he thought that the city was ill advised: on a slight and specious pretext, it was aspiring to conquer the whole of Sicily, a considerable enterprise. He therefore came forward in the hope of deflecting the Athenians.

Thucydides 6.8.4

409 NIKIAS: If there is any man overjoyed to have been chosen to command, who advised you to sail, while looking only to his own ends – especially if he is still too young to command – and seeking to be admired for his stud of horses, but because of the heavy expense involved seeking also to gain from his command, do not allow him to enjoy private splendour at his country's peril. Remember that such men misuse public resources while wasting their own, and that this is a big matter and not one for a young man to decide and act upon hastily.

When I see young men here now sitting beside that same man at his behest, I am alarmed, and in my turn I bid the older men not to be ashamed, if they have one of the younger ones sitting next to them, to seem cowardly by not voting for war.

Thucydides 6.12.2–13.1

For the passage that follows this and precedes the next extract see **203**.

410   The most eager promoter of the expedition was Alkibiades son of Kleinias. He
wanted to oppose Nikias, both because of old political different because Nikias
had just attacked him. He was also exceedingly desirous of a command that he
hoped would enable him to conquer Sicily and Carthage and at the same time,
if he succeeded, to enhance his personal wealth and reputation. Though he
enjoyed high standing with his fellow-citizens, he indulged his desires beyond
what his actual estate could sustain, both in keeping horses and in the rest of
his expenditure. This was later to contribute very greatly to the defeat of Athens.

Thucydides 6.15.2–3

411   So spoke Nikias, thinking that either he would deflect the Athenians with the
scale of the enterprise or, if he was obliged to campaign, he would at least sail
with minimum risk. However, the Athenians were not relieved of their desire
for the expedition by the burdensomeness of the preparations; on the contrary,
they became much more eager, and the outcome for Nikias was the reverse of
what he had intended. He was judged to have given good advice, and now the
expedition would be quite safe. A passion to sail fell on all alike. The older men
thought that either they would subdue their opponents or, failing that. so great
a force would suffer no disaster. Those of military age felt a longing for foreign
sights and spectacles, and they had no doubt that they would come home safely.
The mass of the people, including the members of the expedition, expected to
earn pay in the short term and acquire power which would be a source of endless
pay in the future.

Thucydides 6.24.1–3

For the passage that follows this, see **204**.

How Alkibiades restored his influence

412   Thrasyllos sailed home to Athens with the rest of the fleet. Before he arrived,
the Athenians had elected as generals (for 407/06) Alkibiades, though he was
still in exile, Thrasyboulos, who was away from home, and thirdly, from those
at home, Konon. Alkibiades now sailed from Samos with his twenty ships and
the money to Paros, and from there he made straight for Gytheion in order to
find out about the thirty warships that he had heard the Spartans were fitting out
there, and also to find out how the city felt about his return home. When he
realised that it was well-disposed to him, that they had elected him a general,
and that his friends were summoning him privately, he sailed into Peiraieus on
the day when the city was celebrating the Plynteria and the statue of Athene
was veiled from sight – a coincidence which some regarded as an ill omen for
himself and the city: on that day no Athenian would venture to embark on any
serious business.

When he sailed in, the common people of Peiraieus and the city thronged
around his ships, all agog and eager to see the famous Alkibiades. Some said
that he was the best of the citizens and that he alone had been unjustly exiled...

[17] Others, however, said that Alkibiades was solely responsible for their
past troubles and that he might well prove the sole cause of the troubles

threatening the city in the future.

Alkibiades had anchored near the shore, but he did not land at once through fear of his enemies. Instead he stood on the deck of his ship and looked round to see if his friends were present. When he saw his cousin Euryptolemos son of Peisianax, and his other relatives and his friends with them, he landed and went up to the city, accompanied by men who were all set to prevent anyone from arresting him. After he had defended himself before the Council and Assembly, claiming that he had not committed impiety and that he had been unjustly treated, and after more of the same kind had been said, with no one speaking in opposition because the Assembly would not have tolerated it, he was proclaimed supreme commander with full powers as being able to restore the former power of the city. The Athenians had previously been conducting the procession of the Mysteries by sea because of the war, but Alkibiades now led out the whole army and escorted it by land.

Xenophon *Hellenika* 1.4.10–13, 17–20

413   DIONYSOS: I came down here after a poet. What for? So that the city should be preserved and continue to hold its choral competitions. So whichever of you is about to give the city some good advice is the one that I intend to carry off. First, then, what opinions does each of you have about Alkibiades? The city is agonising.
AISKHYLOS: What is the city's opinion of him?
DIONYSOS: Its opinion? It yearns for him, it hates him, and it wants to have him. But you two say what you think about him.
EURIPIDES: I hate a citizen who will prove slow to help his country but quick to do it great harm, and good at looking after himself but useless to the city.
DIONYSOS: Good, by Poseidon. And you, Aiskhylos, what's your opinion?
AISKHYLOS: Best not to raise a lion in the city; but should you have done so, humour its ways.
DIONYSOS: By Zeus the Saviour, it is hard for me to judge. The one spoke poetically and the other plainly.

Aristophanes *Frogs* 1418–34 (405)

Factional politics in the early fourth century

414   At around the same time a trireme sailed out from Athens without the Assembly having decided that it should; Demainetos, the man responsible had, as is said, shared secretly his thoughts on the matter with the Council since some citizens supported him. With them he went down to the Peiraieus, launched the ship down from the shipsheds, went to sea and sailed to Konon. Subsequently a great row broke out since the Athenians were annoyed – as many as were intelligent and respectable – and said that they were bringing down the city by starting a war with Spartans. The Councillors were shocked at the row and summoned the Assembly, claiming that they had no share in the event. When the people met, those Athenians associated with Thrasyboulos, Aisimos and Anytos got up and informed the Athenians that they were running a great risk unless they absolved the city from blame. Among the Athenians the moderates and men of property cherished the status quo, but the many who took a more populist view had their current fears played on by the advisers and sent a message to Milon, the *harmost* of Aigina, that he could punish Demainetos, on the grounds that his actions had nothing to do with the city. Until this point they were constantly stirring things up and doing a great deal that was opposed to the Spartans. [7] For they sent arms and crews to the ships with Konon, and ambassadors were sent to the King of Persia, [*a few words are lost*]...krates, Hagnias and Telesegoros. When Pharax the former Spartan nauarkh captured these men, he sent them to the Spartans who executed them. They opposed Sparta under the encouragement of Epikrates and Kephalos. They in particular wanted the city to go to war – a view they had a long time before they spoke with Timokrates and took the gold. Some claim that the money from him was the cause of the alliance between these men, the Boiotians, and those in the other cities previously mentioned, ignoring the fact that they all had been ill-disposed towards the Spartans of old and had been considering how to get their cities to war.

Hellenika Oxyrhynkhia 6.1–7.2

The *Hellenika Oxyrhynkhia*, a continuation of Thucydides by an author who cannot certainly be identified, and which survives only in fragments, is peculiarly interested in Athenian internal history and describes it in unusual terms that put the emphasis on factions. The passage here, concerning events of 397/6 provides graphic evidence for the extent to which Athens continued, even after 399, to fear further Spartan interventions. But it is also interesting for what it shows about the potentially independent behaviour of the Council and about the political tensions in Athens in the 390s. Konon, who is mentioned here, was an Athenian who was at this time in charge of the Persian fleet; his victory over the Spartans at the battle of Knidos in 394 was a turning point in Spartan power, after which Konon returned to be honoured in Athens.

Politics played out between Assembly and Courts in the middle of the fourth century

415   Apollodoros proposed a decree in the Council when he was a Councillor, and brought a proposal to the people saying that the people should vote whether they thought that the money that was left over from the administration should belong to the stratiotic fund or to the theoric fund. The laws ordered that whenever there was war the money that was left over from the administration it should go to the stratiotic fund. He thought that the people must have the power to do what it wanted with its own money, and had sworn to give the best advice he could to the Athenian people, as you all witnessed at that moment. When the vote happened no one voted that it was not right to use these moneys as stratiotic, but still even now, if any discussion takes place, it is agreed by everybody that Apollodoros suffers unjustly when he proposed what was best. Jurors should justly get annoyed with the person who deceives with his argument, not with those who are deceived. For Stephanos here brought an indictment for illegal proposal and came to the court with false witnesses procured to slander Apollodoros, and made many accusations irrelevant to the charge, and had the decree rescinded. If that is what he thought it right to do, we bear him no grudge for that. But when the jurors were voting to fix the penalty, Stephanos was not willing to compromise even though we begged him; he fixed the amount at fifteen talents, in order to deprive Apollodoros and his children of their civic rights, and put my sister and all of us into the extremest distress and deprivation. For the property of Apollodoros was worth in all no more than three talents, so that he could not pay so great a fine. Yet if the fine was not paid by the ninth prytany it would have been doubled and Apollodoros would have been registered as owing thirty talents to the Treasury, the property that belonged to him would have been confiscated by the state and sold, and Apollodoros himself, his wife and children, and all of us would have been reduced to utmost destitution. What is more, his other daughter would have not been able to marry – for who would ever have taken in marriage without a dowry a girl with a father in debt to the Treasury and without resources? Stephanos would have become the cause for us all of so many troubles when he had never suffered any harm from us. I am most thankful to the jurors in the case for not overlooking Apollodoros' impending ruin and fixing the fine at a talent, so that he was able, with difficulty, to pay it..

[Demosthenes] 59.4–8 (349–39)

Persuading the Assembly in the fourth century

416 You, Demosthenes, reproach me if I come before the people not regularly, but only at intervals.

Aiskhines 3.220 (330)

Plutarch *Perikles* 7.7 tells us that Perikles was likened to the state trireme the Salaminia because he appeared only on big occasions. Other politicians clearly adopted different political habits and expected to be constantly giving advice to the people.

417 I think, men of Athens, that you would give a lot of money in return for what is in the best interests of the city becoming clear on the matter you are now considering. Since this is so, you ought to be willing to listen to those who want to give advice. You would not only be able to take a grip on any useful consideration that is raised, if you listened, but I think it may be your good fortune to find that some who come to speak produce many of the ideas you need impromptu, so that out of everything said the choice of what is in your interest becomes easy.

Demosthenes 1.1 (349)

This and the next three passages are the opening gambits from some of Demosthenes' most famous speeches in the Assembly, in which he tried to galvanize the Athenians into action. They indicate what he thought would most successfully soften the Athenians up to accept his advice. In different ways he starts by indicating the inadequacy of past advice, and the need for the people to listen to new voices.

418 If, men of Athens, the proposal was that we should speak about a novel matter, I should wait until most of the regular speakers had revealed their thoughts. If I were satisfied with some view expressed, I would keep quiet; if not, then I would try to say what I understand. But since we happen to consider now matters about which these men have often spoken before, I think I can reasonably be forgiven for getting up to speak first. For if they had advised the right policy in the past, there would be no need for you to be considering the matter now.

Demosthenes 4.1 (351)

419   I perceive, men of Athens, that the present situation causes a great deal of
annoyance and trouble, not only because we have lost much and there seems to
be no way of putting a positive spin on the matter, but because there is no general
agreement about anything when it comes to thinking about the future, but some
people think one thing and others the opposite. Giving advice is by nature
difficult and invidious, and you, men of Athens, have made it much more
difficult. Everyone else makes a habit of taking counsel before acting, but you
do so afterwards. So, for all the time that I know about, it has come about that
the man who criticizes those whose past advice led to mistakes gets
commendation and appears to speak well, but the current situation and the real
matter for debate eludes you. Nevertheless, even though this is so, I have stood
up because I think and have persuaded myself that, if you will be willing to
abandon shouting and rivalry and to listen, as those who are deliberating about
the city and about so important a business should do, it will be possible to
explain and advocate policies that will improve the present and remedy the past.

Demosthenes 5.1–3 (346)

420   All those who speak, men of Athens, ought to speak not out of enmity or favour,
but reveal what each thinks best, particularly when you are discussing major
public matters. But since some are led to speak out of rivalry, or some other
cause, it is necessary that you, men of Athens, should set aside everything else,
and vote and act for what you think is in the city's interest. The current concern
is affairs in the Chersonese and the campaign which Philip has now been
conducting in Thrace for ten months. But most of the speeches have been about
with what Diopeithes does and is about to do. My view is that there is no need
for me or anyone else to sound off, as to the accusations made against members
of this force, whom you can punish according to the laws at any time, whether
now or later. But it is what the enemy to this city, who is in the neighbourhood
of the Hellespont with a considerable force, is trying to secure at our expense,
and what we will no longer be able to recover if we once are late, that is the
subject which requires instant discussion and preparation, from which we must
not be sidetracked by irrelevant disputes and accusations.

Demosthenes 8.1–3 (341)

16   THEORISING DEMOCRACY

The institutional underpinning of democracy

421   The following practices are democratic: the election of officials by all from all;
government of each by all and of all by each in turn; appointment by lot either
to all offices or to all that do not need experience or skill; no property
qualification for office or only a very low one; no office to be held twice, or
more than a few times, by the same man, or few offices apart from the military
ones; short tenure either of all offices or of as many as possible.

Aristotle *Politics* 1317b18–25

Democracy's slogans

422 The rule of the people has, in the first place, the fairest name of all – equality of rights (*isonomiē*); in the second place, the people do none of the wicked things that monarchs do: officials hold office by lot, and their conduct is subject to examination, and all measures are referred to the popular assembly...the whole is contained in the many.

Herodotos 3.80.6

Herodotos uses here the term *isonomiē* (equality in law), just as in his account of Kleisthenes (**34**) he uses the term *isegoriē* (equality in speech). The term *demokratia* seems not to have been coined until into the fifth century, perhaps not until after the Persian Wars (see Hansen (1986) for further discussion).

423 PERIKLES: We enjoy a constitution which does not emulate the laws of our neighbours; we rather provide an example than imitate others. Because affairs are ordered in the interests of the many and not the few, its name is democracy. All enjoy equality before the law in their private disputes. As for the popular esteem, however, anyone who is distinguished in any way is advanced in public life on merit rather than in rotation. As for poverty, furthermore, if anyone can do the city some service, he is not debarred by the obscurity of his status.

Thucydides 2.37.1

This is an extract from Thucydides' version of Perikles' Funeral Oration.

424 PERIKLES: It is my opinion that if the city is generally sound, it benefits its private citizens more than if it prospers so far as individuals are concerned but fails as a whole. A man may prosper personally, but if his country is ruined, he is ruined along with it no less; whereas if he meets with misfortune in a prosperous country, he is much better protected.

Since therefore a city can support the misfortunes of the individual, but the individual citizen cannot support the misfortunes of his city, it must be right for all to defend her and not to do what you are now doing: shattered by your personal afflictions, you are letting go the security of the city and blaming not only me who advised fighting but yourselves who agreed...

As for myself, I am the same, and my position is unaltered; it is you who change: you took my advice while unharmed and are repenting under adversity. The apparent error of my policy lies in the weakness of your resolution...

It is reasonable that you should rally to the support of the city's prestige which derives from the empire – an empire in which you all take pride...

Thucydides 2.60.2–4; 2.61.2; 2.63.1

These extracts come from Perikles' last speech (summer 430), a speech in which he defends his track-record in the face of Athenians who have become fed-up with his policy of withdrawing inside the walls and allowing the Spartans to ravage Attica.

The advantages and drawbacks of sharing power among many

425 HERALD: Who is sovereign lord of this land? To whom must I relay the words of Kreon, who is lord of the land of Kadmos, now that Eteokles has fallen by his brother's hand at the seven gates, slain by Polyneikes?

THESEUS: First, stranger, you began your speech in error, in seeking here a sovereign lord; for the city is free and not ruled by a single man. The people rule, taking turns in yearly rotation. No advantage is given to riches: the poor man has equality.

HERALD: You give me the edge there, as in a game of draughts. The city from which I come is ruled by one man and a not a mob. No one puffs up the citizens by his speeches and twists them this way and that in pursuit of his own gain. Pleasing and most gratifying at the time, he subsequently harms the city, and then, by concealing his former errors behind fresh slanders, he escapes justice. Besides, without straight speaking, how could the people guide the city straightly? Length of time yields better understanding than haste. Your poor farmer, even if he had some understanding, could not attend to public affairs because of his work. Assuredly it is offensive to decent people when a worthless man enjoys high standing in society after mastering the people with his tongue, although he was nothing before.

THESEUS: Our messenger is clever and an embroiderer of his message. But since you did initiate this debate, listen: it was you who proposed a verbal duel. Nothing is more menacing to a city than a sovereign lord, because then, in the first place, there are no laws the same for all; instead one man rules, having taken the law into his own possession, which means the end of equality. When the laws are written down, both the powerless and the rich enjoy equal justice, and when the powerless are ill spoken-of, they can reply to the prosperous in the same terms. The weaker one defeats the great man, if he has justice on his side. Freedom is found in the words: 'Who has a proposal beneficial to the city and wishes to come forward with it?' Whoever so wishes wins renown, and whoever does not stays silent. What could be fairer to the citizens than that?

Euripides *Suppliant Women* 399–441 (422)

It is one of the peculiarities of Athenian thought that they could imagine Athenian democratic values going back to Theseus – so here the king Theseus is made into a spokesman for democracy and an opponent of monarchy. Euripides seems to expect his audience to see Theseus as merely an informal political leader like Perikles.

The basis of democratic equality

426   ATHENAGORAS: How can it be right for citizens of the same state not to be judged worthy of the same benefits? It will perhaps be said that democracy is neither intelligent nor fair and that those with the money are also the best at ruling. What I say is, first, that 'the people' (*demos*) is the name of the whole state, whereas 'oligarchy' is the name of only a part; secondly, that though the rich are the best at looking after money, the intelligent are the best at deliberation, and the many are the best at listening and deciding, and all elements alike, individually and collectively, enjoy their proper place in a democracy. Oligarchy gives the many their share of the dangers, but as for the benefits, it does not merely want more of them, but it takes and keeps them all.

Thucydides 6.38.5–39.2

Thucydides presents the city of Syracuse as a variant on Athens, but one where the divisions between advocates of radical democracy and of oligarchy are much more pronounced. Athenagoras is his 'democratic' spokesman – we do not know whether there was a Syracusan named Athenagoras (named, presumably by a family that admired Athens) or whether Thucydides coined this name to create a spokesman for views that he had learned that some Syracusans expressed.

427 When the powerful venture to lend money to the have-nots and to assist and benefit them, then at last there is pity and an end to isolation; there is comradeship and mutual aid; there is harmony among the citizens, and other blessings such as no man could enumerate.

Demokritos DK68B255

The Presocratic philosopher Demokritos is most famous for inventing the view that the world was made up of 'atoms', but he was also an important contributor also to ethical and political thought – thought that is itself coloured by his atomism.

Protagoras, political education, and why everyone should have a say in politics

428 SOKRATES: So now we can consult together about our visitor Menon. He has long been telling me, Anytos, that he is eager to acquire the wisdom and expertise which enable men to run estates and cities well, to look after their parents, and know how to entertain both fellow-citizens and strangers and send them off in good style. With this expertise in mind, to whom would it be right to send him? In the light of what we have just been saying, it seems plain enough that we should send him to those who profess to be teachers of excellence and who declare themselves available, at a fixed price, to any Greek who wishes to learn.
ANYTOS: Just who are you talking about?
SOKRATES: I am sure you know that they are those commonly called 'sophists'.
ANYTOS: Watch yourself, Sokrates. I do hope that no friend or acquaintance of mine, citizen or foreigner, goes mad enough to approach them and be ruined: they really are the manifest ruin and corruption of their pupils.
SOKRATES: What do you mean, Anytos? Can they be so different from others who claim to confer some benefit that they not only do not improve whatever is presented to them but on the contrary damage it? And for these services they openly dare to charge fees? For my part, I cannot bring myself to believe you. I know that one of them, Protagoras, made more money from his craft than Pheidias, who created such exceptionally fine works, and ten other sculptors put together. People who mended old shoes or repaired cloaks could not get away with it for a month if they returned the cloaks and shoes in worse shape than they got them: they would soon starve to death. So it would be extraordinary if Protagoras took the whole of Greece for a ride, while he was actually corrupting his pupils and returning them worse that he got them, for more than forty years. I believe that he was nearly seventy when he died and had been practising his craft for forty years, and for all that time and up to the present day he has continued to be well-regarded.
In addition to Protagoras, there were a great many others, some born before him and others still alive. Are we to say, by your account, that they consciously deceive and ruin young men, or are they themselves unaware of what they are

doing? Though some say that they are the cleverest of men, shall we say that they are as mad as that?

ANYTOS: They are far from mad, Sokrates; the mad ones are rather the young men who pay them money and, still more, those with responsibility for them who allow it, and, most of all, the cities who let them in or do not expel them, whether it be a foreigner or a citizen who attempts such a thing.

SOKRATES: Anytos, has one of the sophists done you harm or why are you so hard on them?

ANYTOS: Good heavens, I have never had anything to do with any of them, and I would not allow any member of my family to do so.

*****

SOKRATES: Now it is your turn to say which Athenians Menon should approach. Name anyone you like.

ANYTOS: But why name a particular person? Any fine and upstanding Athenian that he happens to meet will make him a better man than the sophists, if he is willing to take advice.

SOKRATES: Did these fine fellows grow up like this spontaneously? Though taught by nobody, can they themselves teach what they did not learn?

ANYTOS: I suppose they learnt it from forebears who were themselves fine fellows. You don't doubt that there have been good men in our city?

SOKRATES: I believe that there are good politicians in the city now and have been as good in the past. The question before us is whether they have been good teachers of their own excellence.

Plato *Menon* 90e–92b; 92e–93a

The issue of whether political skill can be taught, and whether virtue can be taught, is central to a number of Platonic dialogues and reflects a real debate about in Athens as to whether there were political experts and what it was that made them expert.

429   SOKRATES: Now, I observe that when we gather in the Assembly and the city needs to take action on a matter of building, builders are sent for to advise on the buildings, and when action is needed on shipbuilding, shipwrights are sent for, and likewise with all matters that they think can be learnt and taught. But if anyone whom they do not regard as an expert tries to advise them, no matter how handsome or rich or well-born he is, they still will have none of him, but jeer and hoot, until either the would-be speaker is shouted down and gives way of his own accord, or the archers drag him away or put him out on the orders of the *prytaneis*. This is how they act in what they regard as a technical matter; but when deliberation is needed on some matter of public policy, anyone may get up and give them advice, be he carpenter or smith, cobbler, merchant, shipper, rich or poor, of good family or none. No one brings it up against any of these, as against those I have just mentioned, that here is a man who without any technical qualifications, unable to point to anybody as his teacher, is yet trying to give advice. The reason is that they do not think this is a subject that can be taught.

Plato *Protagoras* 319b–d

On education and political leadership cf. **397**. On keeping order in the Assembly and Council see **137**.

430   Glaukon son of Ariston was striving to be a speaker in the Assembly. He was
eager to lead the city, though he was not yet twenty. None of his friends or
relatives could stop him, though he was getting himself dragged from the
platform and making himself a laughing-stock. Sokrates, who was well-
disposed towards him because of Kharmides the son of Glaukon and because
of Plato, was the only one who stopped him. He came upon him and first made
him willing to listen by saying the following:

'Glaukon, have you got in mind to become a chief adviser for the city?'

'I do, Sokrates,' he said.

'By Zeus, that's a fine thing to do, if anything human is. For clearly if you
manage this you will be able to get whatever you yourself desire and you will
have the capacity to benefit your friends, will exalt your ancestral household,
will increase your fatherland, will be widely known first in the city and then in
all Greece, and perhaps, like Themistokles, even among the barbarians.
Wherever you might be, everywhere you will be admired.' Hearing this,
Glaukon was filled with pride and was happy to remain with Sokrates. So after
this Sokrates said, 'So, this is clear, is it, Glaukon, that if you want to be
honoured you must benefit the city?'

'Absolutely', he said.

'By the gods', said Sokrates, 'please don't hide this, but tell us how you will
make a start on benefiting the city.' When Glaukon was silent, as if he was at
that moment considering where he would begin, Sokrates said 'Just as if you
wanted to increase the household of a friend you would try to make him richer,
will you also try to make the city richer in the same way?'

'Absolutely', he said.

'So would it be richer if it had more income?'

'That seems very likely.'

'Tell me then,' said Sokrates, 'from what sources does the city currently
income, and how much do they bring in? You have obviously considered that,
so that you might increase any that are less than they might be and add sources
of income that are currently overlooked.'

'No, by Zeus,' said Glaukon, 'I haven't considered that.'

'But if you have left that aside, tell me about the city's expenses. It is clear
that you have in mind to cut out any expenses that are excessive.'

'No, by Zeus, I have not had time yet to get round to that.'

'So,' said Sokrates, 'we will put off the issue of making the city richer. After
all, how could someone who doesn't know the city's expenses and income
worry about that?'

'But Sokrates,' said Glaukon, 'it is possible to enrich the city from its
enemies.'

'By Zeus, one certainly can,' said Sokrates, 'if one is stronger than they. If
one is weaker one would simply lose one's present goods.'

'What you say is true', he said.

'So,' Sokrates said, 'the man who will advise on which enemies the city
should make war has to know the strength of the city and the strength of the
enemy, in order that if his city is stronger he can advise trying war, and if it is
weaker persuade it to be cautious.'

'What you say is correct.'

'First, then, tell me the strength of our city in infantry and in naval ships, and then the strength of our enemy.'

'But, by Zeus, I couldn't tell you that off the top of my head!'

'Well, if you have written it down, bring it here', said Sokrates. 'It would give me great pleasure to hear it.'

'No, by Zeus,' he said, 'I haven't even written it down.'

'So,' said Sokrates, 'on war too we will hold off from giving advice to start with. Perhaps it is because of their magnitude that, being at the start of being political leader you haven't examined these questions. But I know that you have already taken concern for the defence of the country, and you know how many guardposts are opportune and how many not, and how many garrisons are sufficient and how many insufficient. You will advise increasing the well-placed forces and removing those that are excessive.'

'By Zeus,' said Glaukon, 'I am going to abolish the lot because they are guarded so badly that things get stolen from the countryside.'

'But if someone removes the guardposts,' said Sokrates, 'do you not think that that will give anyone who wants to the ability to snatch things? And,' he said, 'have you yourself gone and examined this, or how do you know that they are badly guarded?'

'I am guessing,' he said.

'So,' said Sokrates, 'on this matter too we will give advice when we are no longer simply guessing but already know?'

'Perhaps,' Glaukon said, 'that is better.'

'I know you haven't been to the mines so as to be able to say why there is less income from them than there used to be.'

'No, I haven't gone,' he said.

'Well, by Zeus,' said Sokrates, 'the area is said to be oppressive, so whenever you have to give advice on this, that excuse will be sufficient.'

'I'm being mocked,' said Glaukon.

'But I know you have not neglected this next issue, but have considered it – for how long is the grain that comes in from the countryside sufficient to feed the city, and how much is needed each year in addition, so that the city will not running short without your noticing but are able to advise the city about what is needed from a position of knowledge and help keep it safe.'

'You are talking about an enormous task, said Glaukon, 'if one has to look after such things!'

'But, on the other hand,' Sokrates said, 'no one could manage his own household well unless he knows all its needs and takes care to see that they were met. But since the city consists of more than 10,000 houses and it is difficult to look after so many households, how about your starting by trying to increase your uncle's household?'

Xenophon *Memorabilia* 3.6.1–14

The question of what an Athenian politician needed to know was and remains a debatable issue (compare Aristotle, *Rhetoric* 1359a30–1360b3). As often in *Memorabilia* Sokrates is made the champion of an unorthodox view, but a view that continues to have some modern support (cf. Finley 1962 on demagogues as 'indispensable experts'). Xenophon himself attempts to address some of these questions in his pamphlet *Ways and Means*.

431 PROTAGORAS: In the beginning human beings lived scattered, and there were no cities. Because they were all over the place, the weaker among them were the victims of wild beasts. Their craft skills were sufficient assistance when it came to food, but inadequate when it came to fighting against wild beasts. They did not yet have any of the skills in running a city, one of which is skill in war. So they sought to gather together and make themselves secure by founding cities. But when they gathered together they did each other wrong, because of not having skills related to city life, and as a result they scattered again and came to harm. So Zeus, afraid that our race might be completely destroyed, sends Hermes to bring to human beings shame and justice, so that there could be ordered cities and the bonds that create friendship. So Hermes asks Zeus in what manner he should give shame and justice to humans. 'Am I to distribute them in the same way that skills have been distributed, for they have been distributed like this – one man with skill as a doctor is enough for many individuals without that skill, and so with others who possess technical skills. Am I to give justice and shame in this way among men, or am I to give them to everyone?' 'To everyone,' said Zeus, and let all share them. For there would be no cities if a few people were to share them, as with other skills. And make it a law from me that they should execute the man unable to share shame or justice on the grounds that he is a plague to the city.' So indeed, Sokrates, because of this the Athenians above all, when the discussion is about the best way to do carpentry or some other skill, think that just a few should have a part in giving advice, and if someone who is not one of those few gives advice they do not put up with it, as you observe, and as I say is reasonable. But whenever they enter discussions involving the skills of running a city, all of which involves justice and good sense, they quite reasonably put up with everyone speaking, on the grounds that everyone has a share of this virtue, or else there would be no cities.

Plato Protagoras 322a8–323a3

For the view that man achieves his full potential in, and only in, political society see Thucydides 2.37.3, and compare the equation of the man who doesn't take part, with the useless man, in 2.40.2.

432 SOKRATES (acting as a mouthpiece for PROTAGORAS): Remember what we said before, that to the sick man what he eats both appears and is bitter, while to the healthy man it both appears and is the opposite. It is not necessary to make one of these two wiser than the other – that is not even possible – nor should we criticise the sick man for being ignorant because he judges as he does, or reckon the healthy man wise, because he judges differently. Rather, it is a matter of changing one into the other, because the other state is better. So, too, in education, we have to bring about change from a worse state into a better state. The doctor brings about the change by drugs, the sophist by arguments. It is not the case that someone can make a person who judges falsely judge truly. For it is not possible to judge what does not exist, or to judge anything other than what one is experiencing – this is always true. I think that someone judging when his soul is in a pernicious state judges things akin to that condition, but giving him a sound state of the soul causes him to think different things. Some people, because of ignorance, call these appearances 'true', but I hold that the one kind are better than the others, but in no way truer.

Plato *Theaitetos* 166e2–167b

This is a clear statement of a relativist position which Sokrates puts into the mouth of Protagoras. Such relativism offered a reason for taking everyone's view seriously and was therefore linked to radical democracy. For further discussion see Farrar (1988).

The relation of the rule of the people to the rule of law

433   In another kind of democracy the aforementioned arrangements are unaltered, but the many are sovereign and not the law. This comes about when the decrees of the assembly are sovereign and not the law. This is brought about by the demagogues; for when democratic cities are subject to law, the demagogue does not arise, and the best of the citizens predominate; but where the laws are not sovereign, demagogues arise; for the common people become a single composite monarch, since the many are sovereign not individually but collectively.

Aristotle *Politics* 1292a4–13

The question of the place of law in government was a fraught one in classical Athens, particularly at the end of the fifth century. For the separation of law-making from Assembly decrees see above **214**. Modern scholars have often taken the view that fourth-century Athens represented the rule of law (by contrast, above all, to the Arginousai trial – **213** above): see Ostwald (1986), Sealey (1987), Harris (2006).

434   It is said that Alkibiades, before he was 20 years old, had the following discussion about laws with Perikles, who was his guardian and also the political leader in the city.
   'Tell me, Perikles,' he said, 'could you teach me what law is?'
   'Of course, absolutely,' Perikles said.
   'Teach me then, by the gods', said Alkibiades. 'When I hear some men being praised for being legal experts, I think a man would not justly be so praised if he did not know what law is.'
   'What you desire is no difficult matter,' Perikles said, 'when you want to know what law is. Laws are everything that the people, when it has been assembled and has been examined, decrees that one ought to do or ought not to do.'
   'Is this when it has decided that one ought to do good things, or bad?'
   'Good, by Zeus, lad,' he said, 'and not bad.'
   'And if it is not the mass of the people but, as where there is oligarchy, a few who assemble together and decree what it is right to do, what do we call that?'
   'Everything,' he said, 'which the sovereign power in the city decides that it is right to do is called law.'
   'And if a tyrant in charge in the city decrees to the citizens what they should do, is that law?'
   'Even everything that a tyrant who is in power decrees,' he said 'even this is called law'.
   'What constitutes force and the negation of law, Perikles? Is it not when the stronger compels the weaker, not by persuasion but by force, to do what he has decided?'
   'I think so,' said Perikles.

'And all that a tyrant, without having persuaded the citizens, compels them to do by decree is the negation of law?'

'I think so,' Perikles said. 'For I take back what I said about whatever a tyrant decrees without having persuaded the people being law.'

'But all that the few decree, not having persuaded the many but using their power, do we agree that that is a matter of force, or not?'

'I think that everything,' Perikles said, 'that anyone compels anyone to do, without persuading them, whether it is a matter of decrees or not, is force rather than law.'

'And what about all that the mass of the people, having power over those who have money, decrees, without persuading them, would that be force rather than law?'

'Alkibiades,' said Perikles, 'when I was as young as you I displayed cleverness of that sort too...'

Xenophon *Memorabilia* 1.2.40–46

17 OVERTHROWING DEMOCRACY

Why democracy was not more unstable

435   Someone might suggest that no one has been unjustly deprived of civic rights at Athens. I maintain that there are some who have been deprived of civic rights unjustly, but they are few. But it needs more than a few to attack the democracy at Athens, since the situation is that one must not bear in mind people who have been justly deprived of civic rights, but if any have been deprived unjustly. And how could anyone think that the many behave at Athens unjustly, since it is the common people who fill the offices? Men lose their rights at Athens through not ruling justly, or not saying or doing what is just. In view of this one cannot believe that there is anything to fear at Athens from those who have been deprived of civic rights.

Old Oligarch 3.12–13

436   The Spartans decided to remain in Boiotia and to consider their safest line of march. Furthermore, certain Athenians were making secret overtures to them, in the hope of putting an end to the democracy and the building of the Long Walls.

Thucydides 1.107.4

This incident occurs immediately before the battle of Tanagra in 458/7, and so just a few years after Ephialtes' reforms (above **43**) and Kimon's ostracism.

437   In addition, Perikles sent a thousand kleroukhs to the Khersonese, five hundred to Naxos, half that number to Andros, a thousand to Thrace to live among the Bisaltians, and others to Italy, when the site of Sybaris was being resettled, which they renamed Thourioi. He did all this to relieve the city of its lazy and consequently meddlesome mob, to remedy the poverty of the people, and to give the allies a neighbouring garrison to deter revolt.

Plutarch *Perikles* 11.5

The settlements listed here were probably made at various dates between c. 450 and 435 (cf. **72**). The motivations ascribed here to Perikles may not go back to the fifth century. For continued Athenian suspicions of political conspiracy, see above **399**.

The oligarchic coup of 411

438   When the news reached Athens, for a long time they disbelieved even those soldiers who had actually escaped from the very event and were reporting clearly: so complete a destruction seemed incredible. When they finally recognised the truth, they were angry with the speakers who had joined in promoting the expedition as though they themselves had not voted for it.

Thucydides 8.1.1

The news in question here is news of defeat in Sicily. For the vote for the Sicilian expedition see **407**.

439   PROBOULOS: What I desire, by Zeus, to hear from them first is this – what do you want that you have shut and barred our Akropolis?
LYSISTRATE: We want to keep the money safe and stop you fighting with it.
PROBOULOS: Is it because of the money that we are fighting?
LYSISTRATE: Yes, and that all the rest was stirred up. In order that Peisandros and other office-hunters could go and steal it, they were forever stirring up some trouble.

Aristophanes *Lysistrate* 486–490 (411)

For the appointment of *probouloi* see above **47**.

440   Alkibiades gave this advice to Tissaphernes (satrap of Sardis) and the king of Persia, under whose protection he then was, partly because he thought it was the best, and partly because he was working on his return to his own country. He knew that if he did not destroy it, he would one day persuade them to recall him. He thought that his best chance of persuading them lay in letting them see that Tissaphernes was well-disposed to him. And so it turned out. When the Athenian force at Samos discovered that he had influence with Tissaphernes, the trierarkhs and the men of most influence became eager to overthrow democracy. This was partly because Alkibiades had already sent word to the most influential men there to tell the right-thinking members of the force that he would be glad to return and be their fellow-citizen and make Tissaphernes their friend, but only under oligarchy and not the wicked system that had driven him out; but it was mainly their own idea.
[48] The movement began in the camp and from there reached the city later. Some men crossed from Samos to negotiate with Alkibiades. He offered to make first Tissaphernes, and then the king, their friend if they would abandon democracy and so enable the king to trust them. The men of influence, the men likely to suffer most severely from the war, now entertained high hopes of securing the direction of affairs for themselves and of winning the war.
On returning to Samos they formed their supporters into a conspiracy. They openly told the rank and file that the king would be their friend and provide money if Alkibiades were restored and they abandoned democracy. The mass

of men at first objected to what was going on, but they kept quiet because of their hope of abundant pay from the king. After communicating with the rank and file, the oligarchical conspirators reconsidered the proposals of Alkibiades among themselves and with most of their associates. Though the others thought the proposals advantageous and safe, Phrynikhos, who was still a general, rejected them completely. Alkibiades, he rightly thought, cared no more for oligarchy than democracy. All he was thinking about was how to change the institutions of the city in order to have himself invited back by his friends and so to secure his recall. Their own overriding concern should be the avoidance of civil war...

[49] However, the assembled conspirators, consistently with their original view, accepted the proposals and prepared to send Peisandros and others on an embassy to Athens to negotiate for the return of Alkibiades and the overthrow of the democracy there, and so to make Tissaphernes a friend of Athens.

Thucydides 8.47.1–48.4; 49

441   Peisandros and the other Athenian ambassadors from Samos reached Athens and addressed the Assembly. They summarised their views, insisting that if they took back Alkibiades and modified their democracy, they could have the king as their ally and defeat the Peloponnesians. Many speakers opposed them on the score of democracy, and the enemies of Alkibiades shouted out that it would be a scandal if a law-breaker were recalled, and the Eumolpidai and Kerykes protested on behalf of the Mysteries, the cause of his exile, and called on the gods to prevent his return.

In the face of much opposition and abuse, Peisandros came forward. He called each opponent up and asked him this question: Now that the Peloponnesians had as many ships at sea confronting theirs, more cities in alliance with them, and the king and Tissaphernes providing money, of which the Athenians had none left, had he any hope of the city's survival, unless someone could persuade the king to join their side? When they replied that they had none, he then told them plainly: 'It cannot happen, unless we adopt a more moderate form of government and restrict the numbers eligible for office, to make the king trust us. In the present situation we have to pay more attention to the survival of the city than to its constitution. Later on, we can make changes if there is anything we do not like. We have also to restore Alkibiades, who is the only man alive who can carry this through.'

[54] At first hearing the people strongly objected to the mention of oligarchy, but Peisandros spelled out clearly that there was no other means to survival. Partly out of fear, and partly in hope of later change, they gave way. They voted that Peisandros should sail with ten others and make the best arrangements possible with Tissaphernes and Alkibiades. At the same time, persuaded by a false accusation made by Peisandros, the people deposed Phrynikhos and his colleague Skironides, sending Diomedon and Leon to command the fleet instead of them. Peisandros had accused Phrynikhos of abandoning Iasos and Amorges, because he thought that he was unsuitable for the negotiations with Alkibiades. Peisandros also visited in turn all the secret societies that already existed in the city for help with lawsuits and elections. He urged them to draw

together and, after agreeing on a plan, to overthrow the democracy. When he had taken the other steps dictated by the circumstances, to minimise delay, he set off with his ten companions on his voyage to Tissaphernes.

Thucydides 8.53–4

For more of the narrative of the oligarchic coup of 411 see **48**.

442 There was now a struggle between the fleet which was trying to impose democracy on the city and the Four Hundred who were trying to impose oligarchy on the fleet. The sailors immediately held an assembly at which they deposed the existing generals and any trierarkhs whom they suspected; in their place they elected new trierarkhs and generals, including Thrasyboulos and Thrasyllos. They also stood up and encouraged one another, saying, among other things, that it was wrong to lose heart because their own city had seceded. Those who had seceded were inferior not only in numbers but also in all-round capacity to fend for themselves. They, on the other hand, had the whole fleet and could compel the cities of the empire to pay tribute just as if Athens were still their base...

Thucydides 8.76.1–4

443 Now for the first time Alkibiades, in my judgement, rendered extremely valuable service; for when the Athenians at Samos were all set to sail against their fellow-countrymen, in which case Ionia and the Hellespont would certainly have fallen straight into enemy hands, Alkibiades prevented them. At that moment, when no other man would have been able to hold back the mob, he stopped them sailing. His reproaches deflected the anger they felt against the envoys (of the Four Hundred) as individuals. He sent them away with an answer of his own. He did not object to the rule of the Five Thousand, but he told them to depose the Four Hundred and reinstate the old Council of 500. If any cuts in expenditure had been made, rendering it easier to pay those on active service, that had his full approval. He further bade them hold out and not to give in to the enemy. If the city was preserved, there were good grounds for hoping that the two sides might be reconciled, whereas if either of them – whether that at Samos or that at Athens – were once destroyed, there would no longer be anyone to be reconciled to.

Thucydides 8.86.4–7

444 On receiving the news (of the revolt of Euboia), the Athenians nevertheless manned twenty ships and immediately summoned a first assembly in the place called Pnyx, where they had been accustomed to meet in the past. They deposed the Four Hundred and voted to hand over the government to the Five Thousand, which body was to comprise all those of them who could provide their own armour. They also voted that no one should receive pay for holding office; if anyone did, they declared him accursed. Frequent other assemblies were held later on, at which law-makers were elected and other necessary steps towards a constitution taken. During the first phase (of this régime) the affairs of Athens were as well managed as they ever were, at any rate, in my time: the interests of the few and the many were fairly blended. It was this that first restored the fortunes of the city after they had fallen into disarray. They also voted for the recall of Alkibiades and others with him. They sent word to him and the camp at Samos, urging them to act vigorously.

[98] As soon as this revolution began, Peisandros and Alexikles and their supporters and the other leaders of the oligarchy withdrew to Dekeleia, with the sole exception of Aristarkhos, one of the generals. He speedily assembled some the least Greek archers and made for Oinoe...

Thucydides 8.97–98.1

445 DECREE: The Council and the people decided. The Aiantis tribe were *prytaneis*, Kleigenes was secretary (410/09), Boethos was President. Demophantos proposed the following. The decree dates from the Council of 500 appointed by lot, for whom Kleigenes was the first secretary. If anyone overthrows the democracy at Athens, or holds any office when the democracy has been overthrown, he shall be an enemy of the Athenians and shall be killed with impunity, and his property shall be confiscated and a tenth part of it devoted to the Goddess; and the person who kills or helps to plan the killing of such a man shall be pure and free from guilt. All Athenians shall swear over unblemished sacrifices by tribes and demes to kill the man who has done such things.

Andokides 1.96–7 (400)

There have been some doubts (Canevaro and Harris, 2012) over the authenticity of this decree, the text of which is inserted into Andokides' speech *On the Mysteries*. In terms of substance it lies in a tradition of Athenian laws against tyranny and subversion that starts with [Aristotle] *Constitution of the Athenians* 16.10 and continues with **446** and with Hypereides 4.7–8. See Ostwald (1955). For the context of the decree see Shear (2007), (2011).

The overthrow of democracy in 404/3 was a direct consequence of defeat by Sparta. For evidence that the Thirty were not simply Spartan puppets but had thought deeply on some constitutional matters see above **16**, and Osborne 2003/2010.

Fourth-century fears of revolution

446 In the arkhonship of Phrynikhos (337/6), in the ninth prytany, of Leontis, to which Khairestratos son of Ameinias of Akharnai was secretary, and Menestratos of Aixone of the *proedroi* put matters to the vote, Eukrates son of Aristotimos of Peiraieus proposed: For the good fortune of the people of Athens, the *nomothetai* decided: if anyone rises up against the people for a tyranny or joins in setting up the tyranny or overthrows the people of Athens or the democracy at Athens, whoever kills the man who has done any of these things shall be undefiled. And it shall not be permitted to any of the councilors of the Council of the Areopagos, if the people of Athens is overthrown, to go up to the Areopagos or to sit together in the meeting or to deliberate about anything at all. If, when the people of the democracy at Athens has been overthrown, any of the councilors of the Areopagos does go up to the Areopagos or sit together in the meeting or deliberate about anything, he shall lose his civic rights, both himself and his descendants, and his property shall be made public and a tenth of it be given to the Goddess. This law shall be written up on two stone stelai by the secretary of the Council, and placed, one at the entrance to the Areopagos as you enter the council chamber, and the other in the assembly. For the inscription of the *stelai* the Treasurer of the people shall give 20 dr. from the people's fund for expenditure on decrees.

RO 79 (337/6)

This law was made shortly after the Athenians had lost the battle of Khaironeia against Philip II of Macedon. The debates between Demosthenes and Aiskhines show clearly how divided the Athenians had been over what attitude to take to Philip, but this is the clearest evidence that a significant body of Athenians were concerned that one or other faction might use the new situation to attempt to overthrow the democracy. The danger is seen to be primarily centred on the Council of the Areopagos, which was exclusively made up of former arkhons, and this suggests that the danger was thought to lie not with people who had previously kept out of politics but with men who had in the past been centrally involved. The Areopagos had become politically active once more in the previous ten years or so, usually on Demosthenes' side, so there may be a particular political edge to this clause in the new law.

FURTHER READING

There are a number of good general introductions to Athenian Democracy. Brief and up-to-date is Carey (2001). The basic systematic institutional study is Hansen (1991 and later revision). Rhodes (2004) collects classic recent articles covering a similar range of topics to those covered in this book.

Part I: How Athens became a democracy

The classic work on the history of the Athenian constitution is Hignett (1952). Forrest (1966), Ober (1989), Hansen (1991) and others tell the story more briefly; Ostwald (1986) tells it with a particular slant. For what is at stake in how we tell it, see Osborne (2006).

1   What did Solon do?
Blok and Lardinois (2006), Hansen (1990), Irwin (2005), Morris (1996), Mossé (1979/2004), Osborne (1996/2009), Ste Croix (2004) chs. 4 and 5, van Wees (2006), (2013).

2   The Kleisthenic Revolution
Anderson 2003, Andrewes (1977), Levêque and Vidal Naquet (1996), Lewis (1963), Ober (1996) ch.4, Osborne (1996/2009 292–314/276–97), Ostwald (1969).

3   Fifth-century constitutional changes
Badian (1971), Blok (2009), Christ (1992), Forsdyke (2005), Hignett (1952), Ostwald (1986), Patterson (1981), Sinclair (1988), Wallace (1989).

4   The creation of fourth-century democracy
Eder (1995), Hansen (1991), Rhodes (1979–80), (2010).

Part II: Athenian democratic institutions

Sinclair (1988), Hansen (1991).

5   The civic and the religious in Athenian democracy
Bowden (2003), (2005), Furley (1996), Millett (2005), Osborne (2000).

6   Citizenship
Blok (2009), Boegehold (1994), Davies (1977/8), Loraux (1993).

7   Demes
Hopper (1957), Jones (1999), Osborne (1985), (1990b/2010), (2011), Whitehead (1986).

8   Other subdivisions of the demos
Jones (1999), Lambert (1993).

9   The Council of 500
Rhodes (1972), Connor (1974), Hansen (1981).

10   The Assembly
Hansen (1981), (1983), (1987), (1989), Markle (1985), Sinclair (1988).

11   Law courts
Blanshard (2004), Boegehold (1995), Carey (1998), Cartledge, Millett and Todd ed.
(1990), Christ (1998), Cohen (1995), Harris (2006), Hesk (2000), Hunter (1994),
Hunter and Edmondson (2000), Lanni (2006), MacDowell (1978), Osborne
(1985/2010), Todd (1990), (1993).

12   Magistrates and officials
Davies (1994), Develin (1989), Hansen (1980).

13   The Army and Navy
Christ (2001), Hansen (1989) 25–72, Hanson (1996), MacDowell (1986), Ober (1985),
Pélékidis (1962), Spence (1993).

14   Democracy and religion: regulating cult activities and piety.
Bowden (2013), Connor (1989), Furley (1996), Garland (1990), Goldhill (1987),
Kearns (1985), Osborne (1993/2010), (2013), Parker (1996), (2005), Rhodes (2009).

Part III: Democracy in Action

The elite and the mass in democratic Athens
Millett (1989), Ober (1989), Vlassopoulos (2010).

15   Politics in action
Andrewes (1962) 71–85, Connor (1971), Finley (1962), Harris (1995), Henderson
(2003), McGlew (2003), Raaflaub (2003).

16   Theorising democracy
Balot (2006, 2009), Brock (1991), Davies (2003), Farrar (1988), Kraut (1984), Lintott
(1992), Loraux (1986), Ober (1996), (1998), (2008), Raaflaub (1989), Wallace (1994).

17   Overthrowing democracy
Finley (1971), Krentz (1982), Morgan (2003), Ober (1998), Shear (2011), Wolpert
(2002).

Bibliography

Akrigg, B. (2007) 'The nature and implications of Athens' changed social structure and economy' in R. Osborne (ed.) (2007) 27–43.

Anderson, G. (2003) *The Athenian Experiment: Building an imagined political community in ancient Attica, 508–490 B.C.* Ann Arbor.

Andrewes, A. (1962) 'The Mytilene debate: Thucydides 3.36–49' *Phoenix* 16: 64–85.

Andrewes, A. (1977) 'Kleisthenes' reform bill' *Classical Quarterly* n.s. 27: 241–8.

Bäbler, B. (2005) 'Bobbies or boobies? The Scythian police force in classical Athens', in D. Braund (ed.) *Scythians and Greeks: cultural interactions in Scythia, Athens and the early Roman empire.* Exeter, 114–22.

Badian, E. (1971) 'Archons and strategoi' *Antichthon* 5.7: 1–34.

Balot, R. (2006) *Greek Political Thought.* Oxford.

Balot, R. (ed.) (2009) *A Companion to Greek and Roman Political Thought.* Malden, Massachusetts.

Blanshard, A. (2004) 'What counts as the demos? Some notes on the relationship between the jury and "the people" in Classical Athens' *Phoenix* 58: 28–48 .

Blok, J. (2009) 'Perikles' citizenship law: a new perspective' *Historia* 58.2: 141–70.

Blok, J. and Lardinois, A. (2006) *Solon of Athens: new historical and philological approaches.* Leiden.

Boegehold, A. L. (1994) 'Perikles' citizenship law of 451/0 BC', in A. L. Boegehold and A. Scafuro (eds.), 57–66.

Boegehold, A. L. & A. Scafuro (eds.) (1994) *Athenian Identity and Civic Ideology.* Baltimore.

Boegehold, A. L. (1995) *The Lawcourts at Athens: sites, buildings, equipment, procedure, and testimonia.* Princeton.

Bowden, H. (2003) 'Oracles for sale' in P. S. Derow and R. C. T. Parker (eds.) *Herodotos and his World.* Oxford.

Bowden, H. (2005) *Classical Athens and the Delphic oracle: divination and democracy.* Cambridge.

Brock, R. (1991) 'The emergence of democratic ideology' *Historia* 40: 160–9.

Canevaro, M. (2010) 'The decree awarding citizenship to the Plataeans: ([Dem.] 59.104)', *Greek, Roman and Byzantine Studies* 50: 337–69.

Canevaro, M (2013a) *The Documents in the Attic Orators: Laws and Decrees in the Public Speeches of the Demosthenic Corpus.* Oxford.

Canevaro, M. (2013b) 'Nomothesia in Classical Athens: what sources should we believe?' *Classical Quarterly* n.s. 63: 1–22.

Canevaro, M. and Harris, E. M. (2012) 'The documents in Andocides' *On the Mysteries*' *Classical Quarterly* n.s. 62: 98–129.

Carey, C. (1998) 'The shapes of Athenian laws', *Classical Quarterly* n.s. 48: 93–109.

Carey, C. (2001) *Democracy in classical Athens.* Bristol.

Cartledge P. and Harvey, F. D. (eds) (1985) *Crux: Essays Presented to G. E. M. de Ste Croix on his 75th Brithday.* Exeter and London.

Cartledge, P., Millett, P. and Todd, S. (eds.) (1990) *NOMOS. Essays in Law, Politics and Society in Classical Athens.* Cambridge.

Christ, M. (1992) 'Ostracism, sycophancy, and the deception of the demos: [Arist.] Ath.Pol. 43.5', *Classical Quarterly* n.s. 42: 336–46.

Christ, M. (1998) *The Litigious Athenian.* Baltimore.

Christ, M. (2001) 'Conscription of hoplites in Classical Athens', *Classical Quarterly* 51: 398–422.

Clinton, K. (2005) *Eleusis: the Inscriptions on Stone: Documents of the Sanctuary of the Two Goddesses and Public Docuemtns of the Deme.* £ vols. Athens.

Cohen, D. (1995) *Law, Violence and community in Classical Athens.* Cambridge.

Connor, W.R. (1971) *The New Politicians of Fifth-century Athens.* Princeton.

Connor, W. R. (1974) 'The Athenian Council: Method and Focus in Some Recent Scholarship' *Classical Journal* 70: 32–40.

Connor, W. R. (1989) 'City Dionysia and Athenian democracy' *Classica et Medievalia* 40: 7–32.

D'Angour, A. (1999) 'Archinus, Eucleides and the reform of the Athenian alphabet' *Bulletin of the Institute of Classical Studies* 43: 109–30.

Davidson, J. (2007) *The Greeks and Greek Love*. London.

Davies, J. K. (1967) 'Demosthenes on liturgies: a note', *Journal of Hellenic Studies* 87: 33–40.

Davies, J. K. (1977/8) 'Athenian citizenship: the descent group and the alternatives' *Classical Journal* 73: 105–21.

Davies, J. K. (1994) 'Accounts and accountability in classical Athens', in R. Osborne and S. Hornblower (eds.) (1994), 201–12.

Davies, J. K. (2003) 'Democracy without theory' in P. Derow and R. Parker (eds.) *Herodotus and his World*. Oxford, 319–35.

Develin, R. (1989) *Athenian Officials 684–321 B.C.* Cambridge.

Eder, W. (1995) *Die Athenische Demokratie im 4. Jahrhundert v. Chr.* Stuttgart.

Farrar, C. (1988) *The Origins of Democratic Thinking*. Cambridge.

Finley, M. I. (1951) *Studies in Land and Credit: the Horos inscriptions*. New Brunswick [Reprinted with introduction by P.C. Millett, New Brunswick and Oxford, 1985].

Finley, M. I. (1962) 'The Athenian demagogues', *Past and Present* 21: 3–24. [Reprinted in M. I. Finley (ed.) (1974) *Studies in Ancient Society*. New York and London: 1–25; in M. I. Finley (1985) *Democracy Ancient and Modern*. Second edition. London: 38–75, and in P. J. Rhodes (ed.) (2004)].

Finley, M. I. (1971) *The Ancestral Constitution*. London [Reprinted in M. I. Finley (1975) *The Use and Abuse of History*. London].

Flemming, D. (2004) *Democracy's Ancient Ancestors: Mari and early collective governance*. Cambridge.

Forrest, W. G. (1966) *The Emergence of Greek Democracy 800–400 BC*. London.

Forsdyke, S. (2005) *Exile, Ostracism, and Democracy: the politics of expulsion in ancient Greece*. Princeton.

Furley, W. (1996) *Andokides and the Herms: a study of crisis in fifth-century Athenian religion*. London.

Garland, R. (1990) 'Priests and power in classical Athens' in M. Beard and J. North (eds.) *Pagan Priests*. London, 73–91.

Garnsey, P. D. A. (1985) 'Grain for Athens' in Cartledge and Harvey (eds.) (1985), 62–75; reprinted with addendum by W. Scheidel in P. Garnsey (1998) *Cities, Peasants and Food in Classical Antiquity*. Cambridge, 183–200.

Goette, H. R. (1993) *Athens, Attica and the Megarid: an archaeological guide*. London.

Goldhill, S. (1987) 'The Great Dionysia and civic ideology' *Journal of Hellenic Studies* 107: 58–76 [Reprinted in J. Winkler and F. Zeitlin (eds.) (1990) *Nothing to do with Dionysos?* Princeton].

Hansen, M. H. (1974) *Eisangelia. The Sovereignty of the People's Court in Athens in the Fourth Century BC and the Impeachment of Generals and Politicians*. Odense.

Hansen, M. H. (1980) 'Seven hundred archai in Classical Athens' *Greek, Roman and Byzantine Studies* 21:151–73.

Hansen, M. H. (1981) 'Initiative and decision: the separation of powers in fourth-century Athens' *GRBS* 22: 345–70

Hansen, M. H. (1983) *The Athenian Ecclesia. A collection of articles 1976–83*. Copenhagen.

Hansen, M. H. (1985) *Demography and Democracy: the number of Athenian citizens in the fourth century B.C.* Herning.

Hansen, M. H. (1986) 'The origin of the term *demokratia*' *Liverpool Classical Monthly* 11: 35–6.

Hansen, M.H. (1987) *The Athenian Assembly in the Age of Demosthenes*. Oxford.

Hansen, M. H. (1989) *The Athenian Ecclesia II. A collection of articles 1983–89*. Copenhagen.

Hansen, M. H. (1990) 'Solonian democracy in fourth-century Athens' in J. R. Fears (ed.) *Aspects of Athenian Democracy*, 71–99. Copenhagen.

Hansen, M. H. (1991) *The Athenian Democracy in the Age of Demosthenes* (trans. J. A. Crook), Oxford.

Hanson, V. D. (1996) 'Hoplites into democrats: the changing ideology of Athenian Infantry' in J. Ober and C. Hedrick (eds.) *Demokratia. A conversation on democracies ancient and modern*. Princeton, 289–312.

Harris, E. M. (1995) *Aeschines and Athenian Politics*. Oxford.

Harris, E. M. (2006) *Democracy and the Rule of Law in Classical Athens. Essays on law, society and politics*. Cambridge.

Harvey, F. D. (1990) 'The sykophant and sykophancy: vexatious redefinition?' in S. C. Todd, P. A. Cartledge and P. C. Millett (eds.) (1990) 103–21.

Hedrick, C. W. (1990) *The Decrees of the Demotionidai*. Atlanta, Ga.

Henderson, J. (2003) 'Demos, demagogue, tyrant in Attic Old Comedy' in K. A. Morgan (ed.), 155–79.

Hesk, J. P. (2000) *Deception and Democracy in Classical Athens*. Cambridge.

Hignett, C. (1952) *A History of the Athenian Constitution to the end of the fifth century B.C.* Oxford.

Hopper, R. J. (1957) *The Basis of the Athenian Democracy*. Sheffield.

Hunter, V. J. (1994) *Policing Athens. Social Control in the Attic Lawsuits 420–320 BC*. Princeton.

Hunter, V. J. and Edmondson, J. (eds.) (2000) *Law and Social Status in Classical Athens*. Oxford.

Irwin, E. (2005) *Solon and Early Greek Poetry. The Politics of Exhortation*. Cambridge.

Johnstone, S. (2011) *A History of Trust in Ancient Greece*. Chicago.

Jones, N. F. (1999) *The Associations of Classical Athens. The Response to Democracy*. New York and Oxford.

Jones, N. F. (2004) *Rural Athens under the democracy*. Philadelphia.

Kearns, E. (1985) 'Change and continuity in religious structures after Cleisthenes' in P. A. Cartledge and F. D. Harvey (eds.) (1985) 189–207.

Kellogg, D. L. (2013) *Marathon Fighters and Men of Maple: Ancient Acharnai*. Oxford.

Knox, R. (1985) 'So mischievous a beaste? The Athenian Demos and its treatment of its politicians' *Greece and Rome* 32: 132–61.

Kraut, R. (1984) *Socrates and the state*. Princeton.

Krentz, P. (1982) *The Thirty at Athens*. New Haven.

Kroll, J.H. (1972) *Athenian Bronze Allotment Plates*. Cambridge, MA.

Lambert, S. D. (1993) *The Phratries of Attica*. Ann Arbor.

Lane Fox, R. (1994) 'Aeschines and Athenian politics', in R. Osborne and S. Hornblower (eds.) (1994) 135–55.

Lanni, A. (2006) *Law and Justice in the Courts of Classical Athens*. Cambridge.

Lévêque, P. & P. Vidal-Naquet (1996) *Cleisthenes the Athenian: an essay on the representation of space and time in Greek political thought from the end of the sixth century to the death of Plato*. Atlantic Highlands [Translated and edited by D. A.Curtis. French original 1964].

Lewis, D. M. (1963) 'Cleisthenes and Attica' *Historia* 12: 22–40 [Reprinted in P. J. Rhodes (ed.) (2004)].

D. M. Lewis (1966) 'After the profanation of the mysteries', in E. Badian (ed.) *Ancient Society and Institutions: studies presented to Victor Ehrenberg* (Oxford, 1966) 177–91.

Liddel, P. (2007) *Civic Obligation and Individual Liberty in Ancient Athens*. Oxford.

Lintott, A. (1992) 'Aristotle and democracy' *Classical Quarterly* n.s. 42: 114–28.

Loraux, N. (1986) *The Invention of Athens. The Funeral Speech in the classical city*. Cambridge, Massachusetts.

Loraux, N. (1993) *Children of Athena. Athenian ideas about Citizenship and the division between the sexes*. Princeton.

MacDowell, D. M. (1978) *The Law in Classical Athens*. London.

MacDowell, D. M. (1986) 'The law of Periandros about symmories', *CQ* n.s. 36: 438–49.

McGlew, J. F. (2003). *Citizens on Stage: Comedy and Political Culture in the Athenian Democracy*. Ann Arbor.

Markle, M. M. III (1985) 'Jury pay and Assembly pay at Athens' in P. A. Cartledge and F. D. Harvey (eds.) *Crux: Essays in Greek history presented to G.E.M. de Ste. Croix on his 75th Birthday*. Exeter and London, 265-97 [Reprinted in P. J. Rhodes (ed.) (2004), 95–131].

Millett, P. C. (1989) 'Patronage and its avoidance in classical Athens' in A. F. Wallace-Hadrill (ed.) *Patronage in Ancient Society*. London and New York, 1–33.

Millett, P. C. (2005) 'The trial of Socrates revisited', *European History Review* 12: 23–62.

Mitchell, L. G. (2000) 'A new look at the election of generals at Athens' *Klio 82*: 344–360.

Morgan, K. A. (ed.) (2003) *Popular Tyranny: Sovereignty and its Discontents in Ancient Greece*. Austin.

Morris, I. (1996) 'The strong principle of equality and the Archaic origins of Greek democracy' in J. Ober & C. W. Hedrick (eds.) *Dēmokratia: a Conversation on Democracies, Ancient and Modern*. Princeton, 19–48.

Mossé, C. (1979) 'How a political myth takes shape: Solon, "Founding Father" of the Athenian democracy' in P. J. Rhodes (ed.), 242–259.

Noussia-Fantuzzi, M. (2010) *Solon the Athenian: the poetic fragments*. Leiden.

Ober, J. (1985) *Fortress Attica: defense of the Athenian land frontier 404–322 BC*. Leiden.

Ober, J. (1989) *Mass and Elite in Democratic Athens: Rhetoric, Ideology, and the Power of the People*. Princeton.

Ober, J. (1996) *The Athenian Revolution. Essays on Ancient Greek Democracy and Political Theory*. Princeton.

Ober, J. (1998) *Political Dissent in Democratic Athens. Intellectual Critics of Popular Rule*. Princeton.

Ober, J. (2008) *Democracy and Knowledge: innovation and learning in classical Athens*, Princeton.

Ogden, D. (1996) *Greek Bastardy in the Classical and Hellenistic Periods*. Oxford.

Osborne, M. J. (1981-3) *Naturalization in Athens*. Brussels.

Osborne, R. (1985) *Demos: the invention of Classical Attika*. Cambridge.

Osborne, R. (1985) 'Law in action in classical Athens' *JHS* 105: 40–58 [Reprinted with endnote in R. Osborne (2010) 171–204].

Osborne, R. (1990a) 'Vexatious litigation in classical Athens: sykophancy and the sykophant', in S.C. Todd, P.A. Cartledge and P.C. Millett (eds.) (1990) 83–102 [Reprinted with endnote in R. Osborne (2010) 205–28].

Osborne, R. (1990b) 'The demos and its divisions' in O. Murray and S. Price (eds.) *The Greek City: From Homer to Alexander*. Oxford, 265–93. [Reprinted with endnote in R. Osborne (2010) 39–63]

Osborne, R. (1993) 'Competitive festivals and the polis: a context for dramatic festivals at Athens' in A. Sommerstein, S. Halliwell, J. Henderson and B. Zimmermann (eds.) *Tragedy, Comedy and the Polis*. Bari, 21–38 [Reprinted in P. J. Rhodes (ed.) *Athenian Democracy*. Edinburgh, 207–224, and with endnote in R. Osborne (2010) 325–40].

Osborne, R. (1996) *Greece in the Making 1200–479 B.C.* London [Reprinted 2009].

Osborne, R. (2000) 'Religion, Imperial Politics, and the Offering of Freedom to Slaves' in V. Hunter and J. Edmondson (eds.), 75–92 [Reprinted with endnote in R. Osborne (2010) 229–43]

Osborne, R. (2006) 'When was the Athenian democratic revolution' in S. Goldhill and R. Osborne (eds.) *Rethinking Revolutions through Ancient Greece*. Cambridge, 10–28.

Osborne, R. (ed.) (2007) *Debating the Athenian Cultural Revolution: Art, Literature, Philosophy and Politics 430–380 B.C.* Cambridge.

Osborne, R. (ed.) (2008) *The World of Athens: an Introduction to Classical Athenian Culture*. 2nd edn. Cambridge.

Osborne, R. (2010) *Athens and Athenian Democracy*. Cambridge.

Osborne, R. (2011) 'Space and memorialization in the Attic deme' in S. D. Lambert (ed.) *Sociable Man: Festschrift for Nick Fisher*. Swansea and London, 25–43.

Osborne, R. (2013) 'Democracy and religion in classical Greece' in J. Arnason, K. Raaflaub and P. Wagner (eds.) *The Greek Polis and the Invention of Democracy: a politico-cultural transformation and its interpretations*. Oxford, 274–97.

Osborne, R. and Hornblower, S. (eds.) (1994) *Ritual, Finance, Politics: Athenian democratic accounts presented to David Lewis*. Oxford.

Ostwald, M. (1955) 'The Athenian legislation against tyranny and subversion' *Transactions of the American Philological Association* 86: 103–28.

Ostwald, M. (1969) *Nomos and the Beginnings of the Athenian Democracy*. Oxford.

Ostwald, M. (1986) *From Popular Sovereignty to the Sovereignty of Law: law, society and politics in fifth-century Athens*. Berkeley, Los Angeles and London.

Parker, R. (1987) 'Festivals of the Attic Demes', in T. Linders and G. Nordquist (eds.) *Gifts to the Gods*. Uppsala.

Parker, R. (1996) *Athenian Religion: a history*. Oxford.

Parker, R. (2005) *Polytheism and Society at Athens*. Oxford.

Patterson, C. (1981) *Perikles' Citizenship Law of 451-0 BC*. New York.

Pélékidis, C. (1962) *Histoire de l'ephébie attique des origines à 31 av. J.-C.* Paris.

Raaflaub, K. A. (1989) 'Contemporary perceptions of democracy in fifth-century Athens' *Classica et Medievalia* 40: 33–70.

Raaflaub, K. A. (2003) 'Stick and glue: the function of tyranny in fifth-century Athenian democracy' in K. A. Morgan (ed.) 59–93.

Raaflaub, K. A., Ober, J., and Wallace, R. W. (2007) *Origins of Democracy in Ancient Greece*, Berkeley.

Reinmuth, O. W. (1971) *The Ephebic Inscriptions of the Fourth Century B.C. Mnemosyne* Supplement 14.

Rhodes, P. J. (1972) *The Athenian Boule* [Revised edition 1985]. Oxford.

Rhodes, P. J. (1979) 'Eisangelia in Athens' *Journal of Hellenic Studies* 99: 103–14.

Rhodes, P. J. (1979–80) 'Athenian democracy after 403 B.C.' *Classical Journal* 74: 305–23.

Rhodes, P. J. (1991) 'The Athenian code of laws, 410–399 B.C.' *Journal of Hellenic Studies* 111: 87–100.

Rhodes, P. J. (ed.) (2004) *Athenian Democracy*. Edinburgh.

Rhodes, P. J. (2009) 'State and religion in Athenian Inscriptions' *Greece & Rome* 56: 1–13.

Rhodes, P. J. (2010) 'Stability in the Athenian democracy after 403 B.C.' in B. Linke, M. Meier and M. Strothmann (eds.) *Zwischen Monarchie und Republik*. Stuttgart, 67–75.

Robinson, E. (1997) *The First Democracies: early popular government outside Athens. Historia Einzelschriften* 107, Wiesbaden.

Robinson, E. (2004) *Ancient Greek Democracy: readings and sources*. Oxford.

Robinson, E. (2011) *Democracy beyond Athens: popular government in the Greek classical age*. Cambridge.

Ruschenbusch, E. (2010) *Solon: das Gesetzeswerk-Fragmente: Übersetzung und*

Kommentar. Stuttgart.

Ste. Croix, G.E.M. de. (2004) *Athenian Democratic Origins and Other Essays* [D. Harvey and R. Parker (eds.)]. Oxford.

Seaford, R. (1994) *Reciprocity and Ritual: Homer and tragedy in the developing city-state*. Oxford.

Sealey, R. (1987) *The Athenian Republic: democracy or the rule of law?* University Park.

Shear, J.L. (2003) 'Prizes from Athens: the list of Panathenaic prizes and the sacred oil' *Zeitschrift für Papyrologie und Epigraphik* 142: 87–108.

Shear, J. L. (2007) 'The oath of Demophantos and the politics of Athenian identity' in A. Sommerstein and J. Fletcher (eds.) *Horkos: the Oath in Greek Society*. Exeter, 148–60.

Shear, J. L. (2011) *Polis and Revolution: Responding to Oligarchy in Classical Athens*. Cambridge.

Sinclair, R.K. (1988) *Democeracy and Participation in Athens*. Cambridge.

Spence, I. G. (1993) *The Cavalry of Classical Greece: a social and military history with particular reference to Athens*. Oxford.

Strauss, B. (1993) *Fathers and Sons in Athens: Ideology and Society in the Era of the Peloponnesian War*. London.

Thomas, R. (1994) 'Law and lawgiver in the Athenian democracy' in R. Osborne and S. Hornblower (eds.), (1994) 119–34.

Todd, S. C. (1990) '*Lady Chatterley's Lover* and the Attic orators: the social composition of the Athenian jury' *JHS* 110: 146–73.

Todd, S. C. (1993) *The Shape of Athenian Law*. Oxford.

Todd, S. C. (1996) 'Lysias against Nikomakhos: the fate of the expert in Athenian law' in L. Foxhall and A. Lewis (eds.) *Greek Law in its Political Setting*. Oxford, 101–31.

Traill, J. S. (1986) *Demos and Trittys. Epigraphical and topographical studies in the organisation of Attica*. Toronto.

van Wees, J. G. B. (2006) 'Mass and Elite in Solon's Athens: the property classes revisited', in J. Blok and A. Lardinois (eds.) *Solon of Athens: new historical and philological approaches*. Leiden, 351–89.

van Wees, J. G. B. (2013) *Ships and Silver, Taxes and Tribute. A Fiscal History of Archaic Athens*. London.

Vlassopoulos, K. (2010) *Politics: Antiquity and its Legacy*. London.

Wallace, R. W. (1989) *The Areopagus Council to 307 BC*. Baltimore.

Wallace, R. W. (1994) 'Private lives and public enemies: freedom of thought in Classical Athens' in A. L. Boegehold & A. Scafuro (eds.), 127–55.

Watson, J. M. (2010) 'The origin of metic status at Athens' *Cambridge Classical Journal* 56: 259–78.

Whitehead, D. (1986) *The Demes of Attica 508/7–ca.250 B.C. A political and social study*. Princeton.

Whitehead, D. (1994) 'Cardinal virtues. The language of public approbation in democratic Athens', *Classica et Medievalia* 44: 37–75.

Wilson, P. J. (2000) *The Athenian Institution of the Khoregia: the chorus, the city and the stage*. Cambridge.

Winkler, J. J. (1990a) 'The ephebes' song: tragoidia and polis', in J. J. Winkler and F. I. Zeitlin (eds.) *Nothing to do with Dionysos? Athenian drama in its social context*. Princeton, 20–62.

Winkler, J. J. (1990b) *The Constraints of Desire: the anthropology of sex and gender in ancient Greece*. London.

Winters, T.F. (1993) 'Kleisthenes and Athenian nomenclature' *Journal of Hellenic Studies* 103: 162–165.

Wolpert, A. (2002) *Remembering Defeat: civil war and civic memory in ancient Athens*. Baltimore.

GENERAL INDEX

All references are to page numbers.

Aiskhylos 21, 90, 149.

Akharnai (deme) 40, 41, 51, 74, 105, 124, 165. For the play *Akharnians*, see Index of Passages s.v. Aristophanes.

Akropolis, Athenian 6, 62, 66, 98, 113, 122–5, 128, 162.

Alkibiades, son of Kleinias 104, 160–161; as politician: 60, 113, 135, 146, 148; as general: 79, 106, 113, 136, 147, 148–9; involvement in Mutilation of the Herms (see also Eleusinian Mysteries; Herms), and exile: 22, 24, 129–131, 162–165.

Apodektai 64, 99, 113.

Areopagos 11; Council of: 5, 10, 11, 20–21, 26, 98, 112, 165–166; as law-court: 2, 10, 20, 64, 88.

Arginousai, battle of 61, 79, 83, 106, 133, 160.

Aristotle 1, 2, 10, 11, 21, 30, 34, 44, 55, 64, 158; see also Index of Passages.

[Aristotle], author of the *Constitution of the Athenians* 1, 2, 29; see also Index of Passages.

Arkhestratos 11, 21, 106.

Arkhons xix, 6, 15, 16, 19, 21, 25, 45, 64, 86–8, 98, 101, 121, 127, 166; see also Basileus.

Assembly, meeting place of 71; attendance at 28, 70, 72, 76, 134; factions in 72–3; abuse and domination of 23, 24, 60, 74, 77–8, 149; constitutional role of 7, 28, 29, 36, 55, 59, 63, 65, 70, 73–83, 132–6; decision-making by 32, 33, 36, 37, 60, 61, 62, 65, 70, 72, 73, 75, 77–8, 91, 106, 127, 134, 138, 141–2, 147, 149–151, 156–7; and religion (see also Religion) 32, 33, 37, 75 127; as a law-court (see also Law-Courts) 79–85.

Athene 7, 32, 43, 51, 58, 64, 71, 81, 98, 99, 122–6, 128, 148.

Basileus xix, 12, 45, 88, 121, 125.

Council of 400, Solonian 5, 18, 19; in 411 24, 57, 164.

Council of 500 23; Kleisthenic invention of 17; deme quotas for 40; qualification for membership of 57, 102, 135; proportion of Athenians serving in 134; attendance at 33; oath of 19, 59;

behaviour in 7; organisation of 56, 58; responsibilities of 55; debates in 58–9, 143–5; supervises Assembly 61; prepares business for Assembly 60–2, 75, 79, 80–3, 135–6, 150, 165; limitation on powers of 5, 18, 21; decisions subject to review by the Assembly 5, 18, 149–50; oversight of citizen enrolment 35; oversight of magistrates 45, 63–7, 149; oversight of navy 66, 67–8, 113, 116–7; oversight of cavalry 68, 108; and *nomothetai* 26, 27, 84; religious activities of 57, 58, 64–5, 69, 122–8; and cities of empire 65–6; as court 66, 68–9, 108; honoured 61–2; see also *Proedroi, Prytaneis*.

Demarkh 18, 38, 43, 44, 65, 116, 124, 125, 129.

Demes 16, 18, 29, 37–42, 44–5, 47, 50–51, 53–4, 65, 71, 74, 85–6, 101–2, 104, 109, 129, 131, 138, 140; and tribes 17; constitutional rôle of xxiii; 17–19, 21, 26, 34–5, 43, 46, 91, 134, 136; legal rôle of 34–5, 45, 48, 165; and warfare 101, 110, 115–6; and festivals 38, 118; and religion 42–3, 118, 124–5, 127, 165; see also Akharnai.

Dionysia, festival of 28, 38, 45, 46, 71, 78, 119, 121, 122.

Dionysos 71, 90, 119, 121, 126, 128, 149, 150; see also Dionysia

Dokimasia, see Examination.

Drakon, lawgiver 5, 12, 19, 26, 50.

Eleusinian Mysteries 32, 43, 69, 79, 91, 121–4, 126–7, 129–31, 149.

Ephialtes 1, 2, 5, 10, 11, 20, 21, 57.

Epimeletai xix, 45, 46, 47, 52, 78, 116.

Eukleides (archon 403/2) 14, 25, 26, 27, 34, 45, 59.

Eumolpidai (*genos*) 12, 121–3, 125, 126, 131, 163.

Euripides 31, 149, 154; see also Index of Passages.

Euthunai, see Scrutiny.

Examination (*dokimasia*) xix, 10, 22, 35, 63, 66, 68, 87, 93, 108, 128, 153,

Genē xx, 6, 16, 18, 31, 32, 44, 47, 48, 50, 51, 52, 65, 188, 121, 122, 134.

Generals (*strategoi*) xx; invention of 19;

Printed in the United States
by Baker & Taylor Publisher Services